The Undisclosed Punjab

India Besieged by Terror

THE UNDISCLOSED PUNJAB

INDIA BESIEGED BY TERROR

Birbal Nath, IPS (Retd.)

Former

Director General of Police	:	Punjab
Director General	:	Border Security Force (BSF)
Director General	:	Central Reserve Police Force (CRPF)
Member	:	Central Administrative Tribunal (CAT)

Manas Publications

New Delhi-110002 (INDIA)

MANAS PUBLICATIONS
(Publishers, Distributors, Importers & Exporters)
4402/5A, Main Ansari Road
(Opposite HDFC Bank)
Darya Ganj, New Delhi-110 002 (INDIA)
Off. © 23260783, 23265523, Res. © 23842660
Fax: 011-23272766
E-mail: manaspublications@vsnl.com
www.manaspublications.in

ISBN 978-81-7049-323-5
Rs. 495/-

Typeset at
Manas Publications

Printed in India at
Rajdhani Printers, Delhi
and Published by Mrs Suman Lata for
Manas Publications, 4402/5A, Main Ansari Road
(Opposite HDFC Bank)
Darya Ganj, New Delhi-110 002 (INDIA)

Dedicated to the Lotus Feet of the Lord

"त्वमर्कस्त्वं सोमस्त्वमसि पवनस्त्वं पवनस्त्वं हुतवह–
सत्वमापस्त्वं व्योम त्वमु धरणिरात्मा त्वमिति च।
परिच्छिन्नवं त्वयि परिणता बिभ्रति गिरं
न विद्यस्तत्तत्त्वं वयमिह तु यत् त्वं न भवसि"

"The Wise hold this limiting opinion about Thee-
Thou art the Sun, Thou art the Moon;
Thou art the Fire, Thou art the Air;
Thou art the Water, Thou art the Space;
Thou art the Earth and Thou art the Self.
But we do not know that thing, which Thou art not."

To The Departed One,
She, who made all things beautiful,
With her unconditional compassion.

The Distinguished Generals of Indian Army

1. General JN Choudhry (1965 Indo-Pak War)
2. Field Marshal Sam JH Maneck Shaw (The Victorious Hero of Indo-Pak War 1971)

and

The Most Distinguished Police Officers of India

Shri K.F. Rustam Ji, the first Director General of BSF A compassionate and highly patriotic Police Officer.

Shri A.K. Mitra, Director General, Border Security Force, who made BSF a professional force with artistic beauty.

To my friends

* Late Shri Brish Bhan, who was Chief Minister of PEPSU and whose son Shri Ashok Bhan is a Justice of the Hon'ble Supreme Court of India.
* Shri Manzoor Ahmed who taught me what friendship really means.
* Shri Bashir Ahmed who taught me nuances of Urdu Literature.

  Both became victims of Muslim genocide in Patiala in 1947.
* To my late wife, Shrimati Santosh Nath, who converted the desert of my life into a bouquet of flowers and gave me a talented son, Shivengar Jatley; and a very very talented daughter, Geetanjli Pandit, an authority in Human Resource Development.

"Yet each man kills the thing he loves
from all let this be heard
Some does it with a bitter look
Some with a flattering word
The coward does it with a kiss
The brave man with a sword.

—Oscar Wilde's
Ballad of Reading Goal

❖❖❖

"They will be asked
What they did
When their nation died."

—Otto Rene Castillo

Contents

The Primary Actors

Shrimati Priyadarshani Indira Gandhi: She was Prime Minister of India (1966-77 and 1980-84) and assassinated on 31ST October 1984 at 08:10am by her own Sikh Guards SI Beant Singh & Const. Satwant Singh who pumped dozens of bullets into the frail body of the Prime Minister who slumped to the ground at her residence, 1 Safdarjang Road, New Delhi. SI Beant Singh was gunned down by ITBP personnel, who fired upon Satwant Singh, too, who had thrown away his sten gun. Shri Rajiv Gandhi was on a tour in West Bengal. Shrimati Sonia Gandhi rushed to the bullet-ridden body of the Prime Minister at the All India Institute of Medical Sciences, in the vain hope of saving the life of her mother-in-law. SI Beant Singh and Const. Satwant Singh raised slogans that they had avenged the sacrilege of their Sikh Shrine Harmander Sahib, Amritsar by Operation Blue Star. Indeed, it was the blackest day in the history of Sikh Religion since their Guru Tegh Bahadur and Banda Bairagi had laid down their lives through Mughal torture to protect the weak in the Hindu-Sikh polity.

Giani Zail Singh: Called himself a devoted singer of Sikh Religion. Was the President of *Parja Parishad of* princely States of Faridkot, Nabha, Patiala, etc. during the Quit India Movement, launched by Mahatma Gandhi in August 1942. Was Revenue Minister in PEPSU and a Minister in the Sardar Partap Singh Kairon Ministry in Punjab. Later Chief Minister of Punjab. Later Home Minister of India (1980-1982) through his sychophancy of late Sanjay

Gandhi. Used the same tactics to get nominated as Congress candidate for the Presidency of India in July 1982-1987. Sanjay Gandhi thought that he would use Giani Zail Singh. However, Giani Zail Singh was too shrewd for Sanjay Gandhi. In turn/he used Sanjay Gandhi to get into the good offices of Shrimati Priyadarshani Indira Gandhi. Gradually Giani Zail Singh came in his true colours when he tried to pin down Shrimati Priyadarshani Indira Gandhi, Prime Minister of India, and started dictating her in administrative matters beyond the pale of his Constitutional role as Head of the State. Died in the Post Graduate Institute in Chandigarh after a spell of prolonged illness. He betrayed the trust, which the Prime Minister had laid in him. He came in to his true colours jettisoning his earlier sychophancy. (He had earlier said he would sweep the floor if Shrimati Indira Gandhi so desired) He was the arch conspirator who boosted Sant Jarnail Singh Bhindranwale to cow down the Prime Minister and his arch rival Sardar Darbara Singh, the Chief Minister of Punjab (1980 to 1983). Indeed Sant Jarnail Singh was his creation. As Home Minister of India, he prevailed upon the Congress Chief Minister of Haryana in 1981 not to allow Punjab Police to arrest the so-called Santji of Damdami Taxal from Chandukalan, Distt. Hisar, Haryana. Coming from a poor origin, he luxuriated in all the pleasures of the body. As Chief Minister of Punjab, he was considered to have accumulated enough wealth for himself and the coffers of the AICC.

Sant Jarnail Singh Bhindranwale: A meek preacher of Sikh Religion hailing from village Rode, Tehsil Moga Distt. Firozepur, Punjab. He foiled the Punjab Police strategy of arresting him outside Punjab, that is, Chandukalan in Haryana and later in Bombay where Giani Zail Singh, Home Minister of India is said to have himself gone to arrange his escape. Since the Sant was created and wooed by the Home Minister as well as his rival Sardar Darbara Singh, Chief Minister of Punjab, he became conceited and used abusive language towards Shrimati Indira Gandhi, the Prime Minister of India, whose name he put as No. 1 on his Hit List. My name was No. 5 on the same hit list. He died in June 1984 when the Indian Army mounted an unprofessional assault on Sikh Holy Shrine of Harmandar Sahib, Amritsar. He was given to vain bravado of defiance after taking shelter in the Harmindar Sahib, Amritsar and Gurudarshan Prakash Gurdwara Mehta. He carried an arrow, to show as if he was a descendent of 'Dasham Padsha.' He was the first to flee Chandukalan leaving *Guru Granth Sahib* behind and again leaving Bombay (as devised by Giani Zail Singh, the Home Minister of India) leaving his Jatha in Bombay as a camouflage to dupe Major General Sinha of Special Rifles, who had been flown specially to Bombay to effect his arrest. Giani Zail Singh, the Home Minister of India foiled the strategy devised by the PMO and the Home Secretary, Shri TN Chaturvedi, till recently the Governor of Karnataka.

Sardar Darbara Singh: Shri Darbara Singh was Chief Minister of Punjab (age 62) in 1980 with unrestrained libido, which ruined all covert plans to neutralise Sant Jarnail Singh Bhindranwale and his criminal gang. Otherwise, Sardar Darbara Singh was an honest Jat Sikh in financial matters, Chief Minister of Punjab. A warm hearted person, highly hospitable, a Pakka Gur Sikh who had not only the Parkash of *Guru Granth Sahib* in his residence but also carried out the Jaap as taught to him by Sant Jarnail Singh Bhindranwale. He tried to fight Giani Zail Singh by the tactics invented by the latter but was no match for the Giani Ji. President's Rule was imposed on Punjab in 1983 whereafter he shifted to New Delhi and died due to heart ailment. The day President's Rule was imposed on Punjab, Rashtrapati Bhawan at Raisina Hill New Delhi was brilliantly lit up by Giani Ji.

Bhai Amrik Singh: The President of All India Sikh Students Federation. A Fire Brand. A devotee of cult of gun. He escaped arrest on two occasions because Sardar Darbara Singh had warned him. Died during Operation Blue Star. Had a tendency to get flustered under pressure.

Rajiv Gandhi: The most handsome Prime Minister (1944-1991). A victim of intrigue in his cabinet. Could not match strategy of Vishwanath Partap Singh, his Defence Minister and later Prime Minister of India.

Arun Singh: A capable management expert, a friend and colleague, of Rajiv Gandhi. Fell victim to the intrigues of New Delhi.

Tarsem Singh: A Naxalite of Kapurthala Distt. Involved in a number of shootouts. Escaped to Germany via Nepal and Bangkok. His flight was arranged by the Sikh separatists abroad.

Tejindar Khanna: Sri Tejindar Khanna at present Lt. Governor of Delhi, was the Principal Secretary to the Chief Minister of Punjab in 1980-1983.

Ajit Singh Atwal: A very honest DIG, a brave Sikh officer, who was inveigled to the steps of the Harmandar Sahib by a misguided brigadier where he was assassinated by the criminal gang of Bhindranwale.

SS Bains: The brave Sikh SSP of Amritsar.

MMK Wakli: MMK Wakli, the Home Secretary in the crucial period and later Lt. Governor of Delhi.

TN Chaturvedi: TN Chaturvedi, Home Secretary, Government of India (1980-1983). A bureaucrat who was given charge of Home Ministry to checkmate the unconstitutional moves of the then Home Minister Giani Zail Singh.

Jathedar Santokh Singh: Jathedar Santokh Singh of Delhi. Giani Zail Singh created this monster who put Punjab on fire on September 20, 1981, night by his fiery speech at Gurudwara Gurdarshan Prakash Mehta on the eve of the arrest of Sant Bhindranwale.

Secretary RAW: Wanted the Prime Minister Shrimati Indira Gandhi to give orders in writing regarding covert action against Bhindranwale gang holed up in the Akal Takht.

Dr. Sohan Singh: Member, Panthic Committee.

RN Kao: RN Kao, Kashmiri Pandit, Senior Adviser on Security in the Cabinet Secretariat.

Wadhawa Singh: Resident of Sandhu Chatha, Police Station Sadar, Kapurthala. A paid agent of Pakistan ISI who organised training camps for Sikh militants in Pakistan. He is still in Pakistan. ISI is paying for his stay in case Sikh separatism in India can be revived.

Sardar Gurcharan Singh Tohra: Sardar Gurcharan Singh Tohra, Permanent President of SGPC who provided shelter to Sikh militants. Given to use foul language.

Chief Ministers of Punjab (India)

No.	Name/Party	From	To
1.	Dr. Gopi Chand Bhargava (Congress)	August 15, 1947	April 13, 1949
2.	Bhim Sen Sachar (Congress)	April 13, 1949	Oct. 18, 1949
3.	Dr. Gopi Chand Bhargava (Congress)	October 18, 1949	June 20, 1951
4.	President's Rule	June 20, 1951	April 17, 1952
5.	Bhim Sen Sachar (Congress)	April 17, 1952	Jan. 23, 1956
6.	Pratap Singh Kairon (Congress)	January 23, 1956	June 21, 1964
7.	Dr. Gopi Chand Bhargava (Congress)	June 21, 1964	July 6, 1964
8.	Ram Kishan (Congress)	July 7, 1964	July 5, 1966
9.	President's Rule	July 5, 1966	Nov. 1, 1966
10.	Giani Gurmukh Singh Mussafir (Congress)	November 1, 1966	March 8, 1967
11.	Justice Gurnam Singh (Shiromani Akali Dal)	March 8, 1967	Nov. 25, 1967
12.	Lachhman Singh Gill (Shiromani Akali Dal)	Nov. 25, 1967	August 23, 1968
13.	President's Rule	August 23, 1968	Feb. 17, 1969

No. Name/Party	From	To
14. Justice Gurnam Singh	Feb. 17, 1969	March 27, 1970
15. Parkash Singh Badal (Shiromani Akali Dal)	March 27, 1970	June 14, 1971
16. President's Rule	June 14, 1971	March 17, 1972
17. Giani Zail Singh	March 17, 1972	April 30, 1977
18. Parkash Singh Badal (Shiromani Akali Dal)	June 20, 1977	Feb. 17, 1980
19. President's Rule	Feb. 17, 1980	June 6, 1980
20. Darbara Singh (Congress)	June 6, 1980	Oct. 10, 1983
21. President's Rule	Oct. 10, 1983	Sept. 29, 1985
22. Surjit Singh Barnala (Shiromani Akali Dal)	Sept. 29, 1985	June 11, 1987
23. President's Rule	June 11, 1987	Feb. 25, 1992
24. Beant Singh (Congress)	Feb. 25, 1992	August 31, 1995
25. Harcharan Singh Brar (Congress)	August 31, 1995	Jan. 21, 1996
26. Rajinder Kaur Bhattal (Congress)	Jan. 21, 1996	Feb. 12, 1997
27. Parkash Singh Badal (Shiromani Akali Dal)	Feb. 12, 1997	Feb. 26, 2002
28. Amarinder Singh (Congress)	Feb. 26, 2002	March 1, 2007
29. Parkash Singh Badal (Shiromani Akali Dal)	March 1, 2007	Present

– 1 –

Why Read this Book?

Our libraries are glutted with numerous books on Punjab. The question arises: why add another one? The author has been an avid reader of all literature on Punjab and found that the problem of Punjab has been dealt with in these books or magazine articles either partially or in a partisan spirit.

It is not to say that there has not been illuminating literature altogether on Punjab. I have found the analysis of Sikh aspirations by Shri Madhu Limaye very much near the truth. His article in the *Sunday* (21-27 Oct. 1987) "Sikhs: an alien people? The seeds of separatism were sown eight decades ago" was very near the truth. *The Sikh Struggle* by Ram Kumar Narayan and George Sieberer and *Sikh Separatism* by Rajiv A. Kapoor are excellent expositions.

However, to have a complete picture, we must recognise the significant facets of Sikh religion and Sikh psyche as shaped by their religion as also their history, particularly with reference to their persecution by Mughals, and their satraps in Punjab leading to the development of a Persecution Syndrome and Martyrdom Complex among the Sikhs. This book presents the inside story of the mayhem through which Punjab and Northern India went through from 1981 onwards.

Plato has said that the state of a man's knowledge on any subject may be under one of the following three categories: (i) Ignorance, (ii) Belief, and (iii) Knowledge. I would like to add two more categories, that is, (iv) Half Truths, and sometimes, (v) (DFD) Disinformation Fed Deliberately through various media designed to cover up or whitewash the unpalatable.

The unpalatable truth is that the Akalis had always hankered and worked for a Separate Homeland for the Sikhs. This political aspiration was never articulated unambiguously and was thus never discussed honestly at any forum. This demand for a glorious Khalsa Raj remained embedded in the mind of the Akali leadership like a festering wound and they, and the S.G.P.C., never allowed any opportunity to go unexploited in the pursuit of their obsession for Khalsa Raj, However, they never garnered enough courage to state this aspiration in clear and unambiguous words because Sikhs were never in clear majority in a geographical unit before 1966. Shiromani Gurdwara Prabandhak Committee (SGPC) the religious limb of the Akalis, had worked assiduously for decades to ensure a cultural and religious divide between the Sikhs and Hindus of Punjab. They have been remarkably successful in bringing about this divide.

The Akalis and the SGPC have been given to separatist and threatening rhetoric and postures from the day Constitution of India was approved and adopted. The Akali representatives in the Constituent Assembly refused to append their signatures to the Constitution of India, in protest against non-provision of a Sikh state within India.

In their design, the Akalis were helped immensely by Punjabi Hindus, whose stark communalism in disowning Punjabi language as their mother tongue led to the ghastly happenings of 1980s.

There were many factors which transformed Sant Jarnail Singh Bhindranwale, basically a weakling, into a Frankenstein of 1980s. The most decisive being the Pro-Tobacco agitation launched by the communal Hindus of Amritsar in May 1981. Can anyone defend the disgraceful and abusive procession parading the bazars of Amritsar and virtually abusing Sant Jarnail Singh Bhindranwale, for his advocacy seeking a ban on smoking in Amritsar? Bhindranwale retaliated by calling names to the Prime Minister and all the Hindu officers of Punjab police. His abuses were rightly ignored by the Government. However, he felt emboldened and spiced his further abuses by hype and gestures of bravado.

I am a Punjabi, I am also a Sikh in the sense that I read and feel uplifted by Sikh Scriptures.

I was Director General Police, Punjab from Sep. 1980 to Sep. 1982. Later I worked as Director General Border Security Force under Mrs. Indira Gandhi from October 1982 to September 1984. Thus, I have been in a position to examine various events and policies from a close range in the turbulent history of Punjab from 1981 onwards. I explain below how I came in contact with Mrs. Indira Gandhi as early as in July 1959 through a fortuitous circumstance.

Pt. Jawaharlal Nehru, Mrs. Indira Gandhi, Sanjay and Rajiv came in July 1959 for a restful holiday to the "Retreat" at Mashobra near Shimla. Mashobra was a part of Mahasu District of Himachal Pradesh.

Thus, when the Nehru family came for a vacation to the "Retreat" at Mashobra, I was asked to take charge of their security arrangements. Their sojourn in Mashobra was announced without any prior information. There was no advance programme or information that they would visit and stay there. I had gone to Chopal for the annual inspection of the police stations. One goes from Shimla to Theog and then to Kotkhai. The route from Kotkhai to Chopal passed through a dense jungle, which had to be traversed on foot. The forest is stalked by leopards and bears in search of prey.

It was 11 p.m. when the Station House Officer brought me a message asking me to return to Headquarters as soon as I had received the message and report at the "Retreat" at Mashobra. It was not possible at that time to embark upon the return journey through the jungle. However, I left Chopal at 4 a.m. and reached the Retreat at 10 a.m. It was 9th July 1959. Those days, Shri A. Dutt, the Inspector General, was in charge of the Prime Minister's Security. As soon as I reached the Retreat, I reported to Shri Dutt. He was greatly agitated at that time. He told me that the Prime Minister and Mrs. Indira Gandhi were highly annoyed with the security arrangements made at the place. The Nehru family had taken serious objection to the deployment of uniformed police for security in a jungle resort where they had come for rest. They had desired that all the policemen be removed from security duties. As Principal Security Officer, Sri Dutt was worried as to how we could make security arrangements in that vast forest without the police? I told him not to worry. I collected policemen in batches and replaced their uniforms with civilian clothes resembling those of the forest employees. I gave them gardening implements and deployed them as gardeners and forest guards.

Those days Mrs. Indira Gandhi was the President of the All-India Congress Committee (AICC) and, according to the newspapers, she was engaged in securing the collapse of the communist government of Kerala headed by Sri E.M.S. Namboodiripad. The newspapers had further said that she was very imperious.

The Himachal Pradesh Lt. Governor Raja Bajrang Bahadur Singh of Bhadri and I were sitting in the verandah next morning when we noticed Sanjay and Rajiv trying to slither down a frayed fire escape rope, from the first floor to the verandah where we were sitting. Mrs. Indira Gandhi was sitting in the front lawn and reading a book. Suddenly, the fire escape rope snapped and the two children came hurtling down. We rushed towards them. I had to grab Sanjay to save his life and Raja Bajrang Bahadur did the same with Rajiv. Mrs. Indira Gandhi had also seen this incident and rushed towards us. She was relieved to see that none of her two sons was hurt. She reluctantly mumbled some thanks. This was the beginning of my association, merely a police officer, with one who was to become the Prime Minister of India in January 1966. This association lasted till she lived, and later with Sh. Rajiv Gandhi till his assassination in May, 1991. Through those turbulent days I stayed close to the Gandhi family. I still recall those days with pride. I had given the idea of a Special Protection Group (SPG). It got stiff opposition from many concerned quarters, which thought their authority would be undermined if such a force was set up. But I was at last successful in my efforts and was able to create it. This Group has helped in protecting our Prime Ministers against terrorist conspiracies and created a number of Institutions for the Police in the country on modern scientific lines such as the National Crime Records Bureau.

To resume the account, we have to revert to 1946 and 1947 - the days of the Partition of India.

M.A. Jinnah had told Dorothy Norman: "If I had not been a fanatic, there would never have been Pakistan." The Sikh separatists tried to follow Mr. Jinnah's credo in the 1980s.

So far as India is concerned, history is bound to ask those who were entrusted the task of leading the country before and after the achievement of Independence: "What actually did you do or failed to do to check the attack on the integrity of the country."? In the words of Otto Rene Cartillo:

They will be interrogated
by the simplest of our people
They will be asked what they did
When their nation died ...
What did you do when the poor suffered
When tenderness and life
Burned out in them .....

Pakistan was created among scenes of unprecedented butchery. So far as Punjab was concerned, it was almost a civil war - the Hindus and Sikhs knifing the jugular of Muslims and raping and abducting their daughters, mothers, and wives, in what is called East Punjab and Delhi, and the Muslims doing the same to Hindus and Sikhs in what is known as West Pakistan. After the creation of blood spattered Pakistan in 1947, it took Indian Punjab almost four decades to erupt like a volcano of fire and death, of course with the hostile and active abetment of Pakistan bent upon dismembering India, for another partition of the country on the basis of the Sikh religion.

Indira Gandhi's family has suffered deaths and losses. The second victim of the bloodiest violence, which Punjab has seen, have been the Sikhs and Hindus of Punjab and Sikhs at some places like Delhi and the Terai in Uttar Pradesh.

At every step the Sikhs felt pilloried by the Hindu vernacular press of Jallandhar. As if this was not enough, one of the Seven Stars in the Nirankari firmament took upon himself to teach a lesson to the Damdami Taksal of Chowk Mehta and Sikh devotees of Akhand Kirtani Jatha. The Seventh Star pounced upon these genuine Sikh Missionary Schools and heaped ridicule on them. The Nirankaris killed 13 of the Sikh evangelists of Damdami Taksal and Akhand Kirtani Jatha on the eventful Baisakhi day of 1978 to embarrass the Akali Ministry of Sardar Parkash Singh Badal and challenge the dormant martyrdom complex of the Sikhs so that devastation descended upon Punjab, Delhi and other parts of Northern India, disrupting traditional old Hindu-Sikh ties, inviting India's implacable foe Pakistan to shred India's unity.

India's integrity has been saved by the sacrifice of Mrs. Indira Gandhi, the Prime Minister of India, proclaiming to the world India's grim determination to protect its integrity even if the Prime Minister had to sacrifice her own life for it. The second defender of India's integrity was the Sikh peasantry who had ultimately come to realise that their "boys" were no more "martyrs" but had become criminals and smugglers and the so-called "crusaders" trained and equipped by the Pakistani ISI had turned upon Sikh honour and had started gang-raping Sikh womenfolk and taken to looting. Thus, the Sikh peasantry, which had provided shelter to these Pakistani trained marauders from 1983 to 1991, started co-operating with the Punjab police, which under the dynamic leadership of Shri K.P.S. Gill, had acquired a new elan. Under his command the Punjab Police was given betters arms. They were courageously led too by those who were in fields. It was this Sikh peasantry which has scuttled the Pakistani dream of using the Sikh sword for dismembering India.

Both the Sikhs and the Indira Gandhi family have been maligned. Facts, however, speak to the contrary. Truth shall prevail. The disclosures made in this book will show the truth.

Some friends who have gone through the script of this book have told me that it reads like a paen of Sikhism and the personality of Indira Gandhi. Let it be so, if the facts point to these conclusions. There should be no compromising of fact. I love Sikhism and I revere Indira Gandhi even now because of her compassion for the down-trodden.

Pakistan had never forgiven Indira Gandhi for her dismemberment of East Pakistan in January, 1971 and India's breakthrough in the field of nuclear technology by detonating a small nuclear device in Pokhran in 1974. Pakistan has not given up the phantasmagoria of crushing India, camouflaging their strategy by accusing India of not having reconciled herself to the existence of Pakistan. The fact is that India has accepted the reality of Pakistan but not the Two-Nation Theory. If every religious sect in India, is to be treated as a, nation, entitled to their own homeland, India would then be balkanised and offer the much sought opportunity to Pakistan to reconquer these slices of India being inhabited by 'kafirs'.

I am aware that as a retired Director General of Police, I have to maintain secrecy of sensitive issues and policies. However, it will be self-defeating to make secrecy a shibboleth; Admiral Stansfied Turner, who was Director of Central Intelligence Agency (CIA) during Jimmy Carter's presidency of U.S.A. faced a similar dilemma when he wrote about his work in CIA in his book *Secrecy and Democracy*.

But a retired public servant has to be fair. Accordingly, I have omitted names of leaders, and officers and kept back very sensitive information; yet the assassination of Shri Beant Singh, the former Chief Minister of Punjab on 31st August, 1995, amply shows that embers of hatred are still being stoked.

Like revolutions, extremism first starts in human minds. The Sikh mind has been seared by a deep sense of alienation against both the rampaging militants and oppressive Government machinery. The beautiful land of Punjab is enmeshed in a hundred strands of emotion, fear, mistrust and terror, so that only a multi-dimensional effort embracing competence and probity, political sagacity and the ambience of Punjabi culture can heal the outrage Punjab has suffered.

This book describes the personalities, who fashioned the era, and the policies which spelt disaster. It shows the admixture of religion and politics putting the verdant land of Punjab on fire. Should it not be read by every student of history?

– 2 –

Punjab—The Land and the People

In accordance with the accepted principle of redrawing state boundaries on a linguistic basis, the present state of Punjab was carved out of the erstwhile state of Punjab on November I, 1966.

Before 1947, Punjab, the land of the five rivers, extended from river Indus in the west to the outskirts of Delhi. As a result of Radcliffe Award, it was divided into two parts: the Western Punjab went to Pakistan and the Eastern Punjab to India. This partition of the state resulted in the migration of millions of refugees from Pakistan to India and vice-versa.

Patiala and East Punjab State Union comprising the erstwhile Princely States of CIS-Sutlej tract, were merged into Punjab on Nov. I, 1956. But again, the state of Punjab was reorganised in 1966, giving birth to the new state of Haryana with vast areas of Shimla and Kangra going to Himachal Pradesh.

The present century has witnessed the cataclysmic shrinkage in size of the once sprawling Punjab. In 1901, Punjab started from Peshawar and included old Delhi. The North Western Frontier Province (NWFP), Punjab (Pakistan), Union Territory of Delhi, Haryana and Himachal Pradesh, are the major states born out of Punjab in the three-quarters of the present century.

The state of Punjab lies roughly between 29° and 32° north latitude and 73° and 77° east longitude. The state is situated in the northwestern corner of the Indian Union and is surrounded by Jammu and Kashmir in the north, Himachal

Pradesh in the east, Haryana and Rajasthan in the south and Pakistan in the west.

Punjab has an area of 50,491 sq. kms, which is roughly 1.6% of the country's total area. Physiographically, Punjab can be divided into two regions, namely the sub-montane strip and the alluvial plains. The sub-montane tract is the narrow strip of territory stretching between the Himalayas and the Indo-Gangetic plains into which run the spurs of the Himalayas. The upper portions of the districts of Gurdaspur, Hoshiarpur and Ropar, lie in this sub-montane strip. The rest of the nine districts and the lower portion of the largest natural region of the state is plain. The desert belt of Rajasthan extends into the southern districts of Bhatinda, Faridkot and Ferozepore. The soil conditions in the State, therefore, naturally vary from tract to tract. There are 3 snow-fed rivers in the State: the Sutlej, the Beas, and the Ravi (which flow within Punjab over a limited distance), which are important sources of irrigation. These rivers are not navigable.

More than 95% of the total area is flat, plane, sloping gently from about 900 ft. ASL in the northeast to about 550 ft. in the southwest. Physiographically, it is divisible into 3 parts:

(a) The Shivalik Hills, in the North-East.

(b) Foothill zone, dissected by closely spaced seasonal torrents called Choes.

(c) The flat terrain with fertile alluvial soils. Traditionally speaking, the present area in the Punjab falls under 4 tracts, i.e., Majha, Bist Doab, Malwa and Bhattiana.

Majha

The present districts of Gurdaspur and Amritsar form a good chunk of Majha, the major part of which now lies in Pakistan. The word Majha in the local usage means "Middle One", i.e. Majhla or Majha. Starting from Jamuna in the east to the Indus in the west, the Sapta Sindh region comprised 7 Doabas. The Bari Doaba (the tract between Beas and Ravi rivers) formed the Central Doaba, hence the tract seems to have been given the name of Majha. Many of the inhabitants of this tract prefer to add the word "Mahail" to their initials.

Bist Doaba

The districts of Jallandhar, Kapurthala and Hoshiarpur lie between the Beas and Sutlej rivers. This compact and limited area is a homogeneous unit as far as the land, climate, economy, culture and dialect are concerned. Hence this Doaba is a true geographic unit, and for this reason, we very often refer to this area alone as the "DOABA" in our day-to-day dealings, whereas other inter-fluvial areas are only occasionally referred to as Doabas. Many inhabitants of Doaba take pride in calling themselves Doabias.

Malwa

The area lying south of the river Sutlej bounded by the Ghaggar stream in the East and sandy infertile tract in the South-West is known as Malwa. The districts of Ludhiana, Patiala, Sangrur, Faridkot and Ferozepore (except Abohar tract) fall in the Malwa region. According to historians, this fertile plain resembles in fertility the Malwa plain of Central India; hence it was given the name of Malwa. At present no inhabitants call themselves Malwa but it appears that the surname of Malhi probably is the corrupted form of Malwi.

Bhattiana

Bhattiana is the region lying in the south-west of Punjab that fell to the lot of India after partition. The area, extending from Fatehabad-Sirsa along the south-western parts of Bhatinda and Ferozepore, forms the part of ancient Bhattiana, most of which now lies in the Bagar tract of Rajasthan. The same Bhatti Rajputs who inhabited this area in the past and who fought many successful battles against the Muslim onslaught, and ultimately most of who fell prey to Muslim conversion, are the inhabitants of Bhattiana. This sandy tract is otherwise infertile and far away from any of the perennial streams, and the hard ways of life made the inhabiting people hardy and resistant, people who could resist the foreign invaders too.

History and Punjab's Geography

The history of India from the earliest recorded times is closely linked with the history of Punjab. Punjab was the area of the ancient battles chronicled in the *Mahabharata*. Grammarian Panini, Porus, Chandragupta Maurya and Harsha were born in this region. Punjab has always been the land of rishis, avatars, pirs, gurus, martyrs, generals and freedom fighters.

Between the second century BC and the middle of the sixth century AD came the Parthians, Scythians and Huns. Then came the Turks, Slaves, Khilji, Tughlaq, Sayyad and Lodhi dynasties till 1520 AD, when Babar, the first Mughal Emperor, laid the foundation of the empire, which held sway until the early 18th century. One of the principal driving forces of the "Arabs, Turks and Afghans" was religious zeal. This sometimes turned into religious persecution, which assumed gigantic proportions but was checked by the appearance of the Bhakti Movement, the chief exponent of which in Punjab was Guru Nanak, the founder of Sikhism.

Punjab was the northern land gateway to the Indo-Gangetic plains and, for many centuries, it had borne the brunt of the attacks of the invading hordes from the Asian heartlands. These experiences had a decisive influence on shaping the Punjabi character, making for self-reliance, initiative and constant vigilance against external danger. These also imbued the Punjabis with courage and patience to face and overcome adversity.

If there is one word, which can summarise the Punjabi character, it is "vitality". This vitality has enabled the Punjabis to overcome the barriers of geography, poor natural resources and deep emotional wounds inflicted by internecine conflicts.

Sikh Jats, who belong to the agriculturist class, form the bulk of population of the present Punjab.

They are sturdy, self-willed and industrious and are among the finest peasants and soldiers of India. "The Sikh Jat is generally tall and muscular, with well-shaped limbs, an erect carriage and strongly marked and sharp handsome features." Nothing can be said definitely about the origin of Jats.

The Khatris and Aroras are next in number. The Khatris who are generally energetic and educated, are mostly fair-complexioned and have good features. Trade is their main occupation. They claim to be in the direct line of Kshatriyas of the Aryan race. The Aroras also claim to be of Khatri origin. Sir George Campbell maintains that both these castes belong to the same ethnic stock. Next to them in numbers are the Brahmins and Vaishyas, who are split up into several sub-castes and are found almost all over the Punjab.

Among the minor agricultural tribes, Sainis and Kambohs are the most prominent ones. They are admirable cultivators, skillful and industrious. The Sainis claim their origin from the Rajputs and some of the Kambohs from "Kamboj Desh" in Afghanistan. According to legends, the latter came into India in the *Mahabharata* period to take part in the Great War on the side of Kauravas and then settled down in India.

The landless agricultural labour in Punjab consists mostly of Mazhabi Sikhs and Rai Sikhs. Rai Sikhs are mainly the residents of the border tract of Ferozepore district.

Language and Dialects

Punjabi, like the people of Punjab, is a forceful language with a sturdy idiom. Though the Punjab today is comparatively small, Punjabi as a language is spoken over a large area including West Pakistan. Punjabi, which is the main language of the Punjab, has got many dialects. Over the ages, various tracts in Punjab remained isolated for a long time because of geographical barriers and lack of communication and each dialect developed in isolation.

The Punjab was the place in India where Aryans first came and settled and it was on the banks of the rivers of the Punjab that they composed their most ancient literature.

The language of the *Rig Veda* is known as the Vedic language and this, in a way, may be regarded as the oldest form of Punjabi.

Punjabi, as we know it, emerged from a corrupt form of Sanskrit (Apabhransha) in the 11th century AD. From then onwards Punjabi literature in the form of folk songs, tales, proverbs, and riddles began to take shape. It attained maturity in the 12th century in the time of Farid Shakarganj. Baba Farid's shlokas are available in the *Adi Granth* and his language and idiom are very much similar to the modern Punjabi language.

Dialects

The Punjabi language has many dialects for which there are obvious reasons. Political influence went a long way to determine the development of dialects. Political boundaries of the Punjab kept changing from time to time. Consequently, the different tracts of the Punjab came under various influences at different times and absorbed the changes brought on by those influences.

Pre-Historical Period

A cursory reading of ancient Indian history rightly convinces the reader that the history of our nation is closely bound to the history of Punjab. Traditionally, Mata Kaushalya, mother of Lord Rama, was born at Ghuram, about 24 kms from Patiala. Punjab was the arena of the ancient battle chronicled in the *Mahabharata*.

Mohenjodaro-Harappa

In very ancient times, Punjab constituted a part of the vast Indo-Iranian region. The Hindukush mountains and the northwestern ranges formed the boundary between the Indian and Iranian territories. From times immemorial, people from both sides had been inter-mixing. This resulted in a vital fellowship of people and cultures. According to archaeologists, historians, geologists and other scholars, "The earliest traces of human habitation in India were found in Punjab from 5 to 6 lakh years ago in the Soan Valley, between the Indus and the Jhelum rivers ... The excavation at Harappa and Mohenjodaro in the year 1924 unearthed buildings, sculptures, seals, ornaments and pottery, which throw a new light on the history of Punjab. The archaeologists are of the opinion that most probably in the third millennium before Christ, a very advanced and urban civilisation existed in this part of India. Thus, India is recognised, alongwith Persia, Mesopotamia and Egypt as one of the most important areas where the civilising processes were initiated and developed." (Sir John Marshall)

The unearthing at Mohenjodaro (Mound of the Dead) and Harappa are mere symbols of the ancient Indus Valley civilisation. There is no doubt about the fact that the Indus Valley civilisation ranks in antiquity with the old civilisations that flourished in the fertile valleys of the Tigris, the Euphrates and the Nile. This means that the civilisation flourishing in the fertile valleys of Indus and its tributaries also witnessed the growth of ancient civilisations of Assyria, Babylonia and Egypt. The art of building excellent urban centres was known to the people of the Indus Valley civilisation. Those people led a highly developed cultural life. People possessed a sound know-how concerning textiles, both cotton as well as woollen, jewellery, pottery, gold smithy, iron-smithy, carpentry, masonary, etc. The sculptors of that age produced the best specimens of art on stone. Trade, internal as well as external, had reached the pinnacle of glory. Besides, a religion of very high order prevailed in this part of India.

Punjab Under the Aryans

After about 1000 years following the disappearance of the Indus Valley civilisation, the Aryans migrated to Punjab. We find a mention in *Rig Veda* that two Aryan tribes, namely Yadu and Turvasa were brought by Lord Indra from a distant land. "It is probable that the Aryans came from Asia Minor and adjoining areas and the Punjab was their earliest home in India. Their conquest of the Indus Valley and penetration into the basin of the Ganges belong to pre-history. The evidence of their first settlements in this country is to be found in the Vedas and the great epics."

Punjab was inhabited by aborigines who were mostly nomadic and lived off the land. They were dark-skinned and lived in a classless society. The Aryans had to resort to arms against the aborigines to maintain their conquest and to expand their realms towards southeast. Once the Aryans succeeded in crossing the Sutlej, they felt secure. Thus, they settled down in Malwa of the Punjab to lead a free and comfortable life. After having settled in this part, the Aryans established their hold over the entire territory of the Punjab. The scholarly class among the Aryans engaged itself in philosophical and literary pursuits. Their endeavours led to the foundations of the Sanskrit literature. Punjab became a great seat of learning. In the well-known university of Takshshila (Taxila), different disciplines of learning were pursued. This university attracted scholars not only from northern India but also from Afghanistan and China.

King Cyrus by this time had established a mighty Persian Empire on the ruins of Assyria. King Darius (B.C. 521-485) extended the horizon of Persian Empire to Punjab. He annexed the areas of Peshawar and Rawalpindi. These areas came to be known as Gandhara and formed a significant part of the Persian Empire. The river Indus divided this territory into two parts. The kingdom of Pushakalavati (in the present district of Peshawar), was a trans-Indus realm. Traditionally speaking, the great epic of the *Mahabharata* was first recited in the capital of Taxila.

Invasion of Alexander (327 BC)

In the year B.C. 326, Alexander, the great Macedonian emperor, invaded this part of India. The country, east of the Indus was ruled by three sovereigns. The Kingdom of Taxila lay between the Indus and the Hydaspes (Jhelum), and that of Porus extended from Jhelum to Accsines (Chenab), the dominions of Abesares lay among the mountains. With the sole exception of Ambhi, all other rulers put up a stout and stubborn resistance to the Greek invader. Porus decided to fight and brought an army of 30,000 foot soldiers, 7,000 horses, 300 armed chariots and 200 war elephants. Alexander crossed the Jhelum nearly 30 miles southwest of the town of Jhelum and defeated Porus after a hard battle. The 7'6" tall Porus, though defeated, was not disgraced.

Alexander succeeded in pushing his way to the Beas. In his dream of annexing the entire world, he wished to press forward to the Gangetic Valley. However, his war-weary troops resisted any such move. After erecting twelve towers marking the limit of his march, he withdrew to Babylonia, where he met his end in the year B.C. 323. The heroic fight given by Porus of Punjab, was not in vain. It put caution and fear into the minds of Greek soldiers who decided to call it a day.

A glimpse of the history of the Punjab is relevant for our study.

Punjab Under Islam (977 AD): The Crescent Rises

By the eight century AD, Islam had emerged as a new addition to the world community of religions. The seedling of this new sect sprouted in Arabia and it was nurtured in the same soil for about a couple of centuries. Thereafter the Arabian hordes started pushing in all directions with the aim of spreading Islam and occupying new lands. "The sword," said Muhammad, "is the key to paradise and hell. Whoever fell in battle is forgiven his sins. He who perished in a holy war went straight to heaven. There, the gallant martyrs live forever a life of happiness and bliss, free from all sorrows and liable to no inconvenience from excess... " Such liberal promises were enough to kindle the frenzy of the desert populace of Arabia.

Mahmud Ghaznavi (1001 AD to 1030 AD)

The advent of eleventh century AD witnessed a new wave of foreign invasions on our country through the Punjab across its western passes. With the initiation of Mohammadan inroads from the northwest under the noted iconoclast Mahmud Ghaznavi, rulers of Kabul and Sind were slowly and gradually supplanted and the way was paved for the foundation of the Muslim regime in the Punjab. Ghaznavi returned to this land of world famous riches over and over again through the fertile plains of the Punjab. In all, he made 17 attempts including those on Multan, Kangra, Thanesar,

Kannauj, Gwalior and the celebrated shrine of Somnath. Wherever he went, his path lay through the Punjab and this part of the country was laid waste by the hordes of plunderers. The Hindu Kingdom of Shahiya, which ruled the Punjab at that time, was completely extinguished and the entire territory trembled with the horror and terror Ghaznavi had spread. It was only his death in 1030 AD which put a stop to his barbaric acts, but the demoralisation and havoc wrought by him still lingered on. During a brief period ranging from the year of Ghazanavi's death to 1075 AD, the devastated land of the Punjab tried to recuperate but destiny had a far bigger upheaval in store for it.

Mohammad Ghauri (1176 AD to 1205 AD)

Another Muslim invader, Shahab-ud-din Mohammed Ghauri captured Multan in 1075 AD. He erected a strategic fortress at Sialkot. The successors of Mohammad Ghauri founded the Sultanate of Delhi which held sway in the Punjab for several hundred years.

Tamerlane (1398 AD)

Punjab and Delhi faced another fateful event in the invasion of Amir Timur, popularly known as Tamerlane (Timur the Lame) in 1398 AD. This terrible military leader came down upon the north-western India from Samarkand. In no time he reached Delhi and wielded his sword ruthlessly. It is said that the word 'mercy' did not exist in his dictionary and he spared none. Wherever he went he looted, plundered and pillaged the territory brutally and ordered wholesale massacre of the local populace. After getting the desired amount of booty, he started his march back home through the Punjab. Again, on his way back, he devastated whatever lay in his way. Having no desire himself to stay permanently in India, he left behind very powerful governors.

This history of India from Timur's death to Babur's advent is the story of struggle for supremacy among various Muslim rulers. This struggle for succession also hastened the downfall and decay of Delhi Sultanate.

Mughals (1526-1857)

Babur was a Chogutai Turk and was associated with two cruel and barbaric military leaders by blood. His father was a descendant of Timur while his mother was connected with Changez Khan. Babur marched from Kabul and occupied the Punjab in 1526. Thereafter he met the forces of Ibrahim Lodhi, the last ruler of Lodhi dynasty, at Panipat. Here, in a historic battle, Babur defeated the troops of Ibrahim Lodhi and thus made way for the establishment of Mughal rule in India. By the time he laid down his life to save the life of his ailing son Humayun, Babur had practically occupied the whole of northern India. After him, the Mughal dynasty had the great architects of the Mughal empire, in Humayun, then Akbar, Jahangir, Shahjahan and Aurangzeb. With the exception of Humayun, who had to tumble throughout his life, the other Mughals brought the outlying areas of the Indian peninsula within their suzerainty. The whole of the Punjab remained a full-fledged province of the Mughal empire and its people acquired a new culture, the Indo-Mughal culture.

Decay of Mughal Empire

History, like everything, has its own periods of growth and decline. Though the Great Mughals worked assiduously to maintain the glory untarnished, after Aurangzeb the Mughal dynasty did not produce able and painstaking rulers. Because of its famed riches, India continued to attract avaricious marauders.

Nadir Shah (1739 AD)

Mughal empire once again afforded an opportunity to such invaders, who were moved by the lust for the fabled wealth of India. This time the invaders came from Persia and not Central Asia. Nadir Shah marched towards India in the year 1738. He did not meet any resistance en route to Delhi. Like a whirlwind, Nadir Shah overran the Mughals on the historic battlefield of Panipat. Nadir Shah dealt a very severe, shocking and humiliating blow to the pleasure-loving Mughal Emperor Mohammad Shah in 1739. The ruthless aggressor, who was crowned with success, carried back a large booty including the crown pearls, the world famous Kohinoor Jewel and the Peacock Throne. The death blow dealt by Nadir Shah left the decadent Mughal empire prostrate.

Ahmed Shah Abdali (1747 AD)

Ahmed Shah Abdali, an officer in Nadir Shah's army, had accompanied him in his campaign against India. He had minutely seen the inherent weaknesses of the Mughal empire. After the assassination of Nadir Shah in 1747, Ahmed Shah Abdali became an independent ruler of Afghanistan. He very proudly called himself Darri-i-Durran, i.e. the pearl of the age, and, his clan came to be known as Durrani. This barbaric predator attacked India four times between 1748 and 1751 and inflicted very grievous injuries on the Punjab which was also incorporated in the Durrani empire.

Punjab had seen many a bloodbath, but partition in 1947 rocked it with human blood, and the period from 1983 to 1992 saw the spectre of terrorism hitting the Punjab. In the name of religion, pacifists turned fanatics and human life became one of the cheapest commodities.

Partition of Punjab (India) - 1947

Before partition of India, Punjab had five commissionaires and 29 districts as follows:-

1. Ambala Division

   Districts

   1. Ambala.
   2. Karnal.
   3. Rohtak.
   4. Hissar.
   5. Gurgaon.
   6. Simla.

2. Jallandhar Division

   Districts

   7. Kangra.

8. Hoshiarpur.
9. Jallandhar.
10. Ludhiana.
11. Ferozepore.

3. Lahore Division
Districts
12. Gujranwala.
13. Sheikhupura.
14. Sialkot.
15. Gurdaspur.
16. Lahore.
17. Amritsar.

4. Rawalpindi Division
Districts
18. Gujrat.
19. Jhelum.
20. Rawalpindi.
21. Attuck.
22. Mianwali.
23. Shahpur.

5. Multan Division
Districts
24. Montgomery.
25. Lyallpur.
26. Jhang.
27. Multan.
28. Mujjaffargarh.
29. Dera Gazi Khan.

On partition in 1947, the entire Rawalpindi and Multan divisions went to Pakistan and also Gujranwala, Sheikhupura, Sialkot and Lahore districts of Lahore Division. The Shakargarh tehsil of Gurdaspur district also went to Pakistan and now forms a tehsil of Sialkot district. Some parts of Lahore district such as Patti, Khemkaran and Khalra came to India and form part of Amritsar district. Similarly some parts of Ferozepore district went to Pakistan.

International Boundary

The international boundary between India and Pakistan in the Punjab needs to be explained due to its irregular pattern with enclaves on both sides. The international boundary is closely related to the Punjab river system. The Indus basin consists of Indus, Jhelum, Chenab, Ravi, Beas and Sutlej rivers. The three Western rivers, i.e. Indus, Chenab, Ravi carry more than 80% of total water discharge of the Indus basin. The Punjab Boundary Commission, presided over by Sir Cyril Radcliffe, was instructed "to demarcate the boundaries of the two parts of the Punjab on the basis of ascertaining the contiguous majority areas of the Muslims and the non-Muslims. In doing so, it will also take into account other factors."

Out of 29 districts of united Punjab, 14 districts were named disputed districts including Gurdaspur and Ferozepur - where rivers Ravi and Sutlej flowed. Gurdaspur district had four tehsils - Batala, Shakargarh, Gurdaspur and Pathankot. Shakargarh Tehsil was across the river Ravi and was allotted to West Punjab (Pakistan). Sir Radcliffe awarded: "The boundary line in Gurdaspur District shall follow the line of that river down the western boundary of the Pathankot tehsil to the point where Pathankot, Shakargarh and Gurdaspur tehsils meet. The tehsil boundary and not the actual course of the river, shall constitute the boundary between East and West Punjab. Similarly in Ferozepur. ... The district boundaries and not the actual course of the Sutlej river shall in each case constitute the boundary between the East and West Punjab."

The river line was not enough to determine the boundary. Location of head works aggravated the problem of border delineation. From Hussainiwala head works, the Depalpur Canal took off into Pakistan. The anomalies of the Radcliffe Award constitute a baffling complexity and Pakistan has been alleging that the Award was changed at the last minute according to the wishes of Lord Mountbatten, the first Governor-General of India.

– 3 –

Among the Bigots and the British Policy Regarding Unity of India

India is a sub-continent and has diverse religions and multi-lingual and multi-ethnic groups. Indian pluralist society has been rigidly segmented, stratified and is caste-ridden.

But for the Mauryas, the Mughals and the British, there has hardly been a semblance of central authority. However there were common strands, which linked various cultures and areas such as the use of Sanskrit, both in the North and in the South, and the various sects of Buddhists, Jains, Vaishnavas, Muslims and Sikhs spread throughout the length and breadth of the country. That is how India's unity lies in diversity.

India's national unity, as one sees it today, is the aftermath of British rule, which made its central authority felt through the network of railways, common laws, All India Services and, above all, education through the English medium. English language by itself has been a unifying factor. Now the urbanisation, mass media and the process of modernisation have welded its various parts into the whole.

The credit for obliteration of divisiveness goes to Pt. Jawaharlal Nehru who gave the country the credo of unity in diversity. However Pt. Jawaharlal Nehru in his anxiety to unify the country has saddled us with a highly centralised system of governance, denying autonomy to various regional States; this has caused rebel movements in the North such as Kashmir, in the West such as Punjab, and insurgency movements in Nagaland, in Mizoram and Assam in the East. Unless India becomes a truly federal polity and grants autonomy to the federating regional and ethic sub-nationalisms the present concentration of power will continue in New Delhi, straining the fabric of Indian polity.

Pandit Nehru was aided in his task by such scholars as Humayun Kabir, K.M. Pannikar and others who brought out the shared strands of our national heritage. The hydra-headed monster of separatism based on religion and language has, however, not been vanquished completely. Rajni Kothari has rightly stressed that "the pre-existing pluralities have been integrated through political process based on its consensus respecting rival claims, respecting claims on the basis of electoral and competitive criteria, and structuring the diversity of Indian society into a network of linkage."[1]

It has been argued that the concept of nation-state is a European invention and it could not be applied to India. Ronald Indene maintains that democracy and nation-states are human constructs. The historian and Indologist Vincent Smith (1848-1920), a member of Indian Civil Service, has argued that India had some semblance of unity (or a state nation) only under such benevolent despots as Chandragupta.

Says Smith: "In political institutions no evolution took place. No sovereign arose endowed with commanding abilities and capable of welding together the jarring members of the body politic, and Chandragupta Maurya, Ashoka and in a lesser degree the Gupta kings and Harsha of Kanauj had done ..... Even the heavy pressure of Muslim invasions failed to produce effective cohesion of the numberless Hindu states which one by one fell an easy prey to fierce hordes of Arabs, Turks, etc." Indene maintains that I.C.S. scholars were imposing new fangled concepts on an old Hindu civilisation.

The author has worked in northwest and northeast India, that is, in Punjab, Haryana, Himachal Pradesh, J & K and on the borders of Rajasthan, Gujarat, Bengal and Assam, etc., and has felt harrowed by the virulence of communal frenzy and violence.

—

The author has also seen that violence is the norm during all agitations. It appears that the rigorous ideal of non-violence, which Mahatma Gandhi gave us, has not sunk into our psyche. Then, was the non-violent phase of our freedom struggle a transient and ephemeral phenomenon bordering on a passing aberration?

I was in charge of Ambala District from 1962 to mid-1966 when its boundaries extended to Jagadhari and Yamunanagar at one hand and Ludhiana, Ropar, Nalagarh, Kalka on the other. Chandigarh, the capital of Punjab Govt., was part of this district and its problems were taken care of by a Dy. S.P. only.

In Ambala City in the grain market, there is a Gurudwara and a rectangular open space. During Dussehra, Hindus led by the Jan Sangh, insisted on celebrating their festival outside in the rectangular space and the Sikhs led by Jathedar Kartar Singh Takkar insisted on Akhand Path of *Sri Guru Granth Sahib* in the same open space. Jathedar Kartar Singh was a man of fiery temper whereas Jan Sangh had a few hotheads; both the communities seemed bent upon confrontation. Sardar Partap Singh Kairon was the Chief Minister of Punjab at that time and he sent strict instructions to us (Shri S.S. Bedi, my colleague, was District Magistrate) to stop this mad clash under all circumstances. So I devised an indirect strategy: we engaged the parties in parleys and occupied the vacant ground by pitching police tents throughout the open space. We repeated this strategy every year to frustrate their violent designs. Thus, an insensate Hindu-Sikh confrontation was avoided.

Disturbances were caused by R.S.S/Jan Sangh on the announcement in June 1966 of bifurcation of Punjab to form Haryana and the Punjab that now exists. I and the District Magistrate Shri M.S. Gill (who later became the Chief Election Commissioner of India) got the information that hoodlums were indulging in widespread vandalism in breaking street lights and attacking post offices in Ambala Cantonment. With a small posse of police, we reached the spot and the hooligan teenagers tried to escape into lanes. We were able to arrest a very large number of these lumpens and take them to court.

Such ugly manifestations of communalism after decades of our attainment of freedom were a crying shame.

Since I had served in Himachal Pradesh on deputation for four years, and had felt bewitched by the swaying pines, shimmering snows and meandering rivulets, I had submitted to the Govt. in early 1966 that I may be allotted to the cadre of Himachal Pradesh, when Punjab is re-organised. I was told that my request had been accepted. Yet, suddenly, I was transfered to Amritsar as Senior Superintendent of Police in July 1966. Though it was a coveted posting, yet the situation was grim as it was surcharged with communal tension. There were differences as to what should be the boundaries of the new state of Punjab and common links with Haryana. The new state of Punjab came into existence on 1st November, 1966. Sant Fateh Singh announced that he would go on a fast on 17th December, 1966, and thereafter self-immolate himself on 27th December, 1966. Six of his colleagues - Sant Channan Singh, Senior Vice President of Shiromani Akali Dal and President SGPC, Jathedar Jiwan Singh Umranangal, Jagdev Singh Talwandi, Jagir Singh Phaguwalia, Dalip Singh Talwandi, Jathedar Hari Singh Gill - expressed similar resolves. Huge *kunds* (burning furnaces) were built on Akal Takht in pursuance to this ultimatum for inclusion of Chandigarh and Bhakra works in the Punjab.

Deliverance of this ultimatum created panic and consternation in Amritsar city and the countryside. It was feared that if the ultimatum was carried through, there will be widespread disturbances and loss of lives and property. The government was at its wits' end as usual. I prepared a planned programme of police action. As soon as we started implementing it, confidence was restored among the populace. The presence of police pickets and patrols was a deterrence in itself. Unfortunately, the District Magistrate, Shri S.S. Bedi, developed heart ailment and had to relinquish his charge. However, his successor, Sardar Kulwant Singh Ahluwalia, too, was a man of great courage and cool patience. He proved a great pillar of strength to us. I was aware that despite our massive police arrangements meticulously made, violence was unavoidable if Sant Fateh Singh and his other colleagues, self immolated themselves in the presence of large crowds. Therefore, I devised a two-way strategy: first to induce the Govt. to start negotiations and second to deny crowds to the would-be martyrs. Sardar Gian Singh Kahlon, ICS, one of our finest officers, was our Chief Secretary. (His two daughters are married to Raja Amrinder Singh of Patiala and Shri S.S. Mann respectively.) When he visited Amritsar, I prevailed upon him to persuade the Govt. to open negotiations. Again when the Chief Minister, Giani Gurmukh Singh, visited Amritsar, I could convince him, too, to prevail upon the Govt. of India to start some dialogue. Political problems can be solved only by dialogue: bayonets are no substitutes for human ingenuity and communication skills.

Sant Fateh Singh started his fast on 17th December, 1966. There was no immediate danger to his health though his obesity was a cause of anxiety. He was medically examined and bulletins on the state of his health were ritually issued every morning and evening. As days passed, tension started building up and the man in the street grew apprehensive. I enlarged the police dragnet: this resulted in fire spitting speeches from the pulpit of Akal Takht. I was made the recipient of invective. But my plans kept away the innocent people from being embroiled in communal mischief.

As a part of the overall strategy we had kept the Army in the picture about the situation. General Tuli, G.O.C. 15 Div. took me aside and told me not to involve the Army in a situation of such communal frenzy, because when religious feelings run so high, discipline could snap even in disciplined forces. I wish similar sagacity had been shown by Army top brass in 1984 when they planned Operation Blue Star and Rosewood: the magnificient record of Indian Army would not have been blotted by the ignominy of mutiny by Sikh troops.

As a part of our second leg of strategy, we started checking trains and buses and discouraged people to come to Amritsar, though Akalis were propagating from the sanctuary of Gurudwaras in villages, for people to arrive at the Golden

Temple in large numbers. Ultimately, 26th December, 1966 dawned full of forebodings. At 10 a.m. that day, we clamped a very rigorous curfew in the walled city. Those who have visited Amritsar and know its topography would know that entrance to the walled city is through various gates such as Sheranwala gate, etc. We heavily barricaded all these gates. Then we prevailed upon Railways to suspend all trains arriving into Amritsar. Similarly all bus traffic was allowed till Jandiala Guru on G.T. Road and up to the Kathu Nangal only on Batala Amritsar road. We stopped plying of all other buses, trucks and taxis towards Amritsar. As a result of these measures, the leaders inside the Golden Temple found that they had no followers to witness their martyrdom. Master Tara Singh, who had a large following in Amritsar, was put under preventive detention and we had to arrest Justice Gurnam Singh, the future Chief Minister of Punjab. 27th December, 1966 was the day of self-immolation.

It was a gloomy day with wintry clouds roaming the skies. While life in Civil Lines and other outskirts of Amritsar remained normal with its hurly-burly trading and traffic, the walled city wore a ghostly look. Not a leaf stirred, not a man moved except the police and members of the Peace Committee, which had prominent citizens, such as late G.R. Sethi, veteran journalist, late Shri Durga Dass Bhatia, brother of Shri R.L. Bhatia, Minister of State, and some others. Sant Fateh Singh was to immolate himself at 5.30 p.m. About 2.30 p.m., we got a call from New Delhi that Sardar Hukam Singh and others were flying into Amritsar and we should have them escorted to Golden Temple. As a result of parleys between Santji, his advisors and Sardar Hukam Singh, Sant Fateh Singh broke his fast and gave up the idea of self-immolation. A communal holocaust had been averted. I immediately lifted the curfew to the relief of people who had thronged the city bazars. Inside the Golden Temple, protagonists and antagonists of opening the fast had a fracas.

From Amritsar I went to Srinagar as Deputy Inspector General, Border Security Force in March, 1967. I was happy that I would be performing duties not involving disgraceful communal violence. But my hope was belied soon. A girl named Parameshwari Handoo, who was working as a clerk in the office of Cooperative Society, Residency Road, Srinagar, married one Ghulam Rasool Kanth, an Accountant in the same office. Kashmiri Pandits alleged that this was not a marriage and the girl had been inveigled and coerced into relationship with Ghulam Rasool Kanth. Srinagar erupted into violence like a volcano. The communal violence resulted in arson, loot and acts of wanton destruction. The police could not cope with the situation. Shri D.P. Dhar was the Home Minister of J&K. He invoked the aid of Border Security Force to restore peace. I along with some other officers strove day and night to save lives and property. We fanned into all the alleys along Jhelum from Amira Kadal down Habba Kadal, Fateh Kadal, Zaina Kadal, Ali Kadal, Khanyar, Rainawari and Jawahar Nagar. We witnessed scenes of utter brutality but our presence restored peace soon. Then we formed peace committees so that the two communities could live fraternally with confidence in each other as they had generally done so earlier. But my confidence that the Kashmiri Muslim was a nationalist was shattered: the stories of Kashmiri Muslims being secular had been deliberately created and nurtured. Secularism was dead and crass communalism combined with anti-India feelings stalked this valley of ineffable beauty.

It is an irony of fate that though India owes its unity as on today to the British rulers, it also owes its Partition in 1947 as well to the policies followed by the British. The English, who came to India through treacherous trade treaties and their notorious ruses of divesting Indian rulers from adopting their heir, have left the legacy: unity of India as well as its monstrous Partition in 1947 into two nations.

Having taken note of the fact that the British made a singular contribution to the unity of India, we have to examine their role which led to the partition of the country.

According to the British, the Muslim Rulers had treated Hindus with contempt and behaved towards them cruelly as conquerors do towards their defeated subjects.

Irfan M. Habib describs Pakistani view of Medieval India relying on *A History of the Freedom Movement Vol-I,* 1957, (A semi-official publication of the Pakistan Government):

"The interpretation of medieval Indian history presented by the imperialistic school of the British historians led inevitably to the formation of two schools of Indian historians; the Muslim and the Hindu communal school.."

Irfan Habib held the view that Shibli, among the Muslims, and Tilak among the Hindu, were the precursors of these two schools of historians.

With the invasions of India by Arabs, a permanent division of the people into two camps, that is, Hindus and Muslims ever in conflict with each other, grew.

In *The Punjab Past and Present* edited by Dr. Ganda Singh and published by the Publication Bureau, Punjabi University Patiala, Irfan M. Habib writes (page 11):

"It will admittedly be too simple to regard this separatist view as entirely of modern growth. In medieval times, there were a large number of chroniclers and other writers who justified every act of aggrandisement or misdeed on the part of the ruling class, in the name of religion. It is true that there were also others, men like Amir Khusrau and Abu-I-Fazl, who were swayed with a different sentiment. Their work was great and enduring; but lesser men, like Barani and Badauni, have readily been seized by whole schools of modern historians.

Among these we have, first, the line of imperialistic British historians. They turned to the history of India preceding the British conquest with the avowed purpose of showing that all governments previous to the British had been despotic, intolerant and monstrously cruel, and that the Indian people, ever divided, were fit only to be conquered and should be grateful that their last conquerors were so just and merciful. This attitude lent itself to a peculiar interpretation to medieval Indian history. It was assumed that the 'Muhammadans' were the conquerors and rulers of India in the same sense as the British had been (V.A. Smith, *Oxford*

History of India, 1918, p. 259). But, unlike the British, during and after their conquest, the Muslims (lacking the Christian quality of mercy) frightfully ill-treated the subjugated Hindus."

Of the opposite interpretation there is a longer, but less complete (since the series is continuing) statement in the editorial portions of *The History and Culture of the Indian People*, Bharatiya Vidya Bhawan, Vol. V, 1957, but specially Vol. VI 1960, prepared under the general supervision of Shri K.M. Munshi and edited by Prof. R.C. Majumdar.

Prof. R.C. Majumdar dismisses as absurd the notion that "the Hindus were not at all a subiect race during Muslim rule".

It is evident that researchers and scholars, both in India and Pakistan, considered there was no common ground between Muslims and Hindus, the latter being conquered subjects of the Muslims.

Similarly, the Mughal Empire is regarded as Islamic and Hindus as subjects. Dr. Qureshi holds that the entire political history of the Mughal Empire was a struggle between Islamic orthodoxy and heterodoxy for the mastery of the Empire, which culminated in Aurangzeb who represented the victory of Islamic orthodoxy. This is similar to the Hindu writers' view that the Sultanate period was the period of foreign domination whereas in the Mughal age the struggle was between Hindu nationalism and the reactionaries to restore Islamic supremacy.

Ifran M. Habib assails the concept that Muslims formed one brotherhood and shared the conquests and treated Hindus as subjugated citizens.

The divisions between Hindus and Muslims come from antiquity. When, early in the eighteenth century, the Mughal empire broke up, there was a stampede by the provincial Governors to seize power in their areas. The battle of Plassey, and the grant of Dewany of Bengal by Shah Alam to the East India Company made the British the arbiter of differences between the Hindus and Muslims, which sometimes accentuated antagonism into hostilities.

Thus, communalism has come to us from old times. Modern times and technologies postulate that the different religions and cultures form one mosaic of different colours and beliefs. Irrespective of religious differences, all communities constitute one composite human race and there is no room for religious intolerance in the present age of weapons of mass destruction.

References

1. *Politics in India* by Rajni Kothari, p. 421.
2. *Imagining India* by Ronald Inden, published by Basil Blackwell, p. 8.

– 4 –

The Sikh Religion

Nanak naam chardi kala
Tere bhane sarbat ka bhala

Sikhism, the religion professed by 16 million Indians, living mainly in the Punjab, was founded by Nanak (1496-c. 1539). Its basis is the Unity of God and the equality of all human beings; Sikhism is strongly opposed to caste divisions. Guru Gobind Singh (1666-1708) instituted the Khanda-di-Pahul, the Baptism of the Sword, and established the *Khalsa* ('the pure'), the company of the faithful. The Khalsa wear the five Ks: *kes,* long hair; *kangha,* a comb; *kirpan,* a sword; *kachha,* short trousers; and *kara,* a steel bracelet. Sikh men take the last name 'Singh; ('lion'), and women 'Kaur' (princess'). Sikhs believe in a single God, who is the immortal creator of the universe, and who has never been incarnate in any form. Human beings can make themselves ready to find God by prayer and meditation, but can only achieve closeness to God as a result of God's nadar or grace. Sikhs believe in reincarnation, and that the ten human gurus were teachers through whom the spirit of Guru Nanak was passed on, and lives today in the *Guru Granth Sahib* (holy book) and the Khalsa. Sikhs avoid the use of all non-medicinal drugs, and in particular tobacco.

Sikhism is the youngest of all religions. It was founded by Guru Nanak Devji (1469-1539 AD). He was born on April 15, 1469 in the Bedi Section of Khatri caste. His birthplace is the small town of Talwandi in Pakistan, 30 miles southwest of Lahore. It is a place of pilgrimage of Sikhs, thousands of whom visit it every year. It has been renamed as Nankana Sahib after the name of Guru Nanak Dev. He was the son of Mehta Kalu, a patwari and his mother Tripta was an extermely religious woman.

At that time Punjab was part of Delhi Sultanate ruled by Sikander Lodhi. The country was ruled by tyrannical rulers of whom Guru Nanak wrote "Kings are tigers and their officials dogs". In *Var Majh,* he wrote," "Kings are butchers. Justice has taken wings and fled in this dark night of falsity."

Guru Nanak visited the holy places of Hindus and Muslims that is, Hardwar, Puri, Rameshwaram, Kanya Kumari and then Mecca and Baghdad.

In 1497, Guru Nanak attained to union with God while he was bathing in the Bein stream near the town of Sultanpur Lodhi in Kapurthala district.

Guru Nanak Dev preached union with God, the only one, through love of his creatures and chanting (Japa) of the Divine Name. He campaigned against inequalities, superstitions and gave humanity a legacy of love and compassion.

According to Teja Singh, the concept of Sangat in Sikhism was left by Guru Nanak Dev. Unlike other medieval saints, Guru Nanak never spurned the world. He believed that the world has to be accepted on its own terms. He was married and had two sons. He believed it to be wrong to turn one's back on the world. He referred to the world as a *dharamshala,* or abode of righteousness, to which God sent individuals not for their past sins but in His glory. He encouraged full participation in life activities. Bhai Gurdass hailed the preachings of Guru Nanak Dev in this benighted period as follows:

"Guru Nanak has appeared.

Lo! mist hath vanished and light hath shown in the world." K.S. Duggal writes:

"Guru Nanak erected a bridge between two great cultures, religions and traditions. He changed the society by his sayings, which are found in Granth Sahib, one of the finest and the simplest Bible in the world."

Guru Nanak said. "There is no Hindu, there is no Muslim."

This was Guru's method of denouncing hypocrisy and hollow ritualism. Indeed, he wanted Hindus to be genuine Hindus and Muslims to be devout Muslims. Guru Nanak is held in great esteem by both Hindus and Muslims who speak of him with reverence. The Muslims treated him as Waliallah—a beloved of God, and Hindus felt elevated in baptising one child of their family as a Sikh.

Guru Nanak called himself "Nanak, the lowliest, Nanak, the humble."

Nanak said:

"Among the low, let my caste be the lowest of the lowly." He rejected both Sanskrit and Persian and preached generally in the dialect of the people.

He denounced cruelty as much as the crimes perpetrated in the name of caste.

Of Babar's invasion, the Guru complained to God:

"Though Khurasan has been shielded by thee

Though terror has struck the people of Hindustan. Though, O Creator of all takes to thyself no blame. Thou has sent Yama in the guise of great Mughal, Babar.

Terrible was the slaughter.

The lamenters cried loudly,

Did this not awaken pity in thee, O Lord.

Thou art part of all things equally, O Creator:

Thou must feel for all men and all nations."

Rag Asa

He was the despair of the Hindu priests as well as the Muslim maulvis who had reduced their religions to empty rituals and superstitious ceremonials.

Swami Rama has called Guru Nanak "a pioneer sage, who equally revered the fundamentals of all great religions, established a middle path and rejected the non-essentials embracing the path of love in a practical way."

In *Japji Sahib,* Guru Nanak has left the humanity a prayer of the rarest beauty and divine ambience.

The central mantra of *Japji Sahib* reads as under:

Ek Omkar	The One Reality
Sat Nam	Eternal name
Karta Purakh	Creative Principle
Nir Bhau	Without Enmity
Akal Murut	Eternal Form
Ajuni	The Unborn
Sai Bhang	Self existent
Gur Prasad	Known by Guru's grace

If words can ever describe God, no other words than the above would describe Him. In all the religious scriptures nobody has succeeded in describing the Reality better than as above.

The 29th sloka of Siva-mahimnah Stotra, the Reality (God) is described as below:

नमः नेदिष्ठाय प्रियदव दविष्ठाय च नमः । ।29 । ।
नमः क्षदिष्ठाय स्मरहर महष्ठिाय च नमः । ।29 ।
नमः वर्षिष्ठाय त्रिनयनयविष्ठाय च नमः । ।29 ।
नमः स्र्वस्मै ते तदिदमतिसर्वाय च नमः । ।29 ।

"O Lover of solitude, my salutation to Thee who art very near as also very far, far away. O destroyer of the god of love, my salutation to Thee who art the minutest as also the largest. O Three-eyed One, my salutation to Thee who art the oldest as also the youngest. This my salutation to Thee who art all as also transcending all." Guru Nanak preached in Punjabi dialect.

Guru Nanak brings nectar to parched human souls when he extols the virtue of singing His Name (Japu). As paraphrased by Swami Rama, Guru Nanak says:

"Sing the name of Lord.
Sing the name of Lord in every breath of life.
Joy, Joy, Joy let me offer you.
The finest of intoxicants a drug that can subdue.

Your drinks create a drowsiness, your song but augurs woe.

I offer you a wine divine .....

You will remain awake, immersed in joy.

That God's name strike an inner chord of harmony and bliss.

The infinite, the timeless, God created you for this.

Aum is the form, and one Holy true, of the sound of love divine.

Of the awesome, amazing, Supreme Guru the source of Thee and This.

So repeat these words in your heart to imbue.

The vision of God everlasting:

Ek Omkar Satnam Sri Wahe Guru.

The poetry of Guru Nanak is marked by richness of imagery and a certain measure of lyrical exuberance.

Japji Sahib is chiefly Upanishadic in theme. In Guru Nanak's lyrics, reference to all creeds is found. He was Guru for Hindus and Pir for Muslims.

Guruship among Sikhs was made by Nanak Devji not a matter of heredity. He ignored the claims of his two sons Shri Chand and Lakshmi Das when he elevated Lehna to Guruship. (Shri Chand founded the Udasi sect) Guru Nanak elevated his most devoted disciple as his successor.

The second Guru was Guru Angad, earlier called Lehna Ji, a devotee of Guru Nanak. He was born at Matti-ki-Sarai, a small village in Ferozepur district on March 31, 1504.

"He ascended the throne of Guru Nanak. The Guru's spirit entering the disciple": these are the words in which Bhai Gurdas describes Guru Angad's installation. Sikh tradition is that the divine light of Guru Nanak enters in each of his successor. Accordingly, each successor Guru wrote under the *nom de plume* of Nanak Himself.

Guru Angad's 62 Slokas are included in *Sri Guru Granth Sahib*.

Guru Angad's most important contribution was his simplifying Gurumukhi - a script which has 35 letters. He popularised its use among Sikhs and insisted on teaching children in Gurumukhi.

He died on March 29, 1552.

The third Guru, Amar Das (1552-1574) was born at Basarke in district Amritsar on May 5, 1479. He carried out a vigorous campaign against the pernicious practice of Sati and did a lot to spread Sikh faith. He gave authority to 146 of his apostles (men and women) to spread the Gospel and appointed 22 Manjis.

Guru Nanak had laid stress on Sangat, that is congregational worship and getting together, which forged Sikhs into a community.

Guru Amar Das supplemented Sangat by Pangat, that is, Sikhs should not only congregate both in the morning and evening to pray but they must also eat together with the Guru's slogan Sat Nam Sri Waheguru resounding all over. The concept of Pangat welded Sikhs into a casteless and classless community.

The *Anand* (Song of Joy) Marriage ceremony, which consists of singing 4 *Lavans,* is called *Anand Sahib* - Song of Bliss. It is sung when Sikhs solemnise a marriage.

The 4 *Lavan* composed by Guru Amar Das constitute blissful chants.

The 'Lavans' have double meanings. On the one hand, they are the objectives of the married life of the husband and the wife and, on the other, there is the aim of union of Jeev (person) with God, the Almighty. The Guru suggests that the married life of a man and a woman should be happy and joyful and should be based on the lines on which Jeev (person) attains God, the Eternal Lord. As in 'Parmarath' (godly path), it is directed to give up 'Nirvriti' (renunciation) and attain active worldly life. Similarly marriage is the first step for a woman to enter into secular life. As in Parmarath, (godly path) one has first to face fear, then love, then Vairag (mental detachment) and then attainment of the Eternal Lord.

Similarly, in married life, the wife is faced with the first three stages and then selfless love of the husband. The 4th Guru has beautifully explained these stages in the four *Lavans*, which are as under:

No. 1

Har Pehlari lanwa Parvirti Karm Diriraya Balram jeo,
Bani Brahma Ved Dharam Diroh Pap Tajaiya Balram jeo,
Bhara Dariroh harnam dhiawoh simrat nam driraiya,
Satgur ura aradho sab kil wikh pap gawaiya,
Sahj Anand hova wadhbhagi man har har mitha laiya,
Jan Kahe Nanak Lanwa pehli Anand Kaj rachaya."

"God by this first round hath ordained secular life. Accept the word instead of Brahman religion, instead of Vedas, And God will free you from your sins. Hold fast to religion. Meditate on God's name.

"The salve Nanak has given out the first round and made a beginning of the marriage."

No. 2

Har doojri lanwa Sat-Gur purkh manaya Balram jeo,
Nirbhai Bhai man hoye homai mail gowaiya balram jeo,
Nirmal Bhau paiya har gun gaya har wekhe ram hadoore,
Har atam ram pasariya swami sarb rihya bharpure,
Antir bahir har prabh eko mil hargun mangal gaye
Jan Nanak dooji lanwa chalayi anhad sabad wajas.

"In the second round, God hath caused me to meet the Guru, The fear in heart has departed and the filth of my mind hath been washed away. I have obtained a pure state of singing God's praises and beholding him before me,

Thus heard the sound of the word is everywhere diffuses and filleth every place

Within and without us is the God:

No. 3

Har Teejari lanwa man chao bhiya bairagiya balram jeo
ant janam har mail paiya wadhbhagiya balram jeo
Nirmal har paiya har gun gaiya mukh boli har har bani

Sant ? janam wadhbhagi paiya har kathiye akath kahani
Is it Sat (seven) or Sant
Hirde har har har khun upji har japiye mastak bhag jeo
Jan nanak bole teeji lawe har upjia man bairag jeo.

"God hath appointed the Third round, and pleasure and contemplation of the world are produced in mind.

The saints have caused me to meet God and I have found Him by great good fortune;

The salve Nanak hath given out the Third round, and God's love hath been produced in his heart."

No. 4

Har chauthari lanwa man sehj bhiya har paiya balram jeo
gurmukh milya subhaiye har man tan mitha laya balram jeo
har mitha laiya mere man bhaiya an din har live layee
man chindya phal paiya harnam waji wadhai
har prabh Thakar kah rachaiya dhan hirde name waasi
Jan Nanak bole chauthi lanwa her paiya prabh Abinash.

At the fourth round mental peace, composure and happiness are produced in the heart and I have attained God,

Under the Guru's instructions, I have obtained a good disposition and God, who is dear to my soul and body. God is dear and pleasing to me; I meditate on him night and day...

Guru Amar Das was visited by Mughal Emperor Akbar at Goindwal and, notwithstanding Guru's protests from his courtiers and acolytes, the Emperor granted a number of villages to Guru's daughter Bhani. Before his death, Guru Amar Das asked his son-in-law, Jetha, later called Guru Ram Das, to shift to the land granted to Bibi Bhani by the Emperor. The place came to be called Chak Ram Das or Ram Das Pura. Later on, a large number of businessmen came and settled here at the invitation of Guru Ram Das.

His 907 Slokas are included in *Sri Guru Granth Sahib.*

When the Guru foresaw his death, he called the members of his family and his Sikh followers and said: "God's summons hath come and I am about to depart. God's Will I accept with pleasure. There be no mourning for me. When I have gone, sing God's praises and obey God's Will." Sunder, a great grandson of the Guru, who was present at the time of death, composed a poem, called *Sadd* or Call of Death. It is enshrined in *Sri Guru Granth Sahib* and is recited on occasions of mourning. It reads as under:

THE SADD
(Ram Kali Sadd)

I

Jag Data Saeya Bhagat Wachhal te laeya jeo,
Gur Sabad Samae Awar Nan Jane Kaeya jeo,
Awara nan Jane Sabad gur ke Ek Nam Dhiawhe;
Prasad Nanak Guru Angad Parm Padvi Pawhe,
Aya harkara Chalanwara Harnam Samaiya,
jug Amar Atal thakar Bhagat Te har paya.

"God is the benefactor of the Universe; He loveth the saints and filleth the three worlds,

They in whose hearts the Guru's instruction is contained know none besides God:

Under the Guru's instructions they know none besides; they meditate on the one Name

By the favour of Nanak and Guru Angad, Amar Das obtained the supreme position.

When the message came for him to depart, he was absorbed in God's Name ...

II

Har bhana gur Bhaya gur jawe har prabh pass jeo,
Satgur Kare har pe bainti meri pehj rekho ardas jeo,
Paij rakha harnam Keri har deh nam Niranjena
Ant chaldian haeye beli jam daat Kal Nikhanjeno
Satgurki bainta payi har prabh suniardas jeo,
Har khar kirpa satguru milaya dhan khan kare sab jeo.

"The Guru gladly accepted the will of God to go to Him, The true Guru offered a prayer to God. 'Protect mine honour' this is my supplication.

'Preserve the honour of Thy servant, O bright God, grant me Thy name...

III

Mere Sikh suna put bhaiya mere har bhana sya mein pas jeo
har bhana gur bhaya mere har prabh kare sahas jeo
Bhagat satgur purukh saie jis har prabh bhana bhavey
Anand har prabh waje wajai har ap gal mailway
Tusi put bhai parwar mera man wekha kar irjas jeo
Dhur likheya parwana phire nanihi gur jaey har prab pas jeo

"My disciples, sons and brethren, hear me: I have received God's order to go to Him

The guru was pleased with the will of the Lord, my God congratulated him

He to whom God's order is pleasing is a saint of the true Guru ...

IV

Satgur bhane ape beh parwar Sadaiya
Mat mein pichhe kaiyee ravasi so main maal man bhaiya
Mit paijaimit bigse jis mit ki paij bhaviya
tusi veechar dekha put bhai har satgur parnaya satgur
partakh hande baih raj ap tikaya
Sab sikh bundhu ap put bhai Ram Das paiyi paiya

The true Guru was pleased to sit up and call his family: "Let no one weep when I am gone; that would never please me. When a friend obtaineth a robe of honour, friends who desire his honour are pleased

Consider and behold, my sons and brethren, God clotheth me with a robe of honour...

V

Ante Satgur boliya main pichhe Kirtan karao nirban jeo
Kaso gopal pandit sadio har har katha pareh puran jeo
har katha pariyai har nam suniya beban har rang gur
pind patal, kirya deva phul har sar pawye
har bhaiya satgur boliya har ilya purkh sujan jeo
Ram Das Sodhi tilak deeya gur sabad sach neeshan jeo

"Finally, the true guru spoke, 'After my death, sing God's praises,

Call God instead of a pandit and for the Garar Puran, read God's Word

Read God's work, hear God's name; the guru desireth God's love instead of a lofty bier

Barley rolls, bread on leaves, Hindu obsequies, lamps, and throwing his bones into the Ganges....

VI

Sat gur purkh je boliya gur sikhan man leyi Rajai jeo
Mori put sanmukh joeya Ram Das pairi paiya jeo
Sab pave pairi satguru keiri jithe gur aprakhiya
koi kar bakhili nive nahim phir satgur an niwaiya
har gur bhane di wadiyai dhur likhya lekh rajey jeo
kahe Sundar suno santo sab jagat paire paiye jeo

"As the true Guru spoke, so his disciples obeyed his wishes. His son Mohri became obedient to him, and fell at Ram Das's feet

Then all fell at the feet of the true Guru into whom Guru Amar Das had infused his spirit...

Guru Arjan Dev was not only compiler of the Holy *Granth Sahib,* he also composed Sukhmani Sahib: The Fountain of Eternal Joy, also called the "Prayer of Peace", though under the *nom de plume* of "Nanak" since it is held that Guru Nanak reincarnated himself in the Gurus who came after him.

Sukhmani Sahib is composed of 24 cantos each of which is followed by eight stanzas. Sikhs and Hindus recite the poem early in the morning. Writes K.S. Duggal, " .... it inspires and elevates the heart. It is a lofty and soaring statement of the beauty of the Divine in all things and yet this hymn was written by Guru who had personally suffered and had witnessed the suffering of his people, who lived without indulgence, who fought injustice and was martyred." Yet his faith in affirmative joy and peace is monumentally expressed in this poem.

The verse of Guru Arjan Dev has exquisite haunting melody and verbal charm.

'Sri Guru Granth Sahib' is the sacred scripture of the Sikh faith, and is considered as the inspired word of God. It is also venerated as Sikh Guru, or Sikh holy Takht guide and is the presiding presence in every Sikh place of worship.

Guru Arjan Dev's poetic genius is not only reflected in Sukhmani Sahib but also in the composition of *Guru Granth Sahib.* It has verses of Kabir, a weaver and Muslim by birth, of Baba Fariduddin (1173-1266) the exponent of Quranic sufism. Namdev a calico-printer and washerman, Ramdas, a shoe-maker, Mardana, the Muslim drummer. Thus the Granth remains a repository of devotional hymns obliterating distinctions of caste and religion. It contains compositions of six Gurus and thirty-six sages belonging to various castes, creeds and religions.

The Holy Granth opens with the basic postulate as follows:

There is but one God
His name is truth
He is the creator
He fears none nor does he hate anyone
He is in the image of the Eternal
He is beyond birth and death
He is self existent
He can be attained by the Guru's grace.

The hymns compiled in the Holy Granth have been arranged in various Ragas according to Indian classical music. The hymns in every musical measure are led by Guru Nanak and other Sikh Gurus in chronological order, the compositions of bhaktas following them. Granth Sahib has approximately 6,000 hymns set to thirty-one Ragas. Music is a part of the rituals in a number of religions. However, in Sikhism it has a deep relationship with Sikh prayers.

Adi Granth is written, like a *Janam-Sakhi,* in the Gurmukhi script or medieval Hindi and Punjabi, with terminology drawn from several languages spoken in Northern India at that time and from Persian and Arabic languages. *Sri Guru Granth Sahib* was composed in 1604 and is considered the latest sacred book of Asia.

Sri Guru Granth Sahib is a lengthy volume of more than 1430 printed pages and an apotheosis of Bhakti movement and denies importance to superstitions, which had come to haunt Hinduism at the time and emphasises the importance of internal spiritual growth.

Generally, Sikhism has two complementary streams, one of Guru Nanak, and the second militant concept of warrior-saint bequeathed to Khalsa by the Tenth Guru, Gur Gobind Singh Ji. So far as the latter tradition is concerned, Guru Har Gobind, who had succeeded Guru Arjan Dev was the first to confer militant lineaments on Nanak Panth. Born on June 14, 1595 at Wadali in district Amritsar, he was appointed Guru in 1606 at the age of 11 years by Guru Arjan Dev with injunction that he should sit on the throne fully armed.

His forays into mundane matters were criticised by some.

Bhai Gurdas in his Var 26 says, "The earlier Gurus sat peacefully in Dharamshalas, this one roams the land. Emperors visited their homes with reverence; this one they cast into jail."

Himself brave and powerful, Guru Hargobind was the first Guru to assemble an army and lay stress on physical and armed prowess.

Emperor Jahangir, the murderer of Guru Arjan Dev, was so fond of Guru Hargobind that he invited him to accompany him during his royal tours.

Jahangir visited Darbar Sahib and bowed to it. Queen Noorjahan was a follower of Miyan Mir. She visited Guru Hargobind Ji at Lahore. Guru Hargobind Sahib advised her never to forget death and always remember God.

Guru Hargobind asked the Sikhs to arm themselves to resist injustice and tyranny. This annoyed Jahangir who incarcerated the Guru in the Gwalior fort. However, Jahangir later realised that he had made a mistake and ordered the release of Guru Sahib. The Guru Sahib refused to accept the Emperor's offer till 52 innocent rajas undergoing incarceration in that fort were also released.

Guru Hargobind fought many a battle and was always triumphant. His stewardship of thirty-seven years and ten months is marked by a succession of armed conflicts with Mughal armies, which steeled the Sikhs into a fighting force.

People from commercial classes living in towns came into the fold of Sikhism. They were endowed with intelligence and wealth. They placed their wealth at the disposal of the Gurus. Thus, Guru Ram Das and Guru Arjan Dev could build Harmandar Sahib at Amritsar and the free community mess food was made available to all the devotees.

During the period of Guru Arjan Dev, Sikhism made notable strides in the countryside and a large number of Majha Jats embraced Sikhism.

The rapidly growing Sikh movement caused a reaction among the Muslim orthodoxy. In the early stages of the development of Sikh faith, the Muslim clergy had remained indifferent. But as the faith spread, the Muslims saw a danger. Antagonism between the Sikhs and Muslims grew because both are proselytising religions. In Punjabi University Patiala publication *Sikhism*, the state of conflict between the two faiths is described as below (page 19).

"Islam had entered the Punjab in the wake of the Turkish armies of Mahmood of Ghazni. By now, most of the Western Punjab had been Islamised and in the Eastern Punjab, too, a sizable section of the population had accepted the creed of Islam. With the progress of Sikhism, which was also a missionary creed like Islam, the pace of Islamisation was considerably slowed down, if not halted. The prospect of improved status, which Islam offered to the lower sections of the Hindu society, was now available from Sikhism as well, because Sikhism, too, like Islam made no distinction between the high and the low. In so far as Sikhism was closer to the roots of the Hindu culture, for the Hindu masses it had an edge over Islam. Therefore, those who wanted to change their religion with a view to improving their position in the society, preferred Sikhism to Islam. But it was not merely the entry of new people into Islam that suffered a setback and as a consequence, slowed down the pace of spread of Islam; the spell of the Sikh Gurus was felt even in the ranks of Islam. Some of the Musalmans, generally former converts from Hinduism, began to show more interest in Sikhism than in Islam. It is possible that a few cases of reconversion also took place. All these trends naturally alarmed the orthodox elements of the Muslim population and they became progressively hostile to Sikhism".

References

1. Teja Singh: *Sikhism.* Published by Khalsa Brothers, Amritsar p.128.
2. *Ibid;* p. 133
3. *Ibid;* p. 128
4. *Mainstream,* May 23, 1982
5. Ganda Singh: *The Past & Present,* Vol. VI, pages 144-145.

– 5 –

The Sikh Ethos

The *Chambers Twentieth Century Dictionary* defines ethos as "habitual character and disposition of individual, group, race, etc." Such ethos arises out of an individual's or group's experiences and exposures in various fields — religious, cultural, political and historical. We can call ethos as the religious, cultural and historical spirit, which animates a community.

Sikhs have a definite ethos. They have been galvanised by the sacrifices of their Gurus, that is, 5th Guru Arjan Devji and 9th Tegh Bhadur Ji, the suffering and valour of Guru Gobind Singh Ji and Banda Bahadur. Their daily prayer, called *Ardas* in Punjabi, is full of sacrificial episodes on which their religion is based. After completing each divine service and other religions ceremonies, the Sikhs say a prayer as follows:

ARDAS

(Supplication)

Ek-Omkar-Shri Vaheguru ji ki Fateh
Having first remembered the sword, meditate on Guru Nanak, Then on Guru Angad, Amar Das and Ram Das,
may they assist us!
Remember Arjan, Hargobind, and the holy Har Rai:
Meditate on the holy Har Kishan, a sight of whom dispelled all sorrow.
Remember Tegh Bahadur, and the nine treasures shall come hastening to your homes
Ye Holy Guru, everywhere assist us

May the tenth king, the holy Guru Gobind Singh,
everywhere assist us.
Meditate on the teachings of *Sri Guru Granth Sahib,*
the embodiment of the ten Gurus and utter Waheguru,
Remember Five Beloved Ones, four princes,
who attained salvation and meditate on the deeds of
those who worshipped the Name, plied the sword, ate
and distributed their food in companionship and
overlooked others' faults and utter Waheguru,

Think of all Gurudwaras, the holy places, And utter Waheguru

May the Khalsa be lively in spirit, Exalted in intelligence, And make intelligence the instrument of the Divine will.

Grant the Sikhs the gift of the discrimination, The gift of trusting each other,

The gift of faith,

And above all, the greatest gift of all, The gift of thy name.

May the Khalsa, in all its actions, remember God. And in remembering God bring peace and comfort to the whole world

May divine protection extend wherever the Khalsa resides.

May the supplies and swords of Khalsa be in the ascendant.

May the staying places and banners of Khalsa be eternally blessed

We offer this Ardas in thy presence and at Thy lotus feet. Pardon our errors and mistakes.

May all Sikhs who read and hear Guru's hymns be profited through Nanak.

May thy name, O God, be exalted and all prosper by thy grace.

Sri Waheguru ji ka Khalsa - Sri Waheguruji ki Fateh.

Teja Singh writes that the Ardas can incorporate new events of which Sikhs can be proud. He writes:

"The first seven and the last two lines can in no case be altered or omitted. In all other lines, changes can be made." He further writes: "This prayer has been handed down from the days of the conflict with the Mohammedans, in which the Sikhs suffered martyrdoms that are enumerated in it. Yet, nowhere is shown any sign of bitterness or revenge. There is no reproach or curse on the enemy; only the sufferings are enumerated, which are taken as sacrifices made by the community.

"As it now stands, Ardas can be divided into three parts:[3]

1. Six lines of verse by Guru Gobind Singh, invoking God and the first nine Gurus
2. From line 7 to line 25, rhythmic prose composed by generations of Sikhs, as the events of their history went on leaving their impression on their minds ...
3. The prayer proper, the Composition of which excepting a few words here and there, depends entirely upon the man who is praying."

One has to study the Sikh prayer to arrive at the correct conclusion regarding Sikh ethos. The first six verses from the beginning are from Bhagauti-ki-Var, by Guru Gobind Singh, who is called the Tenth King. Sikhs maintain that Bhagauti is Good and not the Goddess Durga. The Sikh prayer, which is recited daily by devout Sikhs and on all solemn occurrences in Sikh households and Gurudwaras, opens as follows:

"Having first remembered God, the Almighty, think of Guru Nanak, then of Guru Angad, Amar Das and Ram Das. May they assist us everywhere! May the Tenth King, the holy Guru Gobind Singh, the lord of hosts and protector of faith assist us everywhere! Turn your thoughts, O Khalsa, to the teachings of *Sri Guru Granth Sahib*, and call on God!

The next stanza impregnates the Sikh mind with fervour for sacrifice:

"The five Beloved ones, the Master's four sons, the forty saved ones, and other righteous, steadfast along suffering souls: think of their deeds and call on Waheguru."

The above quoted stanza refers to the sacrifice of Guru Gobind's four sons and his five devotees whom he had baptised at Anandpur Sahib in 1699, and the reduction of his force to forty who accompanied him to Chamkaur Sahib.

The one stanza after the next refers to the sacrifices of Guru Tegh Bahadur and Banda Bahadur. It reads as follows:

"Those who for their religion allowed themselves to be cut up limb by limb, had their scalps scraped off, were broken on the wheel, were sawn, or flogged alive, think of their resignation and call on God! Waheguru".

A people who chant these prayers daily are bound to be afire with a martyrdom complex. At every significant occasion in their life they are reminded that they are the inheritors of heroic ancestry and fearless lineage. Such people can withstand repression or persecution with dauntless courage. They are also imbued with a martial spirit as they are daily reminded that their Gurus and their progeny gladly embraced death and torture than submit to tyranny. They, therefore, hearken to their past and refuse to be subdued. Those who want to understand the Sikh militancy ought to know more of their past; their past has layers of persecution and their sacrificial spirit. We must remember Sikhism is the youngest religion and it has the vigour and headiness of youth.

Fifth Guru Arjan Dev (1581-1606) was the first martyred Guru. Until Akbar's rule, Sikhs had enjoyed generous treatment from the Mughal Kings: A charge of sedition on the ground that Guru Arjan Dev had helped Khusrau, the rebellious son of Jehangir, was made against Guru Arjan Dev who was taken to Lahore and subjected to torture and martyred. The cruel and torturous execution of Guru Arjan Dev sent waves of repulsion against the Mughals and gave birth to Sikh militancy through the person of the sixth Guru. At the age of eleven only, Guru Hargobind who on assuming Guruship took his initiation not with 'Seli', the ribbon of renunciation that Nanak had worn and given to Angad, but by wearing two swords, the emblems of spiritual power (Peeri) and temporal authority (Meeri), synthesising 'Bhakti and Shakti'. He ordered all his disciples to carry swords, to keep horses and to manufacture arms. He organised bands of warrior saints. Thus, a new tradition was born.

However, Guru Hargobind was able to charm Jehangir and their relations remained cordial. During Guru Hargobind's regime, Sikhism was transformed from a brotherhood of devotees to a force of warrior saints. Guru Hargobind came to be styled *Sachcha Patshah* or the true king. He adopted all emblems of royalty: the umbrella, the two swords, the crest and the hawk. He also fortified the city Ramdaspur (Amritsar), and was responsible for the erection of *Akal Takht*. He had ordered the construction of the new building at a place a few hundred yards away from Har Mandar. It was completed in 1609 and called *Akal Takht* or the Throne of the Timeless. The Akal Takht faces the Golden Temple. It was while sitting on this throne that Guru Hargobind discussed the political and military problems of the Sikhs. Akal Takht served the purpose of a Supreme Court for the Sikhs as intricate cases and disputes of Sikhs were finally decided here.

The military policy of Guru Hargobind brought him in conflict with the Mughals (under Shah Jahan) because the Guru had started enlistment of freebooters and malcontents of the Imperial army in his ranks. Sikh-Mughal hostilities started with the forcible seizure of an imperial hawk by the Sikhs. The Mughals under the leadership of Mukhlis Khan, who was killed in the battle, defeated the Sikh force. Amritsar was sacked and plundered. After this battle, the Guru thought it prudent to move away from Amritsar. In 1628, he retreated to Kartarpur and built the new town of Sri Hargobindpur near it. Another battle took place three years later near Bhatinda over the disputed possession of horses. The Mughal commander died in this battle, too

The third battle of Kartarpur took place in 1634 in which Kale Khan and Pande Khan were killed. The Guru again retreated to the hills and built the town of Kiratpur. The spiritual and temporal reign of the Guru lasted more than 30 years.

We need not dwell here on the career of each Guru. Guruship of 9th Guru Tegh Bahadur (1664-1675) was resisted by rapacious Sodhies of Baba Bakala and corrupt Masands of

Amritsar. He retreated to the hills and founded the holy township of Anandpur Sahib in 1644 near the ruins of an ancient place called Makhowal. Kashmiri Pandits sought the protection of the Guru against their forcible conversion to Islam.

How Guru Tegh Bahadur embraced his execution highlights the Sikh sacrificial spirit. He met his death with perfect composure singing the divine praise, "Why grieve for that which is inevitable? Everyone who's born must also pass from here."

Guru Gobind Singh, the tenth and the last of the Sikh Gurus, was born at Patna on December 26, 1666. He was only nine years old when his father was executed. After the assumption of the guruship, Guru Gobind Singh left Makhowal, his father's headquarters, and shifted to Paonta Sahib. According to historian Teja Singh and Ganda Singh, the Guru had resolved to fight both the political tyranny of Mughals and religious tyranny of Brahmins. Because of hostilities with hill chiefs and his victory at Bhangani, Guru Gobind Singh returned to Anandpur Sahib, made it his headquarters, and raised four small fortresses, Anandgarh, Lohgarh, Keshgarh and Fatehgarh, around it.

Founding of the Khalsa: 1699

A believer in the right of sword, Guru Gobind convened an assembly on Baisakhi Day at Anandpur Sahib in 1699. It was attended by 80,000 people. When all were seated, the Guru stood up and with a drawn sword, asked, "Is there anyone who would lay down his life for Dharma?" There was no response and the Guru repeated this question three times. At the third call, Daya Ram, a Khatri from Lahore, offered himself for the sacrifice. The Guru took him to an adjoining tent where he had kept five goats. Daya Ram was left there but a goat's head was cut by the Guru with his sword and then he displayed the dripping sword to the assembly. He then called for more volunteers. In this manner five persons in all were taken from that assembly. They had all volunteered themselves to die at the Guru's bidding. They are known in Sikh history as "Panj Piaras". They were: Daya Ram, Dharam Chand, Mohkam Chand, Sahib Chand and Himmat Rai. Then, in the presence of this huge gathering, the Guru initiated them in a novel way. Guru Gobind Singh changed the initiation ceremony and introduced "*Khanda ka Pahul*" or "Baptism of the Sword".

An iron vessel filled with water and sugar cakes (Patashas) was placed before the Guru. This was stirred by a double-edged dagger by one of those five. The sacred hymns of the Gurus and the Adi Granth, Japji, Anand, Chaupai and Sawayya were recited. The water thus prepared was named *Amrit* or Sacred Water of Immortality. It was sprinkled on their faces and they were also given five palmfuls of it to drink. This came to be known as 'Baptism of the Sword". The selected five of Guru Gobind Singh were termed the Khalsa or the purified ones and they had to assume the new names of Singhs. Thus Mokham Chand came to be called Mohkam Singh and so on. They were then asked to wear five K's, viz: (i) Kes (long hair), (ii) Kachha, i.e. a pair of knicker-bockers, (iii) Kara or an iron bangle, (iv) Kirpan or a sword, and (v) Kangha or a comb. Then the Guru exhorted how his Khalsa were to live in this world. They were all equal and could marry among one another without any caste consideration. Relationship with smokers was banned. Idolatry was banned. Thus arose a powerful fraternity of soldier saints. Cunningham says that Guru Gobind Singh through baptism of the sword "roused the dormant energies of a vanquished people". The Guru addressed the gathering as follows on the fateful Baisakhi day of 1699:

"I wish you all to embrace one creed and follow one path, obliterating all differences of religion. Let the four Hindu castes abandon them altogether, adopt the way of cooperation and mix freely with one another." Sardar Khushwant Singh infers from these words that "The principal purpose in Guru Gobind Singh's mind in starting a new path was to shield Hindus against tyranny .... and the extremists who killed Lala Jagat Narain, Ramesh Chandra, Vishwa Nath

Tiwari, Harbans Lal Khanna, Ajit Singh Atwal, Sumeet Singh, K.L. Manchanda and many others had no right to call themselves Sikhs".

Guru's denunciation of the caste system and image worship led to armed conflict with the Raja of Bilaspur in whose territory Anandpur was then situated. In the second battle of Anandpur, forces of Wazir Khan, governor of Sirhind, made the Guru surrender the fort. The Guru left Anandpur in 1704. Guru's entourage was attacked again by the wily Mughals. While crossing Sirsa, his two sons Zorawar Singh and Fateh Singh fell into the hands of Mughals and, on their refusal to embrace Islam, they were bricked alive in a wall near Sirhind. Then came the battle of Chamkaur Sahib when the Guru had only forty Sikhs but they fought with courage. It was in this battle that the other two sons of the Guru, Baba Ajit Singh and Jujhar Singh, were killed. After the battle of Khidera, the Guru settled at Talwandi Sabo to which the Sikhs gave the name of Damdama Sahib. There, the Guru stayed about a year and resumed the work of religious preaching.

In the Sikh prayers, sacrifices made by Guru Gobind Singh and his followers are incorporated thus: "The five beloved ones, the Master's four sons, the forty saved ones, and other righteous steadfast and long suffering souls: think of their deeds and call on God! (Wonderful Lord!)

Guru Gobind Singh was a leader incomparable. He
said "Chirion se mein Baj laraoon,
Swa lakh se ek laraoon,
Tab hee Gobind Singh nam kahaoon".

"By sparrows will I get falcons killed
One will I pit against one and quarter lakh
Then alone I shall bear the name of Gobind Singh".

But nothing can surpass the prowess and steadfastness of Banda Bahadur (earlier Madho Dass Bairagi, a Dogra Rajput) who through his dexterity at arms and leadership established Sikh rule in Punjab for the first time. About his sacking of Sirhind, Latif says Banda and his Sikhs "butchered, bayonetted, strangled, hanged, shot down, hacked to pieces and burnt alive every Mohammedan in the place." The corpse of Wazir Khan was "hanged on a tree and left to the tender mercies of crows and vultures." However, in 1715 Mughals under the command of Abdul Samad Khan surrounded the Garhi in which Banda Bahadur was staying. For several months the Sikhs resisted this onslaught. Ultimately Sikhs surrendered and Banda was made a prisoner, and his band of 740 followers, all chained, were paraded in Lahore, and later in Delhi. At the head of the procession were carried two thousand heads of Sikhs, raised on bamboo poles, their long hair streaming in the wind." For the Muslim population of Delhi it was a great 'tamasha'.

The author of *Ibratnama* says, "Such a crowd in the bazars and lanes had rarely been seen. The Musalmans could hardly contain themselves with joy. But the unfortunate Sikhs, who had been reduced to this condition, were quite happy and contended with their lot. In fact, most of them, as they passed along on their camels, seemed to be happy and cheerful, merrily singing their sacred hymns. If anyone from the lanes called out to them that their own excesses had brought them where they were, they quickly retorted that it had been so decreed by the Almighty and that their capture and misfortune was in accordance with His will. And if anyone said, "Now you will be killed", they shouted, "Do kill us. When were we afraid of death? Had we been afraid, how could we have fought so many battles with you? It was merely through want and hunger that we fell into your hands ...!" All contemporary writers, Indian and English, praise the wonderful patience and resolution with which these men underwent their fate. What a lot who embraced death cheerfully singing hymns! Banda Bahadur was brutally executed on June 19, 1716. We can revert to the Sikh prayer once again. "Those who, to purge the temples of longstanding evils, suffered themselves to be ruthlessly beaten or imprisoned, to be shot, cut up, or burnt alive with kerosene oil, but did not make any resistance or utter even a sigh of complaint: think of their patient faith and call on God! (Wonderful Lord)."

By making sacrifices of various Gurus and disciples as part of the Sikh prayer, Sikhs imbued themselves with an indomitable spirit of resistance and further sought to inculcate a courage of Promethean proportions. They ascribed all suffering and struggle to the Will of God and each Sikh sought to go through his misfortune with joyous acceptance and submission to the Almighty. The salutation introduced by Guru Gobind Singh '*Wahe guru ji ka Khalsa*' and '*Wahe guru ji ki fateh*' (The Khalsa belongs to the Guru and the victory belongs to the Guru) gave them an inspiring battle-cry.

Thus, Sikhs were transformed from mere devotees of God, chanting His praises, into warrior soldiers filled with sacrificial spirit scoffing at death and resisting persecution with arms. This is one of the most conspicuous strands of Sikh psyche or ethos. A Sikh would take to arms to resist what he perceives to be oppression or persecution. To understand the other constituents of Sikh ethos, we have to note a few more historical facts.

Mughal persecution of Sikhs is a saga of Sikh determination and courage and a tale of foul, barbarous atrocities committed on them. After the execution of Banda, the Mughal Emperor Farrukh Siyar decided to exterminate Sikhism. Sikhs had no leader left among them and the weak willed ceased to keep long hair and came to be known as 'Sahaj-dharis' or slow adopters. Other Sikhs could not stay in any town or village of the Punjab and retreated to the hills and forests. Thus, from 1716 to 1720, they lay dormant. After the death of Farrukh Siyar in 1719, Sikhs emerging from their hilly and jungle retreats, settled in towns and villages. They grew bold enough to assemble at Amritsar to celebrate Diwali and the Baisakhi with their usual fervour. However, the assumption of governorship of Punjab by Zakaria Khan in 1726 was the beginning of organised extermination of Sikhs. His soldiers went to the hills and hunted out Sikhs. Prices were fixed for their heads. K.S. Narang writes that the Sikhs were arrested wholesale, they were tortured and beheaded outside the Delhi Gate in Lahore. This place came to be known as Shahidganj. In retaliation, Sikhs took to guerilla tactics and looted treasuries, arms, ammunition and horses. Surprise attacks by Sikhs and plundering of Muslims defeated the policy of persecution of Zakaria Khan. Then he sought to placate them by sending a message to the Sikhs at Akal Takht that their leader should accept the title of Nawab and also receive a Jagir of the value of one lakh rupees a year. Thus, the title of Nawab and Jagir were given to Kapoor Singh Faizulpura. Later on, Kapoor Singh passed the command to Jassa Singh Ahluwalia. However, sporadic persecution continued: one outstanding case was the martyrdom of Bhai Mani Singh who had lived throughout with Guru Gobind Singh and was the High Priest of Golden Temple at Amritsar.

In the Sikh lore, the martyrdom of Mehtab Singh and Sukha Singh are prominent; they took revenge for the desecration of the Golden Temple by beheading the Governor of Amritsar, Massa Rangar, in 1740. Massa Rangar was alleged to smoke and organise dances of nautch girls within the Golden Temple precincts. A fleeing Sikh narrated Massa Ranger's misdeeds to the Sikhs in Bikaner, Rajasthan. When Mehtab and Sukha Singh heard of these misdeeds of Massa Rangar, they vowed to kill him. Riding all the way from Bikaner to Amritsar on their horses, they entered the Golden Temple and beheaded the Governor. A painting in the Sikh Museum in the Golden Temple depicts the exploits of Sukha Singh and Mehtab Singh carrying the head of Massa Rangar on a spear.

During the reign of Yahiya Khan as Governor, the foolish acts of his Diwan Lakhpat Rai led to what Sikhs call the first "Ghalughara" of 1746. The word 'Granth' had been banned, the tank of Amritsar was filled with earth. Every Sikh was to be executed. In the bloody battles of Khanuwan and Basoli, known as the first or small 'Ghalughara', about 7,000 Sikhs were killed and about 3,000 taken as prisoners and executed at Shahidganj. In 1746-47, a civil war started among the sons of Zakaria Khan in which Shah Nawaz Khan emerged as the Governor of Punjab. Shah Nawaz Khan was not in favour with the rulers of Delhi. He thus foolishly invited Ahmad Shah Abdali of Afghanistan to invade Punjab, but later resiled from his commitment given to Shah Abdali. Though Shah Abdali was defeated, anarchy took over in Punjab. In this interregnum, Sikhs strengthened themselves. The Sikhs took full advantage of the anarchy and confusion then prevailing in Delhi and Lahore from 1746 to 1749. Dal Khalsa under Jassa Singh Ahluwalia took possession of Punjab and attracted the peasantry, who were mostly Jats, to embrace Sikhism. When Marathas were defeated by Ahmad Shah Abdali at Panipat in January 1761, a power vacuum occurred in Punjab and bands of Sikhs led by Jassa Singh Ahluwalia, Hari Singh Bhangi and Charat Singh Sukerchakya took to looting and plundering the country all around. Sikhs gained control of Gujranwala and Lahore after defeating their adversaries. This led to the sixth invasion by Ahmad Shah Abdali, in February 1762 when, in the battle near Malerkotla, he killed 12,000 Sikhs, including women and children. This carnage is called "Wadda Ghalughara". He also destroyed Hari Mandir at Amritsar. Abdali's successive invasions paved the way for the rise of Sikh power in Punjab.

Qazi Noor Mohammad, a citizen of Baluchistan accompanied Ahmed Shah Abdali on his seventh invasion of India in 1764 A.D. This invasion was carried out to suppress Sikhs. In his *Jungnama* written in Persian, he described Sikhs as follows:

> "A Sikh, a Singh, in their own tongue, is the king of forest. And so they verily, all are, the lions,
> A Sikh is a virtual lion in the battle field
> A Sikh is of royal blood blue, in time of peace."

In order to resist the Mughal persecution and the Afghan invasions, Sikhs had raised 65 bands. The collective strength of these bands constituted the Dal Khalsa. Later these 65 bands leagued together in 11 or 12 main divisions, which came to be called Misls. Misl is an Arabic word meaning 'equal' or alike'. These Misls were (1) Singhpuria Faizalpuria (2) Ahluwalia (3) Ramgarhia (4) Bhangi (5) Kanheyia (6) Sukarchakiya (7) Phulkian (8) Dullewalia (9) Nakkais (10) Shahids (11) Kasirsinghia and (12) Nishanwalia.

The central organisation of the Sikh Misls was called the *Gurmata*, the National League or the Central Diet. After the death of Guru Gobind, the Sikhs from all over used to meet on certain festival occassions like Dussehra, Diwali and Baisakhi at Amritsar and there at Akal Takht in the presence of the Holy Granth, they used to discuss the common plan of action for the entire community and the will of the entire Sikh community at Amritsar was called in the form of resolution or 'Gurmata'.

Maharaja Ranjit Singh (1780-1839) was the son of Mahan Singh of Sukarchakiya Misl. Ranjit Singh conquered Lahore in 1799. He conquered territories of all other Misls, Malwa region, and extended his empire to Kashmir and Peshawar. Though Ranjit Singh had taken Sikh power to great heights through military conquests, he was no match for the British and the decline of his (Sikh) power began with the Amritsar Treaty he had concluded with Lord Metcalfe on April 25, 1809. It was by all standards a restrictive pact for Ranjit Singh. Ultimately the British annexed Punjab in 1849. Conversion of Maharaja Duleep Singh to Christianity in 1853 showed that the Sikh power had reached its nadir in the vicissitudes of its fortunes. The decline of Ranjit Singh's empire brings out that lust for power and petty intrigues was present among the Sikhs. The defeat of Sikhs at Sobraon in 1846 was due to the betrayal of Lal Singh, the Prime Minister and Teja Singh, the Commander-in-Chief of Sikh Army. They had sold themselves to the British.

The glory of Khalsa Raj is appropriately epitomised in the words of Sardar Khushwant Singh as follows:

" ..... A tiny little minority that dominated the whole area; the first people in one thousand years to roll back the invaders and take back the land ..... Sikh troops have been marching through the streets of Kabul carrying the Sikh flag. More Sikhs went to gallows in the freedom movement than any other people. There is a pride in the Sikhs and one upmanship is inculcated in him. They believe that one Khalsa is equal to the Sava Lakh (One hundred thousand and twenty five thousand people) and that one Sikh is an army."

No examination of Sikh ethos will be complete unless we understand the innate racial characteristics of the classes, which had embraced Sikhism. Most of the Sikh converts were Hindus. Even the names of Gurus were Hindu. In the urban areas, they were Kshtriyas, Aroras and Banias who had taken to Sikhism. Since the days of Guru Arjan Dev, peasantry had also started adopting Sikhism. The peasantry consisted mostly of Jats. There are different views on their origin. They are believed to be mostly Scythian descendants. They are virile and industrious with instincts of tribal kinship. They adopted Sikhism in a big way probably for two reasons. It raised their status in a caste ridden polity. Secondly, peasants love egalitarianism - one of the basic tenets of Sikh Panth. The Panth was super-abundantly influenced by the Jat constituency. According to 1891 census, out of 1.7 million Sikhs 66% were Jats. P.K. Nijhawan writes, "Jats fought bitter internecine battles carrying on vendatta for generations. When the Guru (Gobind Singh) took shelter in Machhi Wara, he devoted his time and energy to convert these people to his religion. It suited both. The Jats got cohesive force in the form of Sikhism and the Guru an army of horse-riding, weapon weilding fierce warriors. Hence, he felt strong enough to write his *Zafarnama*, "The epistle of Victory" in his hour of defeat".

Jats are excitable and prone to aggrandising themselves. Being splendid fighters, the Sikh Jats formed the flower of the Khalsa Army during the days of the Misls and later of Maharaja Ranjit Singh. Later, they brought militancy and factionalism to Punjab politics. P.S. Maini writes: "Jat Sikh mind is a complex of attitudes and emotions that find their present expression in action and engagement. And these include pride and power, revenge and reprisal" *(Cry, The Beloved Punjab)*. This perceptive writer further writes that Sikh Gurus being non-Jat sang hymns of peace of Lord, yet "the Jat psyche ..... is quite capable of laying aside the edicts and ideas of the Gurus. And therein lies our misery and our danger". *(Cry, The Beloved Punjab)*. This very author further writes: "The Sikh empire lay shattered within 7 years of his

(Ranjit Singh's) demise, thanks to the politics of intrigue and treachery; the unbridled lust for power is so irresistible in the Jat Sikh psyche as to throw its better instincts into confusion in moments of temptation and excitement."

From the foregoing account of Sikhism and their subsequent persecution, great deeds of bravery and expansion of Ranjit Singh's empire, we can arrive at the following conclusions:

1. Sikhs are highly devoted to their ten Gurus and *Guru Granth Sahib*.

2. Their history is replete with the incidents of martyrdom. They seek martyrdom when their religion is under attack, Martyrdom of Guru Arjan Dev, Guru Tegh Bahadur, four sons of Guru Gobind Singh, Banda Bahadur Bairagi and Mani Das, etc. has imbued Sikh psyche with a "martyrdom complex". They have perpetuated the tradition of martyrdom through their prayers, which they recite daily and definitely on all significant occasions in life. Thus, the Sikh psyche becomes saturated with martyrdom complex.

3. Guru Hargobind synthesised both *Peeri* and *Meeri* in his person. Thus, the borderline between the spiritual and the temporal was sought to be obliterated.

4. They were mercilessly persecuted by Mughal Governors in Punjab State. So they developed persecution syndrome.

5. Jat Sikhs take to arms in a glorious manner but could also turn into bands afire with feelings of vendetta. They are a proud people who have fought oppression and tasted imperialist glory. In the words of late Dr. Rajinder Kaur, daughter of Master Tara Singh, killed by militants though she herself was a fiery extremist: "Sikhs never accept defeat and this facet of Sikh pysche has been ignored by the authorities dealing with Sikh problem. A Sikh remains a fighter wherever he is stationed"[5].

However, Jat Sikhs are prone to factionalism and given to one-upmanship and, in this game, squander their cohesiveness of purpose. It explains groupism and factionalism in Akali politics. After the death of Maharaja Ranjit Singh, Lahore durbar became the hotbed of intrigues and petty squabbles on the left-over morsels of power. Whether it was Rani Jindhan or Lal Singh or Teja Singh, they displayed vaulting ambition and propensity for basest bargains at the cost of community's good or honour. Another aspect of Sikh ethos thrown up by the disintegration of Khalsa Raj is that Sikhs, when armed, can be stubborn and defiant. These facets can be seen in the mushrooming of militant gangs in Punjab and intra-gang rivalry and killings. As the Sikh soldiers had gone rampaging and mutinying till they were decisively defeated by the British at Sabraon, the present day militants did not give in until their supply lines of arms were denied to them. The militancy of Sikh Army and the accession of Sher Singh to Lahore's throne had prompted the British to cross arms with the Sikhs. Sikhs lost the battle of Mudki on 18th December, 1845 because of Lal Singh's betrayal though they had outnumbered the British army under Lord Gough. Again in the battle of Firozshah on 21st December 1845, Sikh artillery outnumbered British guns and the battle would have gone in favour of Khalsa but the victory turned into a stalemate due to the betrayal by Teja Singh. The brave Sikhs were abandoned by their Chief Ranjodh Singh in the battle of Sabraon on 8th January 1846. Cunnighman writes: "Under such circumstance of shameless treason was the battle of Sabraon fought as in the other battles of the campaign soldiers did everything and the leaders nothing. No Sikhs offered to submit and no disciple of Gobind asked for quarters but Sikh leaders had betrayed them."

Guru Tegh Bahadur went to Delhi and was executed in November 1675 at Chandni Chowk, Delhi. In memory of Guru's martyrdom two Gurudwaras of the same name, Sis Ganj, were built, one in Delhi and another in Anandpur Sahib. Guru Gobind Singh wrote of his father's martyrdom as follows:

"Aurangzeb did not want to see any *Tilak* (holy mark on the forehead) or *Janeu* (sacred thread) on any of his subjects. Aurangzeb ordered conversions to start from Kashmir. The emperor thought that if Kashmiri Pandits were converted, conversion of others would become easier. The Governor of Kashmir gave Hindus notice to voluntarily embrace Islam or face persecution. Faced with the threat of conversion, Kashmiri Pandits started leaving Kashmir. Kashmiri Pandits under the leadership of Pandit Kripa Ram called upon Guru Tegh Bahadur at Anandpur Sahib and narrated to him their tale of misery.

Guru Tegh Bahadur advised the Pandits to return to Kashmir and inform the Governor that they would accept conversion if Guru Tegh Bahadur could first be converted. Guru Tegh Bahadur was summoned to Delhi. Accompanied by Bhai Mati Dass, Bhai Dyala and Bhai Sati Dass, he arrived in Delhi, where he was arrested, caged and beheaded on 11 Nov., 1675. Bhai Mati Dass picked up the Guru's sacred head and dashed to Anandpur Sahib and the remaining part of the Guru's body was cremated at the present site of Gurudwara Sis Ganj in Delhi.

Guru Gobind Singh wrote of his father's sacrifice:

"He broke his potsherd on the Delhi king's head.
And he left for paradise
None else can match Tegh Bahadur's sacrifice.
The people mourned Tegh Bahadur's passing away.
There was wailing in the world but rejoicing in
heaven".

A great poet and stoic philosopher that Guru Tegh Bahadur was, he had addressed the people of Anandpur Sahib before his departure for Delhi as follows:

"Death is a certainty, One must not set one's heart on this world. It is God who sends pleasure and pain, profit and loss, weal and woe; these must be accepted as the will of God".

Corporate Identity of Sikhs

In his book *Who is a Sikh,* W.H. Mcleod quotes Kahan Singh Nabha in *Gurusabad Ratnakar Mahan Kos* with regard to the corporate identity of Sikhs as follows:

1. To observe the Sikh code of conduct (rahit) in the bonds of unity.
2. To accept the corporate community (Panth) as Guru and to serve it with loyal devotion.
3. To proclaim the Guru's teachings to the world.
4. To accept the affection of all Nanak Panthis as adherants of the Sikh religion, regardless of their outward appearance; and to treat people with respect and sympathy.
5. To observe in Gurudwara and other shrines rituals enjoyed by the Gurus.

Mcleod is of the view that the popular formula of Sikhism, "Nam Japo, Kirat Karo, Vand Chhakko" (Repeat the Divine Name, Work hard and Share with others your earnings) does not emanate from Guru Nanak.

Mcleod refers to the controversy about Nanak Panthis as some Sikh scholars want Sikhism to be related only to that area of Sikhism,which is amenable to clear divination, namely the "Khalsa".[2]

Sikh Panth could not have transformed into Khalsa unless the latter Gurus had provided it a structural hierarchy and externalities to distinguish it from their Hindu base. This transformation can be easily assigned to the third Guru, Amar Das, who laid the system of sangats and manjis that is "designated authority" .

Again the death of Guru Arjan Dev in Moghul custody in 1606 marks the inauguration of Sikh militancy under Guru Hargobind who merged the concepts of *Meeri* (Mundane) and *Peeri* (the Spiritual) and initiated armed struggle against the Mughals. He created saint soldiers.

Panthic identity was consolidated by the tenth Guru, Gobind Singh Ji, when he founded *Khalsa* by initiating through *Khande-Ka-Pahul (amrit).* However, the fundamental doctrine remained the same till the last Guru, that is, belief in Akal Purakh, veneration for the personal Gurus and to recognise the presence of the timeless Guru in Adi Granth (*Sri Guru Granth Sahib*).

Sikhism is indeed, an egalitarian faith. Teja Singh observes:

"The gurus have combined the Aryan idea of eminence (of God) with the semantic idea of transcendence."[3]

When Guru Gobind Singh founded Khalsa on Baisakhi day of 1699 at Gurudwara Keshgarh Anandpur Sahib, he changed the complexion of Sikhism not only by changing the externals but by baptising them with sword-crossed sweet water called *Amrit*, into a fighting force.

References

1. *Who is A Sikh?* by W.H. Mcleod, Clarendon Press Oxford, p. 3.
2. *Ibid*. p. 3.
3. *Sikhism* by Teja Singh. Published by Khalsa Brothers, Amritsar, p. 3
4. *Ibid*. pp. 34-35.
5. *Spirit of the Sikh* by Dr. Puran Singh, Part II Vol 2, Published by Publication Bureau, Punjabi University Patiala. p. 16.
6. *Ibid*. p. 18.

– 6 –

The Great Debate on Sikh Identity

Sardar Khushwant Singh writes: "It is still disputed whether Guru Nanak (the founder) intended to reform Hinduism or form a third community or bring Hindus and Muslims together. It would appear that, in his earlier career, he tried to bring the two communities closer to each other. Being himself a Hindu, he was, at the same time, concerned with reforming Hinduism. But as the years went by and his message caught on among the masses, he decided to give his teachings permanency through a sect of his own."

Guru Nanakji has said:

NA MAIN HINDU
NA MAIN MUSALMAN

Writing in the *Midday* of April 18, 1982 (Sunday) under the caption 'With Malice towards One and All', Khushwant Singh wrote: "I have often maintained that as a system of belief, Sikhism is much closer to Islam than to Hinduism. And that, despite the fact that the vast majority of Sikhs are converts from Hinduism and to this day form an integral part of the Hindu Social System, I came to this conclusion because of the Sikh Gurus' emphasis on monotheism, rejection of idol worship and rejection of caste system, all of which are basic to Islam". A similar view is expressed by Macauliffe in his *History of Sikh Religion.* We will revert to some of his views later, but suffice it here, to say this much only that this view is accepted by most of the present day Sikh scholars though Macauliffe's contemporary foreigners had contrarily held that

Guru Gobind Singh lived according to Hindu customs and they had buttressed this view by Guru Gobind Singh's invocations of Durga and Shiva in his various works. But the question of Sikh identity is not centered on the way of living of the great Gurus, but the evolution of Sikh psyche during the community's decline, which led to searching of ways for its resurgence. It was the proselytising activities of Singh Sabha movement and Chief Khalsa Diwan and Tat Khalsa and their propagation of Sikh religion and cultivation of Sikh traditions and encouragement of English education among Sikh youth, that gave rise to the new awareness of Sikh identity because it brought them in confrontation with the Shudhi movement, launched by Arya Samaj and eventually to conflictual assertion of their identity.

Sardar Khushwant Singh in his *History of Sikhs* dwells at length on the threat posed to Sikhism by Arya Samaj. Swami Dayanand, the founder of Arya Samaj, visited Punjab in April 1877 on his mission and it is then that he spoke disrespectfully of Guru Nanak Devji. Swamy Dayanand, born in Gujarat, founded Arya Samaj in 1875 with the objective of purifying Hinduism. He denounced idol worship, child marriage, caste and exhorted the need for re-marriage of widows. He emphasised "the infallible nature of the Vedas ... the Vedas, divinely inspired, were the sole source of teaching. All scriptures compiled after the Vedas were regarded as unacceptable ... " The appeal of the Arya Samaj proved particularly enticing to the English educated segment of Punjabi Hindu society. Actually, Arya Samaj was founded as a fundamentalist thrust to secure purity of Vedic Hinduism and checkmate Christian missionaries. Swami Dayanand's remarks enraged Sikhs, who launched the Singh Sabha movement in Lahore and Amritsar to resist the onslaught of Arya Samaj. It was the conversion of 200 Sikh outcasts to Hinduism by Arya Samajists in 1896 that gave rise to Sikh-Arya Samaj conflict. Earlier, the foundation stone of Khalsa College was laid at Amritsar on March 5, 1892, by Punjab Lt. Governor, Sir James Lyall: funds for the College were collected after the issuance of a Hukamnama from Golden Temple Akal

Takht. Sikh Princes had made handsome contributions for the building of the college.

The Singh Sabha movement not only met the threat of Shudhi Movement launched by Arya Samaj, but in the words of Sardar Khushwant Singh "retaliated by carrying proselytising activities into the Hindu camp. Large numbers of Hindus of Northern and Western Punjab and Sindh became Sahajdhari Sikhs and Sahajdharis were baptised to become the Khalsa." Nonetheless, the Arya Samajists did not abandon their Shudhi Movement. Thus, the more Arya Samaj insisted that Sikhism was a part of Hinduism, more and more Sikhs insisted on their separate identity, which ultimately found vehement expression in the booklet by S. Kahan Singh, the Chief Minister of Nabha State, entitled *Hum Hindu Nahi Hain*. Kahan Singh was joined by the great poet and patriot Puran Singh, who wrote: "The great Hindu culture and its innate influence of Sikh culture cannot be denied." Guru Gobind Singh sent his Sikhs to Benaras to study Sanskrit. He is said to be related to Krishna himself. In retaliation, Sikh reformers expound the course of a separate identity. They came to be known as Tat, or true Khalsa. Dr. J.S. Ahluwalia writes that after the loss of political power in 1849, the crisis took the form of physical survival of Sikhs. To secure this survival, Sikhs transferred their loyalty to the British with whom they collaborated gleefully. After survival came revival. According to him and Sardar Khushwant Singh, the weakness of Sikh identity assertion lay in their numerical minority.

Fundamentalism everywhere harkens to the past glories, which are held as sacrosanct and any breach is sought to be penalised. Thus, fundamentalism, which got Punjab in its hold also sought to penalise so called heretics in the name of preservation of Sikh identity. In such a campaign, the pristine message of love and brotherhood of Sikhism was replaced by fancied grievances and the most potent of human emotive weapon—religious hatred. In the pre-independence days and particularly in the post-independence era, Sikh intelligentsia showed obsessive fears of Hinduism's assimilative power and then erosion of their identity. In his book *Sovereignty of Sikh's Doctrine*, Dr. J.S. Ahluwalia quotes Karl Marx as follows:

"Arabs, Turks, Tartars, Mughals, had successively overrun India but soon become Hinduised." If the invaders adopted some Hindu customs, does it mean they had lost their religion?" Dr. Ahluwalia is patently wrong to buttress this thesis by asserting that Buddhism, which was anti-thesis of Hinduism, stands today assimilated by Hindus. This is a distortion of facts. Buddhism today is a living force all over the world and has not shed its identity. In his scholarly work, Dr. Ahluwalia postulates that Vedantic interpretations of *Guru Granth Sahib* are erroneous. He says: "Sikhism though often mixed up with the Sant tradition of the Hindu Bhakti movement, is metaphysically different from the Advait Vedanta of Shankar as well as from theistic Vedanta of Ramanuja and others". In the introduction to his book, Dr. Ahluwalia mentions that "The Sikhs have acquired a distinct community character with their doctrine and culture defined and since that period, the hiatus between Sikhism and Hinduism had continued to become wider". In chapter 16 of his book, he concludes: "The Sikh problem would not lend itself to an abiding solution even if all of their present and foreseeable demands are accepted fully, absolutely and unconditionally, because these are just symptomatic flash points of a much deeper complex embedded in the Sikh psyche that relates to the very nature of Sikh identity and its expression and forms and structures and their correlation to the structures and the institutions of the secular state". Dr. Sardar Kapur Singh had maintained that Hinduism was the only enemy of Sikhism. But, in fact, there are no specifics to Hinduism. The challenge to all religions and churches comes not from any rival religion but the commercialisation and Westernisation of life. If Sikhs can de-Westernise, they can certainly revert to their hoary pristine glory. Why kill innocent Sikhs and others to prove that you would maintain your identity under all circumstances? In his book *East and West* published by John Murray, London, Northcote Parkinson at page 241 quotes Francis L.K. Hiu from his book *Americans and Chinese* as follows: "The Western world is today the arbiter of mankind's fate. It is paradoxical but true that the reaction against Western physical domination has gone far to complete the conquest of the world by Western culture. To ensure its own survival, the rest of the world has been obliged to imitate the West. It is Western methods, beliefs and goals that have been accepted and utilised to combat Western Control." Let Sikh fundamentalists ponder and stop venting their gory wrath on the innocents.

Again, Hinduism is not a blending machine for heterogeneous religions. India's predominant feature is her capacity for synthesis, as Pandit Nehru emphasised on more than one occasion.

Hindus have relied on Ashoka's edict which reads:

"All sects deserve reverence for one reason or another. By thus acting, a man exalts his own sect and at the same time does service to the sects of other people",

Dr. Ahluwalia provides answer to the dilemma raised by him in his article *Search for Sikh Identity-II* of the *Tribune* Chandigarh May 1, 1985, as follows: "A mere numerical majority in the linguistically re-organised Punjab in 1966 in a system of unitarian political structure was not enough for Sikh minority in the national body politic. It was this dilemma that motivated the taking up of the destiny of Sikh identity to the destination of 'deshkal' (Environs) for 'Khalsaji ka bol-bala' can be only in a theocracy. Ganga Singh Dhillon, who came into prominence since March 1982, puts the issue as follows:

"Some historians like J.D. Cunnigham trace the origin of the cultural separation of the Sikhs and their demand for an autonomous region to the Baisakhi of 1699 presided over by Guru Gobind Singh. The establishment of Sikh commonwealth in 1699 was another milestone in this direction and the quest for re-establishing our identity has been strong ever since the end of Sikh rule over Punjab & Kashmir in 1848." He further asserted that historians like Sir Gokal Chand Narang and Mohammed Latif had called Sikhs a 'Nation'." Some other Sikh intellectuals are less strident. K.S. Duggal writes: "What seems to bother the Sikhs currently is again the question of their identity. There are not a few front-rank intellectuals in the community who fear that, with the onslaught of modernism, the Sikhs may be swept off their feet and lose their identity". However, he provides an answer himself by writing further: "Nothing could be farther than the truth". If the gathering of the devotees at the Sikh Gurudwaras is any indication, faith in the Sikh way of life is growing everyday. We have amongst the Sikhs today, people who would be willing to make any sacrifice for the preservation of Sikh tradition",

Hindus have tried to meet the question of Sikh identity by saying that in a Hindu family one son always became a 'Sikh-Hindu'. Shri I.K. Gujral, the Prime Minister of India, in an interview with Mubarak Singh for the magazine *Art of Living* had said that "the Sikhs and Hindus of the Punjab are the same people, they speak the same language, observe the same customs and traditions".[5] He goes on to say; "All Punjabi Hindus revere the ten great Gurus, the *Granth Sahib* and are proud of the Khalsa Panth. On their side, the Sikhs have made notable sacrifices to preserve Hindu traditions". Late Prof. V.N. Tiwari laid stress on 'Punjabiat', but was gunned down on 3rd April, 1985 despite his passionate espousal of Punjab's cause — or was he eliminated because he had laid emphasis on the composite culture of Punjabiat than the so-called Hindu-Sikh divide?

Dr. Ahluwalia has raised not only the question of Sikh identity but also the need for securing' deskal' for Sikh identity to blossom. If every minority identity is to be given a deskal for its culture to flower, not only India, but US and China inhabited as they are by different ethnic groups, must disintegrate since a multi-cultural or multi-religious polity cannot exist according to Dr. Ahluwalia.

So far as the identity of Sikhs is concerned, if they insist that they are a separate religion, it is their own affair. Any claim made to the contrary by any Hindu can carry no weight. But how would Sikhs delete references to Hindu deities and hymns of Hindu saints from the Adi Granth? This Granth contains hymns of first five Gurus and those of the Ninth Guru. Ms. Gurminder Kaur in her book *Guru Granth Sahib: Its*

Physics and Metaphysics writes: "We have, in the Holy Granth, 36 men belonging to various castes and creeds and vocations ... Among them are Jaidev of Bengal, Surdas of Awadh, Namdev, Trilochan and Parmanand of Maharashtra, Beni Ramanand, Kabir, Ravidas and Bhiken of UP." "Can it be denied that though the *Granth Sahib* has the largest number of hymns from Guru Arjan Devji (2,218) followed by Guru Nanak Devji (974), it has also 292 hymns of Kabir and a host of other Hindu and Muslim saints?" Mr. Arun Shourie in his book *Religion in Politics* quotes K.P. Agarwal, *Adi Guru Granth Sahib Ki Mahima,* Bharat Bharati, New Delhi, to point out that the *Granth Sahib* invokes Paar Brahma above 550 times. It invokes the authority of the Vedas, Puranas, Smritis above 350 times. The name of the Saguna diety - Gobind, Murari, Madhav, Saligram, Vishnu, Krishna etc. - are invoked above two thousand times. In his introduction to *Roots of Hindu Sikh Unity* (by Narain Singh), Bhagat Puran Singh of Pingalwara, Amritsar, refers to the distorted interpretation of the following couplet of Guru Amar Dass by Macauliffe in his *History of Sikh Religion* and he refers to the importance of Vedas in another couplet as:

"The line quoted by Macauliffe hinges for their support on the first part that runs:

ਸਿਮ੍ਰਿਤ ਸਾਸਤ੍ਰ ਪੁੰਨ ਪਾਪ ਬੀਚਾਰਦੇ ਤਤੈ ਸਾਰ ਨ ਜਾਣੀ।।

ਰਾਮਕਲੀ ਮਹਲਾ 3

Many people read in the Smritis and Shastras as to what makes the virtue and what make the vice, but they fail to find the 'Real'. Guru Amar Das, on whom Macauliffe relies, has eulogised the Vedas for the 'Real Thing' in them, as follows:

ਵਦਾ ਸਹਿ ਨਾਮੁ ਉਤਮੁ ਮੁ ਸੁਣਹਿ ਨਾਹੀ ਫਿਰਹਿ ਬੇਤਾਲਿਆ।।

ਰਾਮਕਲੀ ਮਹਲਾ 3

There is in the Vedas the pure Name (The thing that matters) but ignorant men do not listen to it and wander in illusions".

The crux of the matter of Sikh identity was commented upon by late Giri Lal Jain as follow:

"There are, of course, some Hindus wholly unfamiliar with historical developments since the beginning of the century who continue to think of the Sikhs as being part of the larger Hindu fraternity. But no one has ever disputed, indeed no one could possibly dispute, the right of the Sikhs to think of themselves as a separate community. But what advantage does that acknowledgment confer on them? None at all in the non-religious sphere. For the Indian Constitution, like all other modern Constitutions, relies on the concept of the individual and not of the community". Hindus can have no dispute if Sikhs claim to be separate from them. The dispute arises on the question of separate homelands for religious or ethnic communities.

Indeed, the threat to Sikh identity does not emanate from amorphous Hinduism but from the modern technology, which through a matchless array of gadgets and comforts seeks to lure human heart and mind away from religious moorings. Evidently, this threat is not only to Sikhism but to all religions and explains the dominance of present day life by religious fundamentalism and revivalism by way of reaction and reassertion among Muslims and partly among Hindus, too. The success of Ayatullah Khomeini in Iran and such cults as Hare Krishna and Hare Rama in the West are manifestations of the same religious reaction to the modern materialism.

The crisis posed by Arya Samaj to Sikhs on which Sardar Khushwant Singh has dwelt at length was more than adequately met by Singh Sabhas and Tat Khalsa, who received all encouragement from the British, who were interested to keep Sikhs apart from Hindus. Propagation of Sikh faith got a new impetus when Shiromani Gurdwara Prabhandak Committee took over the charge of all the Gurdwaras. Saral Jhingran in *Secularism in India* writes: "I have questioned the concept of the religious community as the basis and all inclusive unit of society. Both communalism and religious fundamentalism draw sustenance from the ubiquitous use of the term "community" for all socio - political discourse. Once the category of religious community as a distinct, independent and relatively autonomous unit of the society is challenged, both communalism and religious fundamentalism lose their *raison d'etre*."

Golwalkar and Damodar Vinayaka Savarkar sum up the position as follows. Golwalkar, the RSS Chief, had this to say on Hindu Identity:

" ... We Hindus have been in undisputed and undisturbed possession of the land over eight or over ten thousand years before the land was invaded by any foreign race". According to T.K. Oomen, Hindus are simply the original and obvious inhabitants of Hindustan, that is India. Hindu society living in this country since time immemorial is the national society here. The same Hindu people have built the life values, ideals and culture of this country and, therefore, their nationhood is self-evident." According to T.K. Oomen, this all-embracing definition does not have a religious content, Hindus being a people of a designated land, as the Germans or Greeks are.

According to Damodar Vinayak Savarkar, Hindus are all those who pursue religions of Indian origin, According to this definition, Islam, Christianity and Zoroastrianism are not Hindu as they came to India from outside but Sikhism, Jainism and even Buddhism are part of Hindu mainstream. In the words of Savarkar: "Sikhs are Hindus in our definition of Hindutva and not in any religious sense whatsoever. Religiously, they are Sikhs as Jains are Jains, Lingayats are Lingayats, Vaishnavs are Vaishnavs but all of us racially and naturally and culturally are one polity and people".

The subject of religious identities seeking territorialities is inexhaustible.

Those Hindus, who persisted to call Sikhs as a sub-sect of Hinduism, have served neither Hindu cause nor the cause of the country. The facts remain that Guru Amar Das and Guru Gobind Singh gave Sikhs a distinct identity. Sikhs have an identity of their own though their Gurus and *Guru Granth Sahib* refer to the Hindu saints and gods. Yet, in the 19th and 20th centuries, Sikhs came to acquire their own customs. The Anand (the Song of Joy) Marriage Ceremony was preached by the third Guru Amar Das. He not only laid different marriage ceremonies but even separate death rituals for Sikhs called the Sadd (Ram Kali Sadd) "Jag Data Soeya Bhagat Wachhal Te Loeyo Jeo, Gur Sabab Samae Awar nan Jane Koeye Teo." .....

Arya Samajist and Brahmanical sections raised a hue and cry saying that the Sikh marriages performed by Anand ceremonies were illegal and the offspring out of such wedlocks should be treated as illegitimate. This led Tikka Ripudaman Singh of Nabha to introduce the Anand Marriage Bill in the Viceroy's Council on 30th October, 1908. On the expiry of the term of the Tikka as member of the Council, the Bill was piloted by Sir Sunder Singh Majithia and was passed into an Act on 22nd October, 1909, as 'Anand Marriage Act' (Act VII of 1909).

Thus, the distinct religious identity claimed by Sikhs cannot be annulled but their violent quest for securing 'deshkal' cannot be conceded, whatever the dimension of violence perpetrated by a misguided section and buttressed by intellectual acrobatic jugglers.

– 7 –

Onward to Khalistan: Raj Karega Khalsa

History of India's struggle for independence shows that vis-a-vis minorities, the Congress posture has been undergoing too many changes whereas the two militant minority organisations, that is, Muslim League and Akali Dal, have been consistent in their stand. Muslim League stuck to its demand for Pakistan and made it a reality. Sikhs sought a separate homeland and are still fighting for it, though their stand was ambiguous at times. Ever since the enactment of Gurudwara Act in 1925, Akalis strove throughout to have Sikhs accepted as a separate entity in India. In pre-independence days, Akalis strove for weightage for Sikhs in the Services and Legislatures. They constituted just one per cent of India's population and they were not in a majority even in one single district of Punjab; yet invoking danger to the Panth from both Muslims and Hindus, the Akalis placed Sikhs at par with Muslims so far as the two minorities were concerned.

In fact Sikhs had emerged as a political entity under Banda Bahadur who was earlier called Lachhman Das and on becoming a Bairagi came to be called Madho Dass. He was born at Rajouri in the Poonch district of Jammu region. He was baptised as a Sikh by Guru Gobind Singh at Nanded. Banda (that is *servant* or *slave* to his guru) launched the Sikh struggle against the oppressive rule of the Mughals. Writes A.C. Bannerji, "His (Banda's) immediate object was to punish Wazir Khan, the Faujdar of Sirhand, who had cruelly murdered the Guru's younger sons, and was probably responsible for the murder of the Guru, and to chastise the Hill Rajas, who had fought for years against the Guru. His limited objectives were soon merged in a bid for acquisition of sovereignty for Sikhs. Sikh warriors under him raised the slogan:

"Agya Bhayi Akal Ki Tabih Chalayo Panth
Raj Karega Khalsa Yaki Rahe Na Koi..."

(The Khalsa shall rule, no opponent shall exist.)

This couplet, which now forms a permanent and inseparable part of the Sikh Ardas, i.e. Prayer, was composed and first sung by the Khalsa during the days of Banda ... Banda's struggle has a complex character. It was a religious struggle in so far as it was inspired by Sikh religious ideas. It was sustained by the tremendous driving power of the moral force generated by the life and teachings of Guru Gobind Singh.[1] According to Cunningham, "A living spirit passes the whole Sikh people, and the impress of Gobind has not only elevated and altered the constitution of their minds, but has operated materially and given amplitude to their physical powers."[2] Banda's legacy was a lasting transformation of Sikhs into a fighting community though his success did not last long. The persecution of Sikhs at the hands of Bahadur Shah and Farrakh Siyar failed to daunt their religious spirit.

Guru Gobind Singh had given a new concept of man called "Khalsa", who fought against all the acts of oppression and discrimination.

According to Dr. Trilochan Singh of Ludhiana, in his article published in *'Vishav Ekta'* of 30th June, 1981, "The Tenth Guru gave a direction to Sikhs to regard Guru Granth Sahib as an embodiment of the Guru and uttered 'Raj Karega Khalsa' as a blessing to Sikhs after the creation of the 'Order of the Khalsa'. He further says that since its composition, it is being recited at the tail-end of every Ardas (Supplication).

Having once ruled Punjab from Jammu to Jamrud, Sikhs have been haunted by the dream of recapturing the earlier glory and once again ruling these lands. However, they adopted different strategies at different times. After the disintegration of their empire through their own petty intrigues and incessant factionalism, Sikhs were in a state of bewilderment. M.J. Akbar writes: "Rarely in history has the fall from the sublime to the ridiculous been as astonishing".[3]

To break the conundrum, Sikhs offered their soldiery in quelling the uprising of 1857. Ghani Jafar, the Pakistani scholar in his widely circulated book outside India, *The Sikh Volcano*, writes: "The colonial power was quick in deciding to canalise the frustrated militancy of the Sikhs to its own strategic ends, political and military. The Sikhs were inducted in large number into the British Indian army to replace those communities, which had 'betrayed' the colonial power by taking up arms in 1857 uprising". This also gave the Sikhs an opportunity to wreak vengeance on East India troops, who had destroyed their empire. Sikh soldiers fought to save the British in North India. In return, the British made the Sikhs their new darlings. The British ascribed the rationale of Sikhs' eagerness to put down the uprising of 1857 as combat between Sikhism and Islam. Thus, when Lawrence raised local levies, Sikhs flocked in large numbers to the British standard and identified themselves with the British cause.

The British rewarded the unwavering loyalty of the Sikhs by laying a network of canals and allotting the best irrigated areas to them. Thus, prosperity returned to Sikh families. This gave an impetus to the rise of their population, too. In his classic book, *A History of the Sikhs*, Sardar Khushwant Singh has shown great concern on the slow rate of growth in Sikh population. At page 146, he has given the figures as follows on the basis of various censuses:-

Year	*Actual Number of Sikhs*
1881	1,1706,165
1891	1,849,371
1901	2,102,896
1911	2,2883,729
1921	3,110,060

The role of the British in encouraging Sikh separatism finds mention in the official handbook published for restricted circulation. Ghani Jafar writes: "Two centuries of British colonial adventure in South Asia have left many distortions in India's political, cultural and economic evolution, but perhaps hardly as unsettling as in the case of Punjab, where the colonial policy of 'divide and rule' went a long way in nourishing religious and socio-economic conflicts within the region."[4]

However, the Sikh-British honeymoon—like any other honeymoon—could not last forever. The first open confrontation was the Gurudwara Reform Movement and the Singh Sabha Movement, which gave impetus to education among the Sikhs and resisted the onslaught of Arya Samaj. Votaries, both Sikhs and Hindus, visited Gurudwaras in large numbers and their offerings were substantial. Nonetheless, the Mahants who were controlling the gurudwaras were prisoners of profligate habits and their acts of wining and debauchery were resented by the more enlightened Sikhs. Sikh resurgence was rising to a new crest and the youth who emerged out of the portals of Khalsa College, Amritsar founded by Lt. Governor Lyall with the funds raised voluntarily and generous contributions by Sikh princes—were attracted to the freedom movement. On the Baisakhi Day 1919, Brigadier General Edward Harry Dyer had blocked the concourse assembled in Jallianwala Bagh, Amritsar in the neighbourhood of Golden Temple and then gunned down hundreds of unarmed men, women and children. 379 persons were killed and over 2000 injured: mostly Sikhs. This barbarous slaughter of the peaceful gathering raised tremors of shock throughout the country. Gandhiji and other national leaders condemned this holocaust. The nemesis came later. Udham Singh, as a 19 year-old orphaned youth, had seen this slaughter, which had made an indelible mark on his mind, and had vowed to avenge these killings. He shot Sir Michael O'Dyer, who was the Punjab Governor. R.E. Dyer had died due to a severe stroke in 1927 itself. However there are black sheep everywhere. Arur Singh, head priest of Golden Temple, had presented a saropa to R.E.H. Dyer, the killer, condoning his smoking and other non-Sikh indulgences.

The martyrdom complex in Sikhs impelled them to free their Gurudwaras from profligate Mahants. Control of the

Golden Temple and Akal Takht was wrested on 12th October, 1920. A General Assembly of the Sikhs was convened on 15th November, 1920 to elect Shiromani Gurudwara Parbhandak Committee and Shiromani Akali Dal was established on 14th December 1920 as an adjunct of SGPC to secure the control of Gurudwaras.

Guru Nanak Ji was born at Nankana Sahib. The main Gurudwara at the Janam Asthan (the birthplace) was under the control of Mahant Narain Dass. He had desecrated the Gurudwara by drinking and debauchery. In February 1921, SGPC decided to wrest control of this Gurudwara from this debauch. Narain Dass collected a large number of mercenaries who opened fire on Akalis as they entered the Gurudwara singing hymns. 85 Akalis lost their lives at the hands of mercenaries, and their bodies were chopped up and burnt. The outrage shocked the country almost as much as the Jallianwala Bagh tragedy. Mahatma Gandhi visited Nankana Sahib and condemned the fiendish killings. Eminent Hindus and Muslims rallied around Sikh cause. Lala Lajpat Rai and Maulana Shaukat Ali made fiery speeches. Mahant Narain Dass was prosecuted and sentenced. SGPC gained control of the historic Gurudwara. SGPC demanded enactment of an Act to transfer control of all Gurudwaras to them. The British were unwilling to accept this demand because on 11th May, 1921, the Akali Dal had committed itself to the cause of freedom by passing a resolution. In 1921, the British seized the keys of the Golden Temple from the President of SGPC. Akalis started a peaceful satyagraha, as advised by Mahatma Gandhi, under the fiery leadership of Baba Kharak Singh. The British were forced to return the keys. Gandhiji called this the first victory of the freedom movement.

On 9th August, 1922, SGPC started its agitation for control of Guru Ka Bagh, which commemorates a visit made by the fifth Guru Arjan Dev to the site. It is nearly 13 miles from Amritsar in Ajnala Tehsil. Sikh Jathas of a strength of 100 volunteers each would take a vow of non-violence in the Golden Temple in the morning and begin their march towards Guru Ka Bagh as also to offer themselves for arrests. Waves of Jathas followed. Police used lathis and physical violence. The Sikhs simply stood there and allowed themselves to be beaten until they fell unconscious. Hindus and Muslims like Swami Shradhanand and Hakim Ajmal Khan once again rallied to the Sikh cause, making speeches at Guru Ka Bagh. The news of British brutality travelled abroad and an American film maker, Captain A.I. Verghese made a documentary called '*Exclusive Picture of India's Martyrdom*'. The Congress set up a committee of inquiry, which concluded that force used by the police was excessive on all occasions. E.F. Andrews visited Guru Ka Bagh and described police brutality as 'inhuman, brutal, foul ... and a moral defeat of England.' Ultimately the police was removed from this site on 17th September, 1922.

In 1925, Sikhs achieved a great victory. The Sikh Gurudwara Act was enacted. SGPC became a repository of Sikh faith and its glorious traditions and purged the management of Gurudwaras of all evil practices. Its proselytising activities were a major factor in the revival of Sikhism and the profound change in the demographic profile of Punjab. (Sikhs became a majority from a minority in the state carved out in November 1966.) It published prodigious Literature on Sikh faith in various languages. It worked with a missionary spirit and the respect, which Gurudwaras inspire would not have been possible without its splendid work, though it is unfortunate that it came to superimpose political aims upon its religious activities.

Sikhs' Role in Freedom Movement

Sikhs have made a significant contribution to India's struggle for freedom. Sikhs' fight for freedom goes back to the nineteenth century when, in 1863, a splinter sect called Kukas organised themselves as a para military sect. They practised swadeshi and boycotted everything British. Inevitably, they invited British wrath and a large number of them were tied to the barrels of cannons and blown off. Their leader, Ram Singh, with 11 of his close followers, was banished to Burma where he died in 1885.

The next landmark in the Sikh struggle against British oppression was the agitation launched against the Punjab

Colonisation Act, 1907, which sought to enhance land revenue and water charges. There was widespread agrarian unrest. Sardar Ajit Singh and Lala Lajpat Rai were prominent among the leaders of the movement. Both were imprisoned in Mandalay in Burma. After their release, Ajit Singh went to Canada and joined the Ghadar Party. The Ghadar Party was started by Sohan Singh Bakala under the inspiration of Lala Hardayal. Their headquarters was in San Francisco. They pledged to end British rule through an armed revolution. It was a secular, revolutionary movement. Soon they were joined by Kartar Singh 'Sarabha', Dr. Mathura Singh and Jwala Singh who were later hanged in India. Their activities received fillip by what has come to be known as the Kamagata Maru episode. *Kamagata Maru* was the name of a Japanese ship which was engaged by Baba Gurdit Singh for transporting Indian emigrants from Canada to India at the outbreak of World War I. The *Kamagata Maru* had a bloody reception when it touched Calcutta.

Sikhs were not allowed to stay in Calcutta. In the confrontation that ensued, 18 passengers were slaughtered. Baba Gurdit Singh and 27 others escaped. Baba Gurdit Singh remained underground for 7 years. Due to the slaughter of innocents who had gathered to celebrate Baisakhi - the birthday of Khalsa - in Jallianwala Bagh, Amritsar in 1919, Punjab became the vortex of political struggle. The Nobel laureate Rabindranath Tagore relinquished his knighthood as a protest against the brutal Jallianwala Bagh slaughter. The Indian National Congress held its annual session at Amritsar in December the same year. It was attended by Mahatma Gandhi, Jawaharlal Nehru and his father Moti Lal Nehru, Madan Mohan Malviya, C.F. Andrews, the Ali Brothers and Hakim Ajmal Khan. Punjabi leaders, who attended it, were Baba Kharak Singh, Lala Lajpat Rai and Sardar Sardul Singh "Caveeshar".

Sikhs had come to find inspiration in Mahatma Gandhi. That is how their Gurudwara Reform Movement had such an excellent record of true non-violence of Satyagrahis. In 1928, Sikh League held a meeting in Lahore presided over by Sardar Kharak Singh, which was attended by Mahatma Gandhi.

Every Indian is familiar with the legendary martyrdom of Bhagat Singh and his two colleagues Sukhdev and Rajguru for killing a British police officer, whose violence had resulted in the death of Lala Lajpat Rai. Ultimately, Bhagat Singh, Sukhdev and Rajguru embraced their death heroically on March 23, 1931 at Hussainiwala near Ferozepore on the banks of river Sutlej where Punjab Government has now built a befitting memorial.

Sikhs have magnificent record of sacrifices made during the course of freedom struggle: for instance, out of total of 121 executed, 73 were Sikhs and out of 2646 imprisoned for life, Sikhs again were 2047.

From 1920 onward, Akali Dal was influenced by Master Tara Singh, a Hindu convert. He was given more to rhetoric and dramatic gestures than carefully planned strategies. The Akalis, who had worked in close cooperation with Congress, broke off from national mainstream politics on the issue of noncooperation with Britain during World War II.

However, Sikh soldiers had nationalist freedom at heart, which manifested itself in a minor mutinous incident which involved Horse Regiment in 1940. Sikh soldiers also played a prominent role in the Indian National Army (INA). Captain Mohan Singh, with 20,000 Sikh soldiers, joined INA to fight the British and free their country.

Up to 1940, Akali leadership had demanded greater representation for Sikhs in the Legislature and administration and promotion of Punjabi language. The demand for weighted representation varied from fifty per cent in the Provincial Civil Service, five per cent at the Centre and at least one Cabinet Minister. The Sikhs hardly formed one per cent of India's population and only 14% in pre-partition Punjab where Muslims constituted 53% of the population.

Sikh Politics During Pre-Partition Days—Origin of Khalistan

The Muslim League under the leadership of Mr. Mohd. Ali Jinnah, at its Annual Conference at Lahore in 1940, gave a firm call for creation of a sovereign Muslim State, which should comprise whole of Punjab and other Muslim majority areas. Muslim League's campaign for Pakistan aroused Sikhs' worst fears of Muslim domination and oppression.

The term Khalistan first emerged soon after the Muslim League Conference of 1940. An All-India Akali Conference was held at Attari in March 1940, which resolved to oppose the demand of Pakistan: if, however, the country were to be partitioned, they demanded a similar State for Sikhs too. It was at this Conference that one Mr. V.S. Bhatti of Ludhiana circulated a pamphlet on Khalistan to be made as a buffer state between Pakistan and India: Khalistan was to comprise the Sikh majority areas (but there was hardly any) and the Sikh Princely' States of Nabha, Patiala, Faridkot, Jind and Malerkotla, which was under a Nawab. Another convention called by Baba Gurdit Singh and Jagjit Singh, editor of 'Khalsa Sewak', demanded that Khalistan should comprise all areas from Jammu to Jamrud. It was Sikh logic that all Sikh territories, which had been wrongfully annexed by the British, be restored to them before the British leave India. It was said that Maharaja Dalip Singh had given these territories to the British purely on 'trust'.

In 1935, the Akali leadership had passed on to Master Tara Singh, whose sole aim was to advance the Sikh cause with an alliance with Congress or without it. The alliance between the Akalis and the Unionists was the handiwork of Penderal Moon, who was Deputy Commissioner Amritsar and Major Short of the 11th Sikh Regiment to whom is ascribed the quip, "Secure the Sikhs and you secure India".

Cripps Mission

Sir Winston Churchill, the British Prime Minister, sent Sir Stafford Cripps, a Member of the British Cabinet, to India in March 1942. But Cripps failed to elicit any co-operation from Congress. The Note by Sir S. Cripps on his Interview with Sikhs on 27th March, 1942 is reproduced below:

"Note by Sir Cripps

L/P&J/10/4: ff 23-5

INTERVIEW WITH A NUMBER OF SIKHS

27 March 1942

Baldev Singh; Ujjal Singh; Master Tara Singh; Sir Jogender Singh.

After reading through the document with some explanation, they naturally raised immediately the question of protection of the Sikh minority and the possibility of having some redistribution of provincial power between the eastern and western Punjab in order to carve out a province in which the Sikhs would have the decisive voice as a large balancing party between Hindus and Muslims. We then went again very carefully through the document and I pointed out to them the successive stage at which they might hope to be able to exert pressure, which would enable them, either to remain part of the single Indian Union or to get some provincial autonomy within the second Union, if such was formed. These stages were as follows. First of all, in the Constituent Assembly Congress would not have a clear majority or at least a very small one and would desire to get the smaller minorities such as the Sikhs on their side by making the most ample provision for their protection in the new Constitution. This would set a standard of minority protection, which might well be satisfactory to the Sikh community 'and might even entail the subdivision of the Punjab, into two provinces or the setting up within the province of the Punjab a semi-autonomous district for the Sikhs on the Soviet model. If this failed and the Constitution did not contain sufficient clauses to satisfy the Sikhs, then in the Treaty which would be negotiated contemporaneously with the framing of the Constitution, we should be able to insist on the insertion of minority protection clauses, in accordance with the definition set out in the document. The form of these would be a matter for negotiation. If, when the Constitution was finally settled, the Muslims decided that they had not got sufficient concessions to enable them to remain within the Indian Union, then it would be necessary for them to obtain a vote of non-accession by plebiscite in the Punjab. Although they would have a narrow majority for this purpose, they would no doubt be anxious to increase that majority as far as possible, both in order to make certain a majority and also to have as favourable an atmosphere for setting up the new second Dominion as possible. The probability would be that they would try to get the Sikh vote to support their action and, in order to do so, would offer minority protection clauses going further than those already offered by the Indian Union and possibly going as far as agreeing to division of the province or the setting up of a semi-autonomous district. There would be the meeting of the second Constitution-making body, in which the Sikh minority would be able to exert its pressure for minority protection, if it had not previously succeeded in getting what it wanted. If at all these points, they had still failed to get protection, then in the negotiation of the Treaty with the second Dominion, the British Government would, in carrying out the words of the document, insist upon adequate protection for the Sikh minority, and that protection would be guaranteed to the extent that, if it were not given, there would be a breach of the Treaty between the Dominion and the British Government and whatever action was appropriate, could follow. I pointed out to them that once our decision to allow the Indian peoples complete freedom in determining their own Constitution was granted, there was nothing further that we could do to provide protection for the minorities, as we could not intervene in the making of the Constitution or in its carrying out, after the Dominion had been set up, beyond insisting upon the observation by the Dominion of its Treaty obligations as regards minorities."

"Although they were obviously anxious, first of all to avoid the setting up of a second Dominion and, secondly, if it were set up, to cut themselves out an autonomous district, I think they appreciated that we had done our utmost in the circumstances to provide protection and they were very pleased when I emphasised to them that this matter of protection to the Sikhs had been particularly discussed in the War Cabinet because of our very great appreciation of the contribution that the Sikhs had made in the past and were making now to the defence of India."

The Akali Party was not prepared to sacrifice Sikh interests in army recruitment. So there came a rupture between the Akalis and Congress in 1942. In June 1942, there was the Sikander Hyat-Baldev Singh Pact and the Akalis chose to support the Unionist Ministry led by Sir Sikander Hyat Khan. The British were elated at these pro-war developments. The Sikhs were rewarded by the inclusion of Sir Joginder Singh as Member for Education, Land and Revenue in the Viceroy's Executive Council.

Viscount Wavell took over as Viceroy of India in October 1945. He was opposed to the partition of India. On his persuasion, the British Government issued a White Paper on India on 14th June, 1945. Wavell convened a conference of all the political parties at Simla on 25th June 1945. In this conference Master Tara Singh put forth, for the first time, the demand for a separate Sikh State. He told the Conference that he was quite prepared to agree to the creation of Pakistan, if Jinnah on his part would agree to the creation of a separate Sikh State.

Cabinet Mission

When the Cabinet Mission comprising Sir Stafford Cripps, Lord Pethick-Lawrence and Dr. A.V. Alexander was to arrive in India, Akali Dal said: "On the eve of the expected far-reaching changes in the constitution of the country ... Panth demands setting up of the Sikh State." Master Tara Singh pressed the Mission for acceptance of Sikh demand but without any effect. So the partition of Punjab was sought by Sikhs and acquiesced to by Mohd. Ali Jinnah as he considered Sikhs would be a permanent liability for Pakistan. A Campbell Johnson writes in his *Mission with Mountbatten* that according to K.M. Pannikar, Sikh Punjab was a British myth (Diary of 26th March, 1947)

Sir Stafford Cripps had told the British Parliament on July 18, 1946 that the Sikhs, in demanding special treatment analogous to that envisaged for Muslims, "ignored the inescapable geographical fact of the situation. The Sikhs are a much smaller community - 5.55 million against 90 million Muslims - and are not geographically situated so that any area could be carved out in which they would find themselves in a majority." Thus, it is clear that the British were sympathetic to the creation of a separate Sikh State but were stonewalled by the logic of geography and demographic realities. The Sikhs, therefore, seeing the very unreason of their proposals, grew tepid in their demand for a Sikh homeland. In his book *Mission with Mountbatten*, Campbell Johnson brings out that Sardar Baldev Singh, Akali representative in the Central Cabinet holding Defence portfolio, called upon the Viceroy on several occasions but there was no mention of the demand for a Sikh State by him, the reason being that ambivalence and confusion prevailed among the Akali leadership at that time. Only Giani Kartar Singh remained an implacable proponent of a Sikh Homeland throughout. Though Akali Dal maintained close relations with the Congress Party, yet its principal concern was securing a position of leverage for the Sikhs as an entity of their own. In 1928, a Committee under the presidentship of Pt. Motilal Nehru had made its recommendations regarding the future Constitution of India, and had recommended abolition of separate communal representation, except for Muslims. The Akali Dal pressed for equating Sikhs with Muslims in any Constitutional arrangement. The Congress gave in to the pressure and "assured the Sikhs that no Constitutional proposal would be acceptable to Congress, which did not give full satisfaction to Sikhs' demands".

Leonard Mosley in his book, *The Last Days of the British Raj in India* writes:

"Their Rome, Mecca, Canterbury, call it what you will, is the fabulous Golden Temple at Amritsar, set in a holy lake. The Sikhs made no bones about their antipathy to Muslims; the Muslims were equally plain in their envy of the Sikhs. What is going to happen to us, asked the Sikhs, when Independence comes? If Jinnah gets Pakistan, the Punjab or, at least Western Punjab to him, we could never live as a minority under the Muslims. But we don't know what will happen to our lands, our houses, our canals and our shrines?"

He further writes:

"It is ironic that inside the compound of the Golden Temple, Granthis at one side were reading aloud the words of the *Granth Sahib*, the Sikh Holy Book, counselling their people to gentleness and goodwill to all men, while a hundred yards away, within the some sacred precincts, men were being exhorted to commit murder." The slogan of "Kill, Kill and Kill" that Master Tara Singh gave on the eve of Partition was to be adopted once again in the same precincts by the extremists in 1983 and onwards.

Sikh Politics after Independence—Demand for Punjabi Suba

After India's freedom, demand for Khalistan was replaced by one for Punjabi Suba - Sikh majority area within India's polity. How this demand for Punjabi Suba crystallised is narrated by Harcharan Singh Bajwa in his book, *Fifty Years of Punjab Politics*. He writes: "In bewilderment, on 23rd January 1948, I took along with me Bhupinder Singh Mann and Giani Kartar Singh and the three of us knocked at the door of Dr. B.R. Ambedkar and solicited guidance from him and quick he was in prescribing a recipe of our peril. He said that in joint Punjab you were in a minority except in two tehsils (i.e., Taran Taran and Moga), which two were non-contiguous. In Eastern Punjab, too, you are in a minority. If you clamour for a Sikh State, it will be a cry in the wilderness. Why don't you ask for a Punjabi-speaking State? Congress is committed to linguistic basis for re-organisation of states. I have told you the way you can have a Sikh state in the cloak of Punjabi Suba". Thus, the foundation-stone for Punjabi Suba was laid by Dr. Bhimrao Ramji Ambedkar and the structure was built by Akali Dal led by Sant Fateh Singh.

States Re-organisation

Before partition, around 40% Sikhs were on the Pakistani side of the border and 60 per cent on the Indian side. After partition of the country, Punjab on Indian side had come to be called East Punjab. In this Punjab, Hindus formed 62.3 per cent and Sikhs 35 per cent. So Sikhs were convinced that if they had to have a Sikh majority state it could only come into existence by acting on the advice of Dr. B.R. Ambedkar since, in its sessions of 1916 and 1920, the Congress Party had accepted the principle of linguistic States after independence. But in the post-independence era, Congress Government was loath to implement its own resolution. In 1953, the government set up the States Re-Organisation Commission chaired by Syed Fazal Ali, and K.M. Panikkar and Hriday Nath Kunzru as members, in order to consider demands for redrawing state boundaries on a linguistic basis. The commission rejected the Akali demand for a Punjabi-speaking state because Hindus, under the influence of Arya Samaj and Jan Sangh, fearing loss of their majority, had got recorded their mother tongue to be Hindi and not Punjabi - it was certainly a cultural fraud because Hindus did speak Punjabi but they had adopted a strategy, which defeated the Akali design to carve out a Sikh majority territory under the garb of a linguistic state. The commission had rejected the Akali claim for a Punjabi-speaking state on the ground that the demand lacked 'the general support of the people inhabiting the area'. This was a major factor in the Hindu-Sikh divide. It embittered Sikhs enormously and convinced them that the Punjabi Hindus would always remain communal and anti-Sikh. Akalis' ambition had been to have a state, which they could always rule. But they were oblivious to the fact that all Sikhs were not Akalis nor Jats who were going to control Akali Dal. Sikhs had their schisms and antagonisms. Sikhs have never been a monolithic community, neither now nor ever during the rule of Maharaja Ranjit Singh nor, in their difficult days subsequently. Denial of Punjabi Suba was, however, perceived by Sikhs as an act of grave injustice to them and a discrimination against their community.

From the start of Independence, the Akali Dal leader Master Tara Singh insisted on official recognition of Sikhs as a separate community. He told the Government, "If you are true nationalists then for the sake of the nation, you must let the Sikhs live honourably. You will err in attempting to extinguish, in the name of nationalism, the distinctive entity of the Sikhs. We value our honour. If we have no separate existence, we shall have nothing to be proud of ...!"

During the debate on the Punjab Re-organisation Bill 1966 in the Parliament, Dr. Kapur Singh, claiming to speak on behalf of the Sikhs, used very picturesque language to describe what he said was the betrayal of Sikhs. In his words, Jawaharlal Nehru had given a solemn assurance to Baba Kharak Singh on the occasion of All India Congress Session at Lahore in 1929, that after independence no constitution will be framed unless it was freely acceptable to the Sikhs.[5] Dr. Kapur Singh, during debates on Punjab Reorganisation Bill 1966, stated that in the month of July 1946, the All India Congress Working Committee had met at Calcutta and re-affirmed the assurances given to the Sikhs and, in his Press Conference held on 6th July there, Pt. Jawaharlal Nehru had spelt out the contents of these solemn undertakings in the following words:

"The brave Sikhs of the Punjab are entitled to special consideration. I see nothing wrong in an area and a set-up in the North wherein the Sikhs can also experience the glow of freedom."

In his words "Here is the brief story of a callous betrayal - the Sikh of India - by those whose flesh of flesh and bones of bones the Sikhs are, and whose ancestors - common ancestors of the betrayed and the betrayers, both - had upheld the highest and the noblest notions and standards of ethical conduct in respect of the subjects of keeping faith with fellow-men and redeeming promises solemnly made.

I quote from *Mahabharat, Adiparvam*, sub-chapter 74 and verse 25:

Yo anayatha santamatmanam anayatha pratipadayete, kin ten na kritam papam caurainatmapaharina.

It means,

"He who has one thing in mind but represents another thing to others, what sin he is not capable of committing? For, he is a thief and a robber of his own self"

Continuing his participation in the debate in the Parliament, Dr. Kapur Singh disclosed that Mr. Mohammad Ali Jinnah had offered to the Sikhs a sovereign Sikh State comprising areas lying to the west of Panipat and east of the left bank of the Ravi river, on the understanding that this State would then confederate with Pakistan on terms favourable to the Sikhs. According to him, the offer was made to Master Tara Singh and Maharaja of Patiala and both of them had declined the offer.

Continuing further, Dr. Kapur Singh accused the Nehru Government of violating the solemn oath taken on the 9th December, 1946, the day the first meeting of the Constituent Assembly was held under the Chairmanship of Babu Rajendra Prasad. Pandit Jawaharlal Nehru had moved the first and the fundamental resolution in which he had said: "Adequate safeguards would be provided for minorities ... It was a declaration, a pledge and an undertaking before the world, a contract with millions of Indians, and, therefore, in the nature of an oath, which we must keep."

Not only had the Nehru Government violated the oath given solemnly on 9th December, 1946 by Pandit Jawaharlal Nehru himself, the Government, according to Dr. Kapur Singh, had disregarded what Gandhiji had said on 16th March, 1931, when he had visited a Sikh congregation in Gurudwara Sis Ganj, Delhi. During this visit Gandhiji was asked what guarantee there was that the Indian National Congress would fully implement the assurances given to the Sikhs in 1929 at Lahore. Gandhiji's reply to this query is published in his *Young India* 1931 and it contained the following: "Sardar Madhusudan Singh has asked for an assurance that the Congress would do nothing that might alienate sympathies of the Sikhs from the Congress. Well, the Congress, in its Lahore Session, passed a Resolution that it would not enter into or be a party to any settlement with regard to the minorities' question that failed to satisfy any of the minorities concerned. What further assurances the Congress can give to the Sikhs, I fail to understand .. I ask you to accept my word and the resolution of the Congress that it will not betray a single individual much less a community. If it ever thinks of doing so, it will only hasten its own doom ... I pray you, therefore, to unbosom yourselves of all your doubts ... What more shall I say? What more can I say than this: 'Let God be the witness of the bond that binds me and the Congress with you'."

Continuing, he said that in 1950 when the Constitution of India was enacted, the Shiromani Akali Dal representatives had declined to append their signatures to the Constitution and had said that "the Sikhs do not accept this Constitution Act; the Sikhs reject this Constitution Act."

Referring to the specifics of the Punjab Reorganisation Bill, Dr. Kapur Singh said that the Shah Commission, constituted on 21st March, 1966, was asked to apply linguistic principles as in the 1961 census figures, to determine boundaries between Punjab and Haryana, which did not involve breaking of the Tehsils. He said that the recommendation of this Commission were violative of the Terms of Reference of the Commission.

If we examine the resolution passed by the Congress at Lahore in 1929, it will be seen that it talks of assurances to all the minorities and not to Sikhs alone. Similarly in his statement made to the Constituent Assembly by Pandit Jawaharlal Nehru on 9th December, 1946, the word Sikh Minority does not occur. It refers to all the minorities in the country. However, Sikhs did constitute a very important minority of India's political spectrum and their satisfaction ought to have been secured by the Congress. Indeed, it was foolish on the part of Congress to bind itself to satisfy each and every minority in the country. On the very face of it, the assurance was basically unrealistic.

Thus, the Sikh grievance was not only against Punjabi Hindus who, under the influence of Jan Sangh (formed in 1951) in two successive censuses of 1951 and 1961, had betrayed Sikhs by declaring Hindi as their mother tongue but also against Congress Government at New Delhi, which had, according to them, resiled from solemn assurances earlier held out to the Sikhs.

With the States Re-organisation Commission's rejection of the Punjabi-speaking State, Master Tara Singh launched a 'morcha' in May 1955, even before the release of the Commission's Report. Batches went out to court arrest. Master Tara Singh offered himself for arrest on 10th May, 1955. On 4th July, 1955, police entered Sarai Guru Ramdas, offices of the SGPC and Shiromani Akali Dal in Darbar Sahib complex, Amritsar in pursuance to the search warrants they had obtained for arrest of proclaimed offenders hiding there. Police fired two shots. This incident aroused widespread resentment among Sikhs so that Shri Bhim Sen Sachar, Chief Minister, Punjab had to apologise from the pulpit of Akal Takht in Golden Temple on 10th November, 1955. Ultimately, Shri Bhim Sen had to step down and he was replaced by S. Partap Singh Kairon. Akalis had gained a minor victory after the morcha in which 8128 persons were arrested in as much as the ban on raising slogans for Punjabi Suba was lifted but the ascendancy of Jat Sikh from Patti to the seat of Chief Ministership was to result in far-reaching transformation of politics in Punjab. Partap Singh Kairon, a graduate in Political Science from the University of Michigan, not only was cognizant of the 'money power' in politics, but also succeeded in disrupting the non-Jat Sikh base of the Akalis.

On Oct. 2, 1956, the Akali Dal, under the chairmanship of Master Tara Singh, resolved to repose confidence in Congress and confine itself to religious, educational, cultural, social and economic betterment of the Sikhs. Akali Dal also amended its constitution and deleted those clauses, which contained the idea of a separate Sikh nation.

An Akali delegation led by Giani Kartar Singh and comprising Sardars Hukam Singh, Gian Singh Rarewala and Principal Jodh Singh met the Prime Minister at Delhi on 24th October, 1956 and evolved the so-called Regional Committee Scheme. Akali Dal decided to join Congress. This was, however, unacceptable to Master Tara Singh. The Congress-Akali alliance won the election of 1957 and Master Tara Singh's splinter group failed to emerge as an electoral entity.

However, the Congress-Akali alliance proved to be short-lived. Urban communal Hindu leaders, who had found no berth in the Kairon ministry, launched a 'Save Hindi' movement. As a reaction, Akalis called Punjabi Suba Conference at Amritsar on 12 Oct. 1958. In January 1960, Master Tara Singh won elections to SGPC. In April, 1960, he launched a morcha for the attainment of Punjabi Suba. Sant Fateh Singh, Vice President Akali Dal, was made Morcha dictator. Akalis offered arrests in large numbers: according to official records, 26,056 arrests were made. Both Sant Fateh Singh and Master Tara Singh went on fast unto death, but broke them on receiving Government assurance of sympathetic consideration of their demands.

Again, in October 1965, Sant Fateh Singh threatened self-immolation for the same cause. He, however, gave it up in view of the outbreak of Indo-Pak hostilities. Sikh peasantry gave an excellent account of their patriotism in maintaining supplies to the armed forces during the war. It was this patriotism of Sikhs, which brought into existence the Sikh majority Punjabi Suba on November 1, 1966. Akalis won the 1967 elections and formed their first ever Akali Government under the Chief Ministership of S. Gurnam Singh, a retired judge of Punjab High Court, who was suave in manners and tried to maintain balance between 'Jathedars' or semi-Sikh priests and the intelligentsia. Akalis again won the mid-term poll in 1969. Their third government was formed in 1977, riding on anti-Congress wave after the Emergency of 1975, when they could garner a good harvest of votes. Akalis had opposed the imposition of Emergency by a morcha under the dictatorship of Sant Harchand Singh Longowal. Though this morcha was a token one, Congress-Akali relations were never to be cordial thereafter.

It has become a cliche to say that so long as Akalis remain in power, they remain moderate but as soon as they lose at the hustings they turn extremists. This truism encapsulates the truth of Akali politics. To exist, they need either power or raise the cry that the Panth is in danger. Their lust for power is insatiable. Their extremism is founded on Sikh psyche, whose twin pillars are persecution syndrome and martyrdom complex. The cardinal fact remains that they should either be kept in power else they would invent fairy tales of discrimination and must create a situation where the central government is painted as the villain and they themselves as martyrs. Akalis seek exclusive power. Power politics in itself is pathological and has been the bane of both Akalis and Congress. The Akalis seek power, which Max Weber defines as: "Power (Macht) is the probability that one actor within a social relationship will be in a position to carry out his own will, despite resistance, regardless of the basis on which this probability rests."

Thus, when the Akalis were out of power, they passed the Anandpur Sahib resolution on 16-17 October 1973. It was modified in October 1978 in a conference at Ludhiana, since Akalis had re-captured power through the battle of the ballot in 1977. Actually, three versions of Anandpur Sahib resolution remained in circulation. However, later, the so-called authenticated version was supplied by Akali Dal under the signature of Sant Harchand Singh Longowal; it appears as Annexure III' to the White Paper on the Punjab Agitation issued by the Government of India in July 1984.

Anandpur Sahib Resolution is called the new Policy Programme of the Shiromani Akali Dal adopted by its Working Committee at its meeting held at Sri Anandpur Sahib on 16-17 October 1973 and approved by the General House of the Akali Dal at its session at Ludhiana presided over by Sardar Jagdev Singh Talwandi (later he challenged the chief ministership of Sardar Parkash Singh Badal and had formed a separate Akali Dal Talwandi Group). It was passed in the form of 12 Resolutions covering all programmes - political, religious, cultural and economic. All economic programmes were designed to benefit Jat Sikh peasantry - the backbone of Akali Dal. Again, the resolutions refer to Sikhs as a "nation" everywhere. The resolutions referred to anti-Sikh policies of the Congress Government. Resolution No. I is very just when it calls for "redefining the central and state relations" as a true federal entity. However, the political goal had the ultimate objective as "the pre-eminence of the Khalsa, *Khalsaji ka bolbala*". Whereas all the other demands on the twelve resolutions could be negotiated and some of the grievances are genuine, the conferment of 'nationhood' on Sikhs and seeking "pre-eminence of the Khalsa" have been objected to as amounting to seeking a theocratic structure in India's democratic polity. It is argued that theocracy is not only an anti-thesis of democracy, which confers equal rights on all citizens, but also a refutation of Sikh ideology, which is through and through egalitarian.

Sikhs claim that they had ruled Punjab from Jammu to Jamrud under Maharaja Ranjit Singh and,when the British annexed Punjab, it was merely a trust with them. Hence, the Punjab should be returned to them. When the Khalsa Army laid their arms before the British, due to the intrigue of their own Prime Minister and Army chief, it was not a case of the kingdom being handed over as trust. Sikh assertion is refuted by Article 3 of Treaty of Lahore concluded between the British Governor and the State of Lahore in March 9, 1846. It reads: "The Maharaja cedes to Honourable Company in perpetual sovereignty all his forts, territories and the Doaba and country, hills and plains situated between the rivers Beas and Sutlej." History cannot be undone and the clock of marching events put backwards. If the argument of some of the Sikh enthusiasts is to be accepted universally, United States of America should revert to U.K. whose former colonies it was and so on. Again, why have innocents in Punjab be put to death? Why should Sikhs not seize Lahore, which was the capital of Maharaja Ranjit Singh's empire? Why should they not capture Peshawar and so on if this Panthic argument is to prevail?

In the 1992 Elections for Punjab Assembly, the Akalis boycotted the polls because the armed extremists had called them to boycott the scene or face their gun power. By the year 1994, the extremists, by and large, had been subdued and the martyrdom of S. Beant Singh, the Congress Chief Minister of Punjab, enabled the elections in February 1997 to be held peacefully. Since extremism had failed, the Akalis joined the electoral battle and rode to power under the same

Indian Constitution, which they had vociferously denounced in and during the ascendancy of Sikh extremism.

References

1. A.C. Bennerji: *The Khalsa Raj,* published by Abhinav Publications, New Delhi, p. 35.
2. *Ibid.* p. 35.
3. *India: The Seige from Within* by M.J. Akbar, published by Penguin, p. 126.
4. *The Sikh Volcano* by Chani Jafer, published by Vanguard, p. 4.
5. Congress Resolution as quoted by Gulati in his book *Akalis* and as further quoted by Rajiv Kapoor in his book *Sikh Separatism,* published by Allen & Unwin, London, p. 201.

– 8 –

Beginnings of The Khalistan Movement

The movement for Khalistan started somewhat actively in the 1970s. The chief proponents of this movement were frustrated Sikh youth, retired Sikh bureaucrats and frustrated Sikh politicians, who had aspired to Cabinet seats in the Akali Governments and, on being denied the same, had started movements for a Sikh Homeland to embarass the Akali Governments under the leadership of Sardar Parkash Singh Badal. It is generally believed in Punjab that all these Khalistani outfits were propped up by the Congress leadership to oust the Akali Governments.

In this connection, we have to study the emergence and the roles of Dal Khalsa and National Council for Khalistan.

Dal Khalsa

This was a small organisation under the name of 'Young Sikh Association', with its headquarters at Chandigarh. On 6th August 1978, a Seminar was convened at Chandigarh, in which all the splinter groups of Sikh ideologues were brought at a common platform. All these units merged in a new organisation named 'Dal Khalsa', a historical name, under which various warring Misls had once been merged. In this seminar the Sikh Sahit Te Sabhiachani Kendar, a miniscule fundamentalist cell, extended its full co-operation. Its office was located in Gurudwara Akal Garh in Sector 35, Chandigarh with S. Jasbir Singh as its Secretary.

In December 1979, a Supreme Body of Dal Khalsa was held at Gurdaspur with following Panchs to guide the Sikhs towards their destiny of Khalistan:

1. Harsimran Singh of Sector 23/0 Chandigarh as Mukh Panch.
2. Gajender Singh of Sector 23/0 Chandigarh as Panch.
3. Satnam Singh of Paonta Sahib Distt. Nahan (Himachal Pradesh) as Panch.
4. Thekedar Jaswant Singh of Distt. Ludhiana. There were few more hardcore Dal members.

The objectives of Dal Khalsa were two-fold:

(i) To protect Sikhism from its opponents.

(ii) To establish Khalsa Raj.

The Dal comprised fanatic urban, mostly non-Jat, Sikhs who later indulged in hijackings and severing of cow-heads and putting them at places of worship of Hindus and causing blasts here and there. It deserves to be noted that this organisation was formed when an Akali ministry was ruling Punjab. Dr. Sohan Singh, the chief of one of the Panthic Committees, played a leading role in the activities of the Dal. Most of the active members belonged to Union Territory of Chandigarh and held their meetings there, but neither UT Administration nor Ministry of Home Affairs, under whom UT Administration functions, took note of the activities of this organisation, which was the first to agitate for Khalistan in an overt manner and indulge in hijacking of aircraft, etc. which we will deal with later.

On 20th January 1980, a Seminar was held by Dal Khalsa under the aegis of Dr. Jagjit Singh Chauhan, ex-minister in the Akali Ministry. On 1st February 1981, Dal Khalsa activists participated in a Seminar of Senior Sikh Sophisticates Forum presided over by Syed Abdullah Bukhari, Shahi Imam of Delhi, and which was held in a Government Building i.e., Panchayat Bhavan. A call for creation of Khalistan was given by the forum, which was attended by Sikh intellectuals and retired Sikh Officers of whom Dr. Sohan Singh was prominent.

Thereafter, Dal Khalsa started indulging in open pro-Khalistani activities. They were seen raising pro-Khalistani slogans during 54th Sikh Educational Conference held at Chandigarh in March 1981. It was not Dal Khalsa that attracted public attention but S. Ganga Singh Dhillon, a U.S. citizen, who lives in a Virginia suburb overlooking the Potamac river, who had prospered through insurance business and had originally hailed from District Shekhupura (now in Pakistan), had been close associate of late Bhan Singh and late Trilochan Singh Reyasti, a protege of Giani Kartar Singh. The conference was sponsored by Chief Khalsa Diwan. In his presidential address at the conference, which was mainly attended by frustrated intellectuals, Dhillon propounded the concept of the Sikhs being a separate nation and not merely a separate community. He pleaded for Associate Membership for the Sikhs in the UNO on the analogy of Uzbeks' Associate Membership of the world body, in spite of their being an integral part of the USSR. His speech and his status as President of the Nankana Sahib Foundation had galvanising effect on Sikh intellectuals; Dal Khalsa decided to step up their pro-Khalistani activities. Interestingly, Ganga Singh Dhillon in his press conference on 18th March 1981, at Amritsar, dis-associated himself from the demand of Khalistan. Though he criticised SGPC and Akali Dal, he had long discussions with Sardar Gurcharan Singh Tohra. In an interview with Inderjit Badhwar of *India Today* on November 30, 1981, he said that he was not a Sikh Jinnah. He was merely asking for a cultural homeland for Sikhs within India. Dhillon said: "Chauhan has crossed that threshold and asked for Khalistan ... I am personally against any partition".

Creators of Dal Khalsa had not reckoned with the characters of Harsimran Singh and Gajinder Singh. Gajinder Singh, a graduate, was a clerk in Education Dept in Punjab when he went on merrily with his seditious activities. He fancied himself to be a writer and a poet and wrote a poetic work entitled "Panj Teer Hor" blasting the Government for anti-Sikh postures. He started publishing a monthly magazine *"Jung"* from Chandigarh in support of a Sikh homeland. When the Prime Minister addressed an election meeting at Dera Bassi in Patiala District during the 1972 election to Punjab Vidhan Sabha, he audaciously distributed pamphlets championing the cause of the Sikh homeland among the audience. He and Harsimran Singh had inscribed "Khalistan to safeguard Sikhism" on the walls in the Sectors 17 & 22 in Chandigarh on 6th March 1974. Gajinder Singh was suspended from Government service in 1976. Harsimran Singh and he, also used to distribute the pamphlets advising Sikhs to boycott Republic Day celebrations as the Constitution had denied Sikhs their birth right, to have a separate homeland. On the formation of Janta-Akali Government in Punjab in 1977, Gajinder Singh tried to re-enter Government service.

Rumours were afloat that Dal Khalsa had been created by the Congress, particularly Giani Zail Singh, to embarrass the Akali Government in power and pave way for its dismissal in case it happened to win the polls in 1979. Five Dal Khalsa activists led by Gajinder Singh Panch from Chandigarh hijacked an Indian Airlines flight going from Delhi to Srinagar to Lahore on 29th Sept. 1981. The hijackers were overpowered by the Pakistani commandos and the 737 Boeing was returned with all its 107 passengers safe to India. The Dal Khalsa activists were not handed over to India. After a number of protests from India, the five hijackers, Gajinder Singh, Jasbir Singh. Tejender Pal Singh, Satnam Singh and Karam Singh were tried and sentenced to life imprisonment on 20th January 1986 by the Special Court of Mr. Fazal Karim at Lahore.

After the hijacking, the Punjab and Chandigarh police cracked down on the Dal and arrested almost all its activists. This was subsequent to a press conference which Harsimran Singh had addressed from the sanctuary of the Golden Temple in which he had boasted that, as Mukh Panch of Dal Khalsa, he would arrange more daring hijackings. The Darbara Singh Govt. then started pressing the Ministry of Home Affairs to declare Dal Khalsa illegal and impose a ban on it. Each time the request was made, the Ministry turned it down. Was it an objective assessment of the Ministry that Dal Khalsa need not be banned or the request was turned down because the Darbara Singh Ministry was to be destabilised? It may be mentioned that on 7th June 1981, Giani Zail Singh, Home Minister, had threatened Darbara Singh Ministry with dismissal, for showing leniency to Khalistani elements. The differences between S. Darbara Singh and Giani Zail Singh had plunged Punjab into a crisis.

The different ways they were dealing with Dal Khalsa and their approach towards it was commented upon by the *Economic and Political Weekly*, May 1982, as follows:

"Thus, while the Union Home Minister was pleading during the Rajya Sabha debate on Punjab incidents that the problem posed by the Dal Khalsa should be met politically ... the state's Chief Minister was saying in Amritsar on that very day that his Govt would once again recommend to the Centre a ban on Dal Khalsa."

Harsimran Singh was arrested by police from Mohali on 12th February, 1982. During his interrogation, he disclosed how he got financial assistance from all the Akali leaders including Dr. Rajinder Kaur and how he started his Khalistani career as early as December 1972. In spite of his known activities for Sikh homeland (Khalistan), his name for Government jobs was sponsored by various Ministers. His main source of inspiration, as of his other colleagues, was Sardar Kapur Singh ICS, a former Minister and Member of Parliament, who had been in the vanguard of Sikh Homeland movement, defining its conceptual framework. Kapur Singh had influenced all the intellectuals of Punjab in this regard.

It is an irony of fate and abysmal depth of political expediency that, whereas the idea for Punjabi Suba was given by Dr. B.R. Ambedkar, the movement for Sikh homeland got a shot in its arm from the Congress leadership, whose obsession was to disrupt Akali rule.

National Council for Khalistan

It was a miniscule organisation of much older people whereas Dal Khalsa consisted of Sikh youth. The Council was created by Jagjit Singh Chauhan of Hoshiarpur and Balbir Singh Sandhu of Taran Taran. Dr. Jagjit Singh had done his MBBS from Amritsar and was a medical practitioner. He was elected to the Punjab legislature three times. Dr. Jagjit Singh was taken as Finance Minister in the first ever Akali Ministry of Punjab formed by Justice Gurnam Singh. He worked in this capacity from 1967-69. After the midterm poll in 1969 he could not find a berth in the second Akali Ministry. In 1971, Dr. Jagjit Singh went to UK, USA and Canada preaching the ideology of a separate Sikh Homeland. On Akalis' return to power in Punjab, he returned to India in 1977 and tried to rehabilitate himself in Sikh politics. However, he did not succeed and failed to get a berth in the government. Frustrated, he founded Inquilabi Akali Dal but without any following. He declared that Sikhs should observe 1980 as the year of Khalistan. He found some support among retired Sikh officers and intellectuals who were impressed by his effort to instal a toy transmitter in the Golden Temple premises in July 1977. However, his real support came from Balbir Singh Sandhu.

Balbir Singh Sandhu had been a teacher in the Guru Arjun Dev Khalsa School, Amritsar. He later joined Bharat Sewak Samaj founded by Shri Gulzari Lal Nanda on the persuasion of Gurdial Singh Dhillon, according to Balbir Singh's own press statement. S. Gurdial Singh Dhillon has been a prominent Congress leader who worked as Speaker of Lok Sabha, later India's High Commissioner in Canada and Agricultural Minister in the Rajiv Gandhi Government for some time. Mr. Balbir Singh Sandhu also worked as the Principal of Panchayati Raj Training Centre at Jallandhar. Since the centre was closed in 1968, he came in touch with Dr. Jagjit Singh, who was also jobless, having failed to find a berth in the Akali Cabinet. However, it was after the return of Dr. Jagjit Singh to Punjab in 1977 that they thought of chalking out a new course of action. Dr. Jagjit though had once called on the author in 1977 and posed that he had abjured politics and would confine himself to preaching Sikhism. Dr. Jagjit Singh and Balbir Singh put their heads together sometime in 1978, when they found that the Akali leadership of Sardar Parkash Singh Badal would offer them no office in the Government. Out of their frustration, they formed the National Council of Khalistan. Dr. Jagjit Singh Chouhan went abroad in May 1980 and gave shape to the Council for Khalistan, not only in UK, his permanent headquarters, but also in USA and Canada, which he visited for the purpose of founding the Council branches as well as collecting funds and establishing contacts with US Senators. He lobbied for Khalistan abroad with uncanny insight into foreign minds.

In India, Mr. Balbir Singh styled himself as Secretary General of National Council for Khalistan (Dr. Chouhan was the President). He showed his adeptness in creating Khalistan symbology: he issued a Khalistan Passport to one Gopal Singh Shahid in the courtyard of Darbar Sahib on Baisakhi day - 13th April 1981. Earlier 30 paisa-stamps bearing the insignia of Khalistan and inscribed ' Akal Saha' had been issued to all leading newspapers in Jallandhar by Dr. Jagjit Singh from his address, Reading Road, UK Camp Office of Khalistan Government on 20th August 1980.

In a meeting convened on 3rd November 1980, Balbir Singh Sandhu informed that a 151 member Khalistan Council was being formed by Dr. Jagjit Singh: 100 would be from Punjab, Haryana, Himachal Pradesh and Delhi, whereas 51 would be belonging to other countries. Later he disclosed that the National Council of Khalistan had started its office at Toronto, Canada, from 4th December, 1980.

Balbir Singh Sandhu, operating from his sanctuary in Golden Temple hostel, tried to unite all splinter organisations propagating Khalistan ideology. One of his calls was to boycott the Republic Day functions. The Dal Khalsa started working in full collaboration with the Council for Khalistan as they had identical objectives to achieve.

The Council for Khalistan claimed that they had established consulates at Washington, New York, Toronto, Winning, San Francisco, Los Angeles, Houston and Yuba City. The Council for Khalistan had very old people on its rolls. Two of them, Ujagar Singh Randhawa and Master Hazara Singh Misriwala, teetering on the verge of death, were asked to cross Indo-Pak border and hoist Khalistan Flag on April 18, 1981. Both were arrested later by the police.

Responsible Akali leaders denounced the acts of Balbir Singh Sandhu as 'antics' and ascribed the creation of Council for Khalistan to Congress leaders to create confusion among Sikhs and malign Akalis. However, it is a fact that SGPC had allotted Room No. 32/25 in Guru Nanak Niwas to Balbir Singh Sandhu and provided him a sanctuary. Balbir Singh was so afraid of arrest that he never left the precincts of Golden Temple. According to Dr. Jagjit Singh, Balbir Singh Sandhu had escaped during Operation Blue Star and had received sanctuary in Pakistan.

As dissidence is endemic in Congress, similar factionalism has afflicted Akali politics with calamitous consequences for the people of Punjab. Their factionalism generates competitive extremism and one-upmanship, which had left Akali Dal in shambles and pushed Punjab into a disaster of unprecedented magnitude. Girilal Jain wrote: "Factionalism is an end in itself for the Akalis as is the lure of office."

Factionalism in Sikh politics can be traced back to the year 1962. Till then, Master Tara Singh had been the unchallenged leader of the Sikhs. However, this very year his supremacy was challenged by Sant Fateh Singh, who captured SGPC as well as the leadership of Akali Dal. Their differences took serious overtones and bedevilled Punjab politics till the death of Master Tara Singh in November, 1967; for instance, both going on fast unto death for attainment of Punjabi Suba. Sant Fateh Singh had emerged victorious carving Punjabi Suba in November 1966. In 1968, both the factions of Master Tara Singh and Sant Fateh Singh's were united under the leadership of Sant Fateh Singh who reigned supreme till his death in 1972.

Akalis had formed the first ever Ministry of their own in early 1967, which came to be known as United Front Government (8.3.67 to 24.11.67). Sant Fateh Singh started frowning on Justice Gurnam Singh, the Chief Minister who, though considered honest, had closed his eyes to the activities of a lady of Ludhiana to mint money for Akali Government patronage. Hardly had the Govt been in power for 8 months, when Sardar Lachhman Singh Gill, a P.W.D. Contractor belonging to Master Tara Singh group, fell victim to Congress allurements and pulled down Gurnam Singh Ministry.

Lachhman Singh Gill's ministry did not last either. Nonetheless, Congress had succeeded in causing disarray in the Akali ranks. A mid-term poll followed in 1969, in which too Congress again failed to emerge victorious. Akalis and BJP formed a coalition Government. It lasted for 14 months. S. Gurnam Singh was expelled from the Akali Party on the charge of being a stooge of the Congress. Congress tried hard to stop the formation of another non-Congress ministry, yet Sardar Parkash Singh Badal came to form a ministry in March, 1970 with two ministers only i.e., Balram Tandon of BJP and S. Balwant Singh.

Other developments were taking place in Delhi. The first elections to the Delhi Gurudwara Prabandhak Committee were held in March 1973 under the Delhi Gurudwara Act of 1971. Jathedar Santokh Singh captured the Delhi Gurudwara Committee. When Giani Zail Singh was the Chief Minister of Punjab, Akali Dal had started an agitation based on four religious demands: the Land Ceiling Act should not apply to Gurudwara lands, SGPC should not be bifurcated as a result of the division of Punjab & Haryana, which Shri Bansi Lal, a shrewd politician and the architect of modern Haryana, had been demanding and elections be held to DGPC Jathedar Santokh Singh played the role of mediator between the Akalis and the Govt. at Delhi. By succeeding in his role, he emerged as a new centre of Sikh power. Paradoxically, he sided both with Congress (I) and Jarnail Singh Bhindranwale. Giani Zail Singh was blamed for propping him up in Delhi's Gurudwara politics. It was alleged that Gianiji had the DGPC. Act amended to reduce the educational qualification of matriculation to enable Santokh Singh to contest.

In Punjab, Sardar Parkash Singh Badal formed Akali Janta Government in 1977. Till 1979, the Government functioned well but thereafter Sardar Parkash Singh Badal lost favour with Jagdev Singh Talwandi, President of Akali Dal. It is a sad comment on factional politics that the President of Akali Dal gave a call for the dismissal of the Akali government. On 26th September, 1979, both Jathedar Talwandi and Gurcharan Singh Tohra approached in this regard S. Sandhu Singh

Bhaura, who was the Chief of Akal Takht. He, alongwith Gurdial Singh Ajnoha of Keshgarh and other Takht chiefs, directed Akali factions to sink their differences.

Ultimately Sardar Parkash Singh Badal, Jathedar Harchand Singh Longowal and Jathedar Gurcharan Singh Tohra emerged triumphant on Akali scene, while Jagdev Singh Talwandi formed a separate organisation, called Shiromani Akali Dal (Talwandi). On the Baisakhi Day of 1981 at Ananadpur Sahib, Jagdev Singh Talwandi called for the creation of Punjab Desh Kal as envisaged in Anandpur Sahib resolution and called for Associate Membership for Sikhs in the United Nations. He launched a symbolic Satyagraha at New Delhi for acceptance of Anandpur Sahib Resolution. People asked whose game was he playing in 1981 and in 1982?

– 9 –

Igniting Sikh Fundamentalism

The Nirankari movement was started by Baba Dyal Das (1783-1855), a saintly contemporary of Maharaja Ranjit Singh. Baba Dayal Das was a bullion merchant in Peshawar. His forefathers had come from Kabul. He was originally a Hindu, but later converted himself to Sikhism. In fact, during the reign of Maharaja Ranjit Singh, a large number of Hindus in Western Punjab and Afghanistan had come under the influence of Sikhism. Those who were baptised joined the Khalsa fraternity. Others continued to describe themselves as Hindus but gave up worshipping Hindu gods and recitation of Vedas and started reading *Sri Guru Granth Sahib* and joining the Sikh congregations at the Gurudwaras. Among these Hindus, there grew a custom of bringing up at least one son as a Keshdhari Sikh. The half-Hindu half-Sikh community of Nirankaris belonged to Khatri, Arora or Bania castes. Most of these people followed Baba Dayal Das. Thus, the Nirankaris comprise non-jat Sikhs and Hindus including some trader castes such as goldsmiths and carpenters, etc. Until 1947, their influence was restricted to Sikh and Hindu communities of Northwest Frontier Province and Kashmir.

Baba Dayal Das had condemned idol worship and making obeisance to holy men and the performance of Brahmanical rituals. According to him, God was formless—Nirankar—hence the name Nirankari. Anand Marriage ceremony is attributed to Baba Darbara Singh and by some to Baba Dayal Das. It consists of circumambulating the *Guru Granth Sahib* four times with the accompaniment of recitation of hymns and shabads from Gurbani - known as Lavan composed by

Guru Ram Das, the fourth Sikh Guru. He later codified Sikh ceremonies from birth to death. The Sikhs owe abiding gratitude to this great leader, whose clarity of thought introduced radical changes in the Sikh way of life.

Nirankaris had their centre at Dayalsar, 4 miles away from Rawalpindi. After the Partition of India, the centre was shifted to Amritsar and later to Chandigarh. After the death of Baba Dayal Das on January 13, 1855, his elder son Baba Darbara Singh took over the mission and was their second Guru up to 1870. He was born in 1814. When his ministry of fifteen years came to an end in 1870 at the age of 56, he appointed his younger brother Rattan Chand (1830-1909) (Sahib Rattanji) as his successor, in preference to his son. Sahib Rattanji pushed the reforms with devotion and dedication. On his pleading, Maharaja Ripudaman Singh of Nabha introduced Anand Marriage Bill in the Imperial Legislative Council in 1908. The bill was passed into an Act in 1909.

Sahib Rattanji was succeeded by Baba Gurdit Singh (1869-1947) who supported Gurudwara Reform Movement and was a member of SGPC before it got legal status. He was a revolutionary of his times.

After Independence, Sahib Hara Singh (1887-1971), the 5th leader of the Nirankaris, established a centre in Sector 21-B, Chandigarh and organised the scattered Nirankaris throughout the country. On his demise in 1971, his eldest son Baba Gurbaksh Singh was appointed to succeed his father and Dr. Man Singh, an eye surgeon and retired Principal of Medical College, Amritsar was nominated by Sahib Hara Singh as an Adviser and President of Nirankari Darbar.

It is, however, the splinter group of Nirankari Mandal with their headquarters at Delhi formed by Baba Avtar Singh, which is much criticised for their alleged anti-Sikh practices. This group had broken away from the original sect during Baba Gurdit Singh's time.

The Sikh-Nirankari controversy escalated in the time of Baba Gurbachan Singh. At present Baba Hardev Singh, son of Baba Gurbachan Singh, is the head of the sect.

Differences of Nirankaris with Sikhs are as follows:

(i) Guru Gobind Singh had ordered that there would be no living Guru after him. He had further directed that *Guru Granth Sahib* be accepted as living personification of all the Gurus and Sikhs should accept the preachings of *Sri Guru Granth Sahib* as the Word of Guru. However, Nirankaris insisted upon calling their head as Gurus. This substitution of *Guru Granth Sahib* by a corporeal Guru, infuriated the Amritdhari Sikhs.

(ii) Relegation of *Guru Granth Sahib* from Guruship.

(iii) In Sampuran Avtar Bani, Avtar Singh called himself Guru and equated himself to Guru Nanak Dev.

(iv) Nirankari chief Avtar Singh maintained that there was no compulsion for the Nirankais to maintain keshas and beard.

(v) The Amrit used by the Sikhs is sanctified by the double edged sword as administered by Guru Gobind Singh Ji on the Baisakhi day of 1699 and is called Khanda-ka Amrit, whereas the Nirankari Mandal substituted in its place the Charan-Amrit, the water with which the feet of the Nirankari Guru had washed.

(vi) Rejection of Nam Simran.

(vii) The Institution of five Beloved Ones (Panch Piara) in Sikhism was replaced by the Institution of Seven Beloved Ones or Seven Stars.

Nirankaris started preaching their doctrines aggressively in Gurdaspur and Amritsar districts when Sardar Niranjan Singh, an IAS officer, was posted as the Deputy Commissioner, Gurdaspur. At the time the Chief Secretary of Punjab also happened to be a Nirankari. The Congress Government of Punjab in the period 1975-76 ignored the complaints of Damdami Taksal from Gurdarshan Prakash Gurudwara at Mehta, on the border of Gurdaspur and Amritsar Districts, concerning their harassment by the Nirankari Officers, particularly Sardar Niranjan Singh, the Deputy Commissioner

Gurdaspur, who was one of the Seven Stars. Thus, the ground for Nirankari-Sikh conflagration was laid by the indifference of Punjab Government led by Giani Zail Singh to the complaints of the Sikh Missions, that is, Damdami Taksal, and Akhand Kirtani Jatha, the latter being located in Gurdaspur district itself. This compelled both the Damdami Taksal and Akhand Kirtani Jatha to take to arms. No amount of sophistry or blame can absolve the Congress Government in Punjab, and the Nirankaris, of their responsibilities for laying the foundation of Sikhs fundamentalism during this period. It is they who transformed Sant Jarnail Singh Bhindranwale into a Frankenstein and it is they who planted doubts in the hearts of the Sikhs regarding their religion being endangered by heretic Sikh sects in collusion with the Congress leadership. The responsibility for the tragedy, which has been forced on the innocent Sikhs and Hindus of Punjab, lies squarely on the shoulders of the Seventh Nirankari Star and the Congress Government under Gianiji, which ruled Punjab from 1972 to 1977. It was they who played with the Sikh sentiments and compelled the Damdami Taksal and Akhand Kirtani Jatha to resort to extremist course of action.

Post 1978 Developments

The two years, 1978 and 1984, form watersheds in the history of benighted Punjab. 1978 saw the rise of Sikh fundamentalism, which got transformed into seccessionism after the Operation Blue Star of 1984. Prior to Blue Star, the cry for Khalistan was raised only by a fringe element but later most of the Sikhs came to feel that their interests demanded carving of a separate homeland.

The simmering conflict between the Nirankaris and Akhand Kirtani Jatha and Damdami Taksal came to boil on 13th April, 1978. Nirankaris had been given permission to hold their Sammelan to celebrate Baisakhi in the Railway Ground of Amritsar by the Akali Government of Punjab headed by Sardar Parkash Singh Badal. Akhand Kirtani Jatha and Damdami Taksal felt betrayed by the Government. When Sardar Jiwan Singh Umranangal, Revenue Minister Punjab, tried to justify this permission, Bhai Amrik Singh who had been smarting for his defeat in SGPC election at the hands of the former, egged on Akhand Kirtani Jatha, whose training camps he had attended and delivered fiery lectures. In the exchange of fire between the Nirankaris and members of the Akhand Kirtani, 13 members of the Jatha were gunned down. In this gun battle, 3 Nirankaris as well as 2 passersby were also killed. The total toll was 18. The most important of Akhand Kirtani Jatha casualty was Fauja Singh, an Agriculture Inspector of the Punjab Government. Then and there his widow Amarjit Kaur vowed to avenge the death of her husband. It appears the police arrived on the scene somewhat late and the DSP, who fired in the air to separate the battling parties, had his name inscribed on the 'hit list' prepared by the militants later. It also transpired that Bibi Amarjit Kaur, widow of Fauja Singh, and Sant Bhindranwale did not see eye to eye; however later they were brought on one platform by the Canadian extremist Talwinder Singh Parmar. Anyway, Nirankaris had put a match stick to Sikh militancy and then posed as innocents.

Punjab Govt registered a case against the Nirankari Chief and his accomplices for the murder of Fauja Singh and others. The trial went on with usual court delays and ultimately Nirankari Chief Gurbachan Singh was acquitted by the Sessions Court of Karnal. Sant Bhindranwale had kept his plans ready. Some militants unsuccessfully sought to kill the Nirankari Guru in Madhya Pradesh through a truck collision. The Nirankari Guru Gurbachan Singh was ultimately killed in his own Nirankari Bhavan at New Delhi on April 20, 1980. The conspiracy had been carefully hatched. The investigation was entrusted to CBI which arrested some culprits and came to the conclusion that Sant Bhindranwale was the force behind the assassination. Interrogating him once in Golden Temple, CBI. did nothing except passing the buck to State Governments, mainly Punjab, a gimmick to embarrass S. Darbara Singh. In this murder case of the Nirankari Chief Gurbachan Singh, only Bhai Ranjit Singh was convicted and others were acquitted. Bhai Ranjit Singh, now the Chief Priest of Akal Takht, got his ultimate reprieve at the hands of Gujral Government.

These two organisations might not have killed any Nirankari or Hindu if the trial of Baba Gurbachan Singh and his Nirankari co-accused had proceeded expeditiously and resulted in their conviction. However, this did not happen and instead some influential Hindus tried to defend the Nirankari Chief, and the fundamentalists proceeded to fulfill a vow taken on Baisakhi day of 1978.

They were also incensed to take the violent course because a Sikh Convention held on May 12, 1978, had requested Akal Takht to issue a Hukamnama to deal with the violence perpetrated by the Nirankaris and the Nirankari Dogma, which was against Sikh preachings.

A seven member committee was formed to assist the Jathedar of the Akal Takht in the preparation of the Hukamnama.

The Hukamnama was issued on June 10, 1978.

The Hukamnama forbade the Sikhs to have any dealing with the Nirankaris. Sikhs were enjoined to observe social boycott of the Nirankari Society.

The most crucial part of the Hukamnama directed the Sikhs to stop the rise of the Nirankaris "in any genuine way". According to followers of Damdami Taksal and Akhand Kirtani Jatha, "in any genuine way" included physical liquidation. Thus, a hit list of 13 Nirankaris was prepared who were suspected of having fired on the followers of Damdami Taksal and Akhand Kirtani Jatha — all these 13 were killed by the motorcycle riding fundamentalist terrorists from September 1981 to the close of 1982.

– 10 –

Instruments of Sikh Fundamentalism

After the carnage of the Baisakhi Day, that is, 13 April, 1978, both the Damdami Taksal and Akhand Kirtani Jatha started training their followers and arming them to wreak vengeance of the Baisakhi Day (1978) killings of their followers at the hands of Nirankaris who had apparently come armed to their Sammelan at Railway Ground, Amritsar on that fateful day –– the killings which were to plunge Punjab into a blood spattered killing ground for more than a decade.

In the violent phase, which descended upon Punjab after August-September, 1981, the Akhand Kirtani Jatha, the Damdami Taksal and Shiromani Gurudwara Parbandhak Committee (SGPC) caused the volcano of Sikh fundamentalism to erupt in an alliance with Dal Khalsa and The Council for Khalistan, the Secessionist limbs of Akali Dal, aided and abetted by Pakistan and caused a serious threat to the integrity of India.

It, therefore, becomes necessary to study these organisations in depth, if we have to draw correct lessons from the tragedy, which overtook the peace loving community of Punjabis in which thousands of Sikhs and Hindus lost their lives and honour.

AKHAND KIRTANI JATHA

It was founded in 1908, by Bhai Randhir Singh of village Narangwal, district Ludhiana. He formed a Jatha and later established a Khalsa High School there. In 1909, he established the Panth Khalsa Dewan. These were the precursors of what is now known as the Akhand Kirtani Jatha, the original name being Panth Khalsa Dewan. Bhai Randhir Singh was a devout Sikh. He believed that it is essential to take steps to retain the purity of the Sikh religion. Being an orthodox Sikh, he did not care for reaction of his superior officers under whom he was serving the Government and went to the extent of turning down offers of promotion so that he could look after the activities of the Panth Khalsa Dewan properly.

Militant Tradition

Sometime during the First World War, he organised a successful agitation to rebuild a portion of the boundary wall of Gurudwara Rakab Ganj at Delhi. Later on, he and his followers also took keen interest in the conspiracy by armed forces of Ferozepur Cantonment to mutiny. Their association and activities were exposed due to which Randhir Singh and others were arrested. Randhir Singh was confined to jail for 15 years.

At the time of partition of the country, members of the Dewan took various steps to protect Sikhs and their relics.

Sometime after 1947, the name of the Panth Khalsa Dewan was changed to Akhand Kirtani Jatha. At that time the following important objectives were outlined:

Objects: *(a)* to propagate Gurbani,

(b) to keep up and nurse tenets and traditions of Sikhism

(c) to undertake social service, (KIRAT)

(d) not to tolerate criticism of Sikhism and its scriptures at any cost

(e) to start taking food in steel utensils.

Dress: They adopted a separate dress for both men and women, which was slightly different from the traditional Sikh dress. Women were required to sport a black head gear and a black 'Dupatta' unlike other Sikh women, who were not required to wear anything on their head. The men were prescribed black Turbans as against Akalis' Blue.

Devotional Postures: There was a great deal of stress on Akhand Path, Kirtan and Naam Jaap.

Randhir Singh died in 1961. The next Jathedar was Mall Singh of Tarn Taran who died in 1979. During Mall Singh's time, particularly during mid-seventies, tension had started brewing between the Nirankaris and orthodox Sikhs. Gurdaspur was on the centre stage where Nirankaris had made attempts to increase their activities with the patronage of the prominent Nirankari Shri Niranjan Singh, who was the then Deputy Commissioner, Gurdaspur. Akhand Kirtani Jatha had a very staunch follower in Fauja Singh, a Government employee having properties in village Chak Mamian, Gurdaspur. His Chak Mamian Farm became an important centre of the Akhand Kirtani Jatha. In March 1977, a training camp was organised there for the members of the Akhand Kirtani Jatha in which, apart from the religious preaching, training in use of firearms was also imparted to enable the devout to defend their religion. In April 1978, when Nirankaris took out a procession in Amritsar city armed with weapons, a clash ensued between Nirankaris and orthodox Sikhs, including members of the Akhand Kirtani Jatha. In the firing 13 people, out of which 11 were members of Akhand Kirtani Jatha, died. This can be taken to be the beginning of Akhand Kirtani Jatha's resolve to take law into their own hands in the name of defending their religion.

Beginning of the Activities

The widow of Fauja Singh, Bibi Amarjit Kaur, became the guiding spirit of the vendetta against the Nirankaris. She organised another training camp at village Chak Mamian, district Gurdaspur, in 1979, at which arms training was imparted and participants were exhorted to defend their religion and traditions at all costs. She also collected huge funds and organised arms collection drive.

Bhai Ram Singh, a retired Squadron Leader of the Indian Air Force, took over the leadership of the Jatha. At this time and onward, the Akhand Kirtani Jatha was able to collect number of arms. All these weapons were kept in a room in

Guru Nanak Niwas, Amritsar (Golden Temple) under the care of Sukhdev Singh Dasuwal.

Special Group for Violent Activities: A special squad for extremist activities was also formed from amongst the trained members of the Akhand Kirtani Jatha. This included:-

(i) Chhattar Singh, S/o Surjan Singh, Khatri, R/o Krishna Nagri, Amritsar.

(ii) Sukhdev Singh Nagoke, Amritsar.

(iii) Surinder Singh Nagoke, Amritsar.

All of them participated in the violent incidents of 1981 and 1982.

DAMDAMI TAKSAL

On the eve of his departure for the Deccan, Guru Gobind Singh ji had nominated Baba Deep Singh and Bhai Mani Singh to look after the Gurudwara Damdama Sahib, District Bhatinda and Amritsar Sahib respectively. (By the way, Guru Gobind Singh never visited Amritsar). Guru Gobind Singh ji had got written the *Guru Granth Sahib* in 9 months. It was written by Bhai Mani Singh. The Guru taught the 48 Sikhs to recite Gurbani Kirtan. The mission was later taken over by Bhai Mani Singh and Baba Deep Singh, whose names figure prominently among Sikh martyrs. Baba Deep Singh got copies made of *Sri Guru Granth Sahib* and placed one each at the Takhts, that is, Akal Takht Sahib, Amritsar, Sri Keshgarh Sahib, Anandpur Sahib, Sri Patna Sahib and Damdama Sahib. Baba Deep Singh embraced death, while fighting against Ahmed Shah Abdali's forces in the Golden Temple area.

'Gurmat Vidhiya Taksal' was founded to make copies of *Guru Granth Sahib* and preaching the same. Bhai Mani Singh at Amritsar had concentrated on interpretation of the *Granth Sahib* and Sikh history through 'Kathas'. The Taksal was created with the objective of having a Jatha of trained people to interpret, recite and preach the *Guru Granth Sahib* and also to train others to do so. Its contribution lies in making copies of Sri *Guru Granth Sahib* and writing commentaries on it and creating 'Pothies' at a time when no printing presses were available.

Taksal got divided into branches and sub-branches. One such branch came to Sant Bishan Singh Murlewala who established himself on the banks of river Chenab in Chopal. Sant Bishan Singh later nominated Sant Sunder Singh as his successor in 1905: Sunder Singh hailed from vill. Bhindar Kalan in District Ferozepore. Thus, the Taksal came to be called Bhindranwala, also Damdami Taksal, also Chakravarti Gurmat Parchar Jatha Bhindran. The following chart shows the succession of various Sants :

Sunder Singh Bhindranwale (1883 - 1930)

Giani Gurbachan Singh (1930 - 1969)

Sant Kartar Singh (1969 - 1977)

Sant Jarnail Singh Bhindranwale (1977 - 1984)

This Taksal was created with the objective of having a Jatha of trained people to interpret, recite and preach the *Guru Granth Sahib* and also to train others to do so. However, soon it was to emerge as a militant organisation.

Giani Gurbachan Singh, in addition to the preachings, also involved himself in the construction of Gurudwaras. He got a sarovar built at Sri Hargobindpur and new Gurudwara at village Bham, and a sarovar at Penjokhra Sahib.

On January 31, 1967, at the tricentenary celebrations of Guru Gobind Singh ji at Patna Sahib, Giani Gurbachan Singh nominated Sant Kartar Singh as his successor. Sant Kartar Singh was born in 1932 at Village Bhure Gohna, Tehsil Patti, District Amritsar. For a short while, he had worked as a Patwari at Muktsar up to 1957. He had come to Giani Gurbachan Singh and had studied the *Guru Granth Sahib* under him. It was Sant Kartar Singh, who constructed Gurudwara Gurdarshan Parkash at Chowk Mehta District Amritsar. He was a fiery character and it is from here that antagonism started between Damdami Taksal and Nirankaris, with Sardar Niranjan Singh, the Deputy Commissioner in neighbouring Gurdaspur being a zealous Nirankari.

During the Emergency imposed by Government of India in 1974, Sant Kartar Singh wanted to take out a procession on the Martyrdom Day of Guru Tegh Bahadur and on being refused permission, he and his Jatha surrounded the residence of District Magistrate, Amritsar and they fired two hundred rounds. Later he died in a car accident.

He left behind not only Gurudwara Gurdarshan Parkash, which was ultimately to become a sanctuary of militants, but also two sons Amrik Singh and Manjit Singh, who became the Presidents of All India Sikh Students Federation. The third legacy of Sant Kartar Singh was Sant Jarnail Singh Bhindranwale, who was the seventh son of Joginder Singh, is of Brar Jat Sikh family in village Rode P.S. Bagha Purana, District Faridkot (earlier Ferozepur). He had studied only up to class five. He tried to excel over his predecessor Sant Kartar Singh in extremism vis-a-vis Nirankaris, and later the Indian Government.

SHIROMANI GURUDWARA PRABANDHAK COMMITTEE—STATE WITHIN STATE

Shiromani Gurudwara Prabandhak Committee came into existence on 15th November 1920, and Shiromani Akali Dal a month later, to look after the management of Gurudwaras, which they were wresting from profligate Mahants: this struggle has been sketched in detail earlier. After the ouster of Mahants, at Nankana Sahib (birth place of Guru Nanak), Guru Ka Bagh (near Ajnala) and at other places with the help of its volunteer force, Akali Dal, and firming up its mass base, SGPC succeeded not only in defeating the designs of the British to regain control of Golden Temple, but compelling the British to vest control of Gurudwaras in a statutory body of the Sikhs. Thus, an Act was framed in 1925, known as Sikh Gurudwara Management Act, by virtue of which regular elections were to be held for constituting the Prabandhak Committee.

Baba Kharak Singh was elected as the first President of the Gurudwara Prabandhak Committee. In the post-Independence days, the Congress leaders like Udham Singh Nagoke, Ishar Singh Mujhali tried to capture SGPC. Baba Kharak Singh was succeeded by Master Tara Singh, the President of Shiromani Akali Dal. He was elected consecutively for four times. After Master Tara Singh, Sant

Channan Singh became the President of the Gurudwara Prabandhak Committee. He occupied this chair for 10 long years till his death in 1972. Ever since, Shri Gurucharan Singh Tohra has been presiding over the Gurudwara Prabandhak Committee, though for a brief period, SGPC was presided over by Baldev Singh Sibia. The presidentship was entrusted to Sardar Baldev Singh to keep the power away from the emerging leadership of Sardar S.S. Mann.

In the elections held in February, 1965, the SGPC contest was between the Akali Dal led by Sant Fateh Singh and the Akali Dal led by Master Tara Singh. Out of 140 seats for which elections were held, 105 seats were won by Akali Dal of Sant Fateh Singh and only 35 by Master Tara Singh's Akali Dal; this defeat in the control of SGPC led to the final eclipsing of Master Tara Singh in Akali politics. Whoever controls SGPC comes to control Akali politics and the political centre for Sikhs remains in the Golden Temple, Amritsar.

In all, the SGPC has 155 members. 140 are elected from Punjab, Himachal Pradesh and Haryana and 10 are nominated. Five Jathedars of 5 Takhts are ex-officio members without having any voting rights.

Section 43 of the Act provides for the Composition of the Board and Section 45 lays down qualifications of elected members and Section 49, which lays down qualifications of the electors, are important to understand the process of elections to this important body, which has been called Parliament of Sikhs as also a State within the State. In view of their importance, these sections are reproduced below:

43. Composition and constitution of the Board:

1. Board shall consist of:
   - (i) One hundred and thirty two elected members;
   - (ii) The head ministers of the Darbar Sahib, Amritsar and the following four Takhts, namely:

     The Sri Akal Takht Sahib, Amritsar, Sri Takht Keshgarh Sahib, Anandpur, the Sri Takht Patna Sahib, Patna and Sri Takht Hazur Sahib, Hyderabad Deccan.

(iii) Twenty-five members, resident in India of whom at least twelve shall be residents of PEPSU, at least nine of other parts of India, than Punjab and PEPSU and not more than four of Punjab co-opted by the members of the Board as described in clauses (i) & (ii).

2. The State Government shall, as soon as may be, call a meeting of the members of the Board described in clauses (i) & (ii) of sub-section (1) for the purpose of co-opting the members described in clause (iii) of the sub-section, and after the members have been co-opted, the State Government shall notify the fact of the Board having been duly constituted and the date of the publication of the notification shall be deemed to be the date of the constitution of the Board.

43. A Constitution of new Board:

1. Whenever a new Board within the meaning of section 51 is constituted, it shall consist of:-

(i) one hundred and forty elected members;

(ii) the Head Ministers of the Darbar Sahib, Amritsar and following four Takhats namely:- The Sri Akal Takht Sahib, Amritsar, the Sri Takht Keshgarh Sahib, Anandpur, the Sri Takht Patna Sahib, Patna and the Sri Takht Hazur Sahib, Nanded and

(iii) Fifteen members resident in India, of who not more than five shall be residents of Punjab, coopted by the members of the Board as described in clauses (i) & (ii).

45. Qualifications of elected members:

1. A person shall not be eligible for election as a member of the Board if such person

(i) is unsound of mind

(ii) is an undischarged insolvent

(iii) is a patit

(iv) is a minister of a Notified Sikh Gurudwara, other than the Head Minister of the Darbar Sahib, Amritsar, or of one of the four Sikh Takhts specified in clause (ii) of sub-section (1) of section 43,

(v) is a paid servant of any Notified Sikh Gurudwara, or of the Board other than a member of the executive committee of the Board;

(vi) being a Keshdhari Sikh is not an Amritdhari;

(vii) takes alcoholic drinks;

(viii) not being a blind person who cannot read and write Gurumukhi.

Explanation - For purpose of clause (viii) a person shall be deemed to be able to:

(a) read Gurumukhi if he is able to recite *Shri Guru Granth Sahib* in Gurumukhi; and

(b) write Gurumukhi if he fills his nomination papers for election to the Board in Gurumukhi in his own handwriting. If any question arises whether a candidate is or is not able to read and write Gurumukhi, the question shall be decided in such manner as may be prescribed.

(2) No person shall be eligible for election as member of the Board if he is not registered on the electoral rolls of any constituency.

(2A) No person shall be eligible for election to the Board if he is less than twenty-five years of age.

3. Notwithstanding anything contained in sub-section (1), no person shall be prevented from standing as a candidate for election as a member or a person elected is, thereafter, found under the provisions of section 84 to be a patit, his election shall be void.

49. Qualifications of electors: Every person shall be entitled to have his name registered on the electoral rolls of a constituency constituted for the election of a member or members of the Board who is a resident in that constituency and...

(i) ...

(ii) is a Sikh, more than twenty one years of age, who has had his name registered as voter in such manner as may be prescribed.

Provided that no person shall be registered as an elector who:

(a) trims or shaves his beard or keshas except in the case of Sehjdhari Sikhs;

(b) smokes;

(c) takes alcoholic drinks.

1979 ELECTIONS TO SGPC

The elections to SGPC held in 1979 were crucial. During these elections, 33 contestants were returned unopposed including Jathedar Gurcharan Singh Tohra, M.P., Jagdev Singh Talwandi M.P., President SA Dal, Mohan Singh Tur and Basant Singh Khalsa, M.P. All the 33 unopposed members were nominees of Shiromani Akali Dal. For 107 seats for which elections were held, there were 349 candidates. These elections are known for the fact that Sant Jarnail Singh had put up 70 candidates under auspices of Panth Khalsa formed by him and Dr. Jagjit Singh. The prestigious contest took place in Beas Constituency from where Jathedar Jiwan Singh Umranangal, General Secretary, SGPC contested as Shiromani Akali Dal candidate. He contested the election after resigning from Punjab Cabinet. He had a straight contest with Bhai Amrik Singh, President, All India Sikh Students Federation and the nominee of Sant Jarnail Singh Bhindranwale. Bhai Amrik Singh was supported by Congress, Jathedar Santokh Singh and Jathedar Rachpal Singh of Delhi. Amrik Singh lost. But he and Jarnail Singh Bhindranwale reciprocated Congress help by helping Congress (I) candidates for Lok Sabha elections in 1980 from Amritsar and Gurdaspur constituencies. However, Bhai Amrik Singh had become an embittered man and his frustration was to turn into an implacable hatred for the establishment.

The SGPC elections are to be held every five years on the basis of adult Sikh franchise and are of crucial importance as the Assembly throws up leadership of the community. "Control of a working majority in 155 person statutory body" says Paul Wallace in an essay Political Dynamics of Punjab, "is the key to Sikh Politics". This has been known as a fact of life to every Punjabi. Because of Akali Dal fattening itself on the resources of SGPC, the latter has emerged as a formidable force on the scene. Originally, Akali Dal was a volunteer force to help SGPC to wrest control of Gurudwaras. However, Akali Dal politics under Master Tara Singh tried to gain momentum of its own.. Akali Dal to date remains a dependent child of SGPC. It can never outgrow its tutelage of the SGPC and break its umbilical cord of sustenance from the SGPC. The largesse, which SGPC has acquired, has made it a prize to be captured by various factions of Akalis, as well as extremists. So when Central Government utilised the services of Jain Saint, Muni Sushil Kumar, he installed Jasbir Singh Rode, nephew of Bhindranwale, as Akal Takht Chief in the hope of winning over AISSF led by Gurjit Singh and others in March, 1988. Since Jasbir Singh had been a vociferous champion of Khalistan according to his own fiery oration at Nankana Sahib in Pakistan in November 1985, the extremists and Akalis came to sabotage the entire peace initiative. It is a pity that the SGPC, which has provided shelter and succour to terrorists, should fall prey to the latter. By making Golden Temple a den of terrorists, SGPC put its own existence in peril. The murder of its Secretary Sardar Bhan Singh by the extremists is a shameful indictment of SGPC policies.

There are as many as 88 Sikh religious shrines, which are directly managed by the SGPC There are another 700 gurudwaras which are managed by it under Section 87 (La) and under Section 87 (lob) of the Gurudwara Act. This means the S.G.P.C controls nearly 800 Sikh religious shrines. The income of the 11 leading shrines managed by the SGPC was Rs. 3,67,68,963.00. The budget of the SGPC was Rs. 6,50,25,312.00 in 1980; it had increased by 577.41% over the past five years. Thus, SGPC has at its command funds unparalleled by any other comparable organisation. It has a large personnel on its pay rolls. These include Granthis (Priests), Dhadis (Ode singers), Ragis (hymn singers) and parcharaks, baptisers and drivers, etc. Thus SGPC has emerged as a State within the State and President of the SGPC acquires the same clout as the Pope in the Vatican. Ragis and Dhadis and Parcharaks carry out propaganda on the lines laid by SGPC. Thus SGPC comes to rule the passions of the laity. It can sway their emotions and condition them accordingly.

Since 1972, when Sardar Gurcharan Singh Tohra assumed the Presidentship from Sardar Mohan Singh Tur, he steered SGPC away from national mainstream and towards extremism. He was a fire-spewing proponent of the line that the Centre has always been anti-Sikh. Even during the Janta regime when Akalis had two ministers in the Central Cabinet, he was given to hectoring than to talking even with the highest.

The progressive increase in SGPC budget clearly belies the trotted theory of erosion of Sikh identity. Progressive increase in offerings establishes the viewpoint, put forth by Shri K.S. Duggal, that despite the influx of foreign gadgetry in Sikh homes they would continue to flock to Gurudwaras in large numbers. Thus, the religiosity of Sikh masses caters to the advantage of SGPC and its policies.

It must be remembered that the number of Gurudwaras has been increasing and a Gurudwara provides an effective pulpit for making fiery speeches by the extremists and as well as sanctuaries to them. Gurudwara remains the pivot of rural Sikh life whence he should normally seek religious inspiration but is exposed to extremist diatribes against Delhi Darbar. Being on the subject of Gurudwaras, we should understand that every Gurudwara is not historic. Historic Gurudwaras are only those where Sikh Gurus had stayed or preached. Other Gurudwaras do not enjoy the same sanctity.

Some jurists have raised the question of legal justification of Gurudwara Act in a secular state. The PREAMBLE to our Constitution states that ours is a SECULAR State. It is, therefore, asked how can the State be burdened with expenditure and supervisory duties for elections to a religious body. There is a demand for scrapping the Sikh Gurudwara Act of 1925 since, SGPC had turned into a Frankenstein of militancy and separatism. The Gurudwara Act offends the Indian Constitution, whereas Article 26 concerning the freedom to manage religious affairs gives every religious denomination the right to manage its own affairs in matters of religion, it does not provide for Govt. setting up an institution on behalf of any religious minority. SGPC, in providing sanctuaries to Sant Bhindranwale, Balbir Singh of Council for Khalistan, AISSF and other terrorists created a wind, which they reaped as the inevitable whirlwind. Sardar Bhan Singh had been murdered by the militants and there had been attacks on a number of SGPC and Akali leaders including Jagdev Singh Talwandi and Sardar Gurcharan Singh Tohra, the then President of SGPC on May 14, 1990. The relationship between the SGPC and Akali Dal has been symbiotic. Observes Rajiv Kapoor: "In its election campaign, the Akali Dal has appealed to the strong sentiments among Sikhs on the achievement of the Gurudwara reforms. It has projected itself as the saviour of Sikh religious institutions from the corrupt control by the non-Sikhs." Akali Dal, with the assistance from SGPC has perfected techniques for arousing religious frenzy, These three outfits, that is, the Akhand Kirtani Jatha, Damdami Taksal and the Shiromani Gurdwara Parbandhak Committee, were to spearhead the backlash of Sikh fundamentalism, which was to cause widespread violence that was ultimately to result in the assassination, later of the Prime Minister of India.

– 11 –

Punjab Government's Policy of Controlled Chaos

When Congress came to power in January 1980 in New Delhi trouncing the shadowy Janta Dal, Akali Government of Punjab under Sardar Parkash Singh Badal was still quite popular. But to Congress, regional parties have been anathema. The Congress political culture never realised the regional sub-nationalism, had to be accorded due recognition in a pluralist polity like India. Accordingly, the Badal Government was dismissed and fresh elections to Punjab Vidhan Sabha were ordered.

In these elections, the Congress party riding the popular Indira wave, which had swept over the whole of India, came to power in Punjab, too. Sardar Darbara Singh was elected leader of the Congress Legislature Party. He became the Congress Chief Minister and seemed to have decided to prove himself the new incarnation of Sardar Partap Singh Kairon and keep the Akalis at bay. In the manner of the legendary Kairon Sahib, who had built Sant Fateh Singh to demolish Master Tara Singh, Sardar Darbara Singh tried to build Jagdev Singh Talwandi to beat Tohra-Longowal-Badal Akali axis. Among the Hindus, he relied upon Sri Virendar of Jallandhar, who published *Partap*, a daily newspaper in Urdu, to counter the influence of Lala Jagat Narain of *Hind Samachar* group of publications. He also cultivated Sri Prem Bhatia of the *Tribune* among the print media in his battle against the faction opposing him. His strategy was to counter moves of his adversaries within the Congress and the Akali Dal by espousing those who were keen to join the rat race.

Factionalism in Congress did not start with the tussle between S. Darbara Singh and Giani Zail Singh. As early as 1956, Bhim Sen Sachar, who in his naivete wanted to play the game of politics by rules, was ousted by the combative S. Partap Singh Kairon through manipulation and magnifying the mistake of allowing police to tear gas the wanted criminals in the hostel area of the Golden Temple in Amritsar. Shri Bhim Sen Sachar, who had been the Chief Minister of Punjab since April 1952, resigned in January, 1956, ushering in a new era of Congress factionalism and manipulative politics.

When Sardar Darbara Singh became the Chief Minister of Punjab, he was determined not to prove himself another lamb like Shri Bhim Sen Sachar.

Giani Zail Singh had left the countryside in Punjab to the mercies of Akali Dal and CPI(M), thus making the victory of Shiromani Akali Dal in 1977 a natural consequence.

Sardar Darbara Singh was the only Sikh Chief Minister who had not been an Akali leader himself earlier. Again, he was so staunch in his anti-Akali-ism that he invited a backlash from the Sikhs. A devout Sikh that he was—he spent four hours in Japa every morning—he became the embodiment of anti-Sikhism like his predecessors and lent support to the rump of Jagdev Singh Talwandi, who had resorted to a symbolic satyagrah at Delhi for the acceptance of the Anandpur Sahib Resolution, which again pushed Harchand Singh Longowal into a corner so that he had to embark upon his Dharamyudh of 45 demands—some genuine and the rest just a farrago of trivia—another demonstration of the fatal competitive extremism created by the Congress Chief Ministers in their zeal to keep Akali Dal off balance. If Darbara Singh had been wiser, he would have desisted from this disastrous course, which ended in his own ouster and the monumental catastrophe for the people of this border state.

Punjab has a long tortuous history of morchas and agitations launched by the Akalis whenever they were out of power. Almost all Congress Chief Ministers in their own way tried to placate, neutralise, weaken or win Akalis over. But the tussle between Sardar Darbara Singh and Giani Zail Singh left the former no room to maneuver. The worst was not only that both Giani Zail Singh and S. Darbara Singh vied with each other in wooing Sant Jarnail Singh Bhindranwale, (Sardar Darbara Singh was said to have learnt Gurbani from Sant Jarnail Singh and Giani Zail Singh was said to touch the feet of Sant Jarnail Singh as a gesture of reverence towards the Sant). But both came to block the settlement, which had been arrived at between the Nirankaris and the Damdami Taksal. The Nirankaris after igniting the spark of conflagration were prepared to abide by the conditions laid by Sant Jarnail Singh: however, Sardar Darbara Singh in his anxiety that the sole credit for the settlement should go to him alone succeeded in raising the ante of Giani Zail Singh, thus resulting in his scuttling the entire move towards peace in Punjab.

The tussle between Giani Zail Singh and S. Darbara Singh had gained such notoriety that it started grabbing headlines in print media. *Mainstream* devoted two articles to the subject. Nikhil Chakravorty wrote on 10th April 1982, in his article captioned *Gilbert and Sullivan in Town*. "Meanwhile a comic-opera situation is developing in Punjab. While Indira Gandhi is having rounds of plain speaking with the Akali leaders, his Home Minister has no compunction in placating the more menacing Akali leader, Sant Jarnail Singh Bhindranwale .... Giani Zail Singh was reported to have touched Bhindranwale's feet during his last visit to the Capital.... His (Bhindranwale) militant followers have been found roaming the streets with unlicensed fire-arms without being touched by Police, which in this Union Territory of Delhi was directly under the charge of the Giani as the Home Minister of India. A disconcerting Gilbertean scenario" (S. Jarnail Singh and his Jatha had gone to Delhi on 3rd April, 1982).

Again in another article captioned *Eyeless in Punjab* Nikhil Chakravorty wrote: "For the last two years and more, Union Home Minister Giani Zail Singh has been known to have been moving heaven and earth to oust Punjab Chief Minister Darbara Singh. Apart from intrigues within the Congress and manipulating the media for this purpose, the Giani has indulged in rather shameless hobnobbing with the Akalis .... For such a politician to be involved in playing soft to Akali intransigence to say the least to fight the Chief Minister belonging his own party .... what is the Home Minister of India?"

Economic and Political Weekly, Special number of November 6, 1981 commented: "Indeed the Sikh community has everything to lose by indulging in simplistic slogan like Khalistan, imported into India by migratory elements .... but it will play the card now because it is seen as the only way to win Sikh hegemony over the state. The paralysis of political management that results from the tussle of the remarkably limited Home Minister, Giani Zail Singh and the secular Chief Minister Darbara Singh has of course crystallised these (Sikh) angers and alienations".

The tussle between S. Darbara Singh and Giani Zail Singh had not only divided the Congress ranks in Punjab but also the bureaucracy as some officers at Chandigarh and Delhi had continued their allegiance to Gianiji. Also some of them were apprehensive how would they fare under President's rule if Gianiji carried out his threat of imposing President's rule on Punjab, as also what would happen if Akalis staged a comeback to power? Such schizophrenia in police and civil servants led to virtual paralysis of the administration that refused to act and preferred playing safe. The officers, who kept national stakes and implications in view, were sought to be lampooned by carrying tales to the newspapers. Bureaucracy in a crisis is never cohesive but the tussle between the Punjab Chief Minister and the Union Home Minister encouraged the communal elements (services had been deliberately communalised by communal parties such as Akali Dal and Jan Sangh during their spells of governance) among them to indulge in their pastime of intrigue and smear campaigns.

Congress fortunes in Punjab nosedived because of frequent changes in the Presidentship of Punjab Congress Committee. S. Darbara Singh was the President of the PCC as well as Chief Minister. Giani faction strenuously campaigned for his removal from PCC Presidentship. I happened to be present when Mrs. Indira Gandhi, the President of AICC, in one of her histrionic ways said that when the government in

Punjab was being so ineffective, how could she entrust PCC to the Chief Minister? The Chief Minister sensed what was coming, and immediately put in his resignation. Accordingly Miss Sarla Parashar replaced Darbara Singh as President Punjab Congress Committee. Later on Shri Hans Raj Sharma came to occupy this position. Then came S. Santokh Singh in lurid light. In reality, there have been numerous changes because Congress in Punjab is a fractured and demoralised lot. Congress in Punjab remains inert till elections are announced, when there is a flurry of activity. Like Akalis, Congress too finds it difficult to exist without power. Its base is always shifting and vote banks go on changing according to emerging power equations.

Congress Chief Minister's style of functioning has a significant impact on the fortunes of the State. Sardar Partap Singh Kairon took Congress to the Jat Sikhs. He was so sure of himself that he brought about the ouster of Master Tara Singh by Jats, thinking that he would be able to manipulate Jats. If Jats did not desert him completely it was because they perceived him to be the architect of rural progress. After supplanting Master Tata Singh, Jat Sikhs took full control of Shiromani Akali Dal and Shiromani Gurudwara Prabhandak Committee. Every Congress Chief Minister had a single point myopic programme: Weaken Akalis by creating or encouraging factions among them, which had led to the rise of total extremism, thus distancing Akalis from the national mainstream. The architect of the myopic policy was Sardar Pratap Singh Kairon but Giani Zail Singh brought in a new variation of this theme. He began to behave as if he was more an Akali and he prided himself in receiving Siropas as the defender of Sikh faith. Mrs. Gandhi was very upset on the turn of the events that were taking in Punjab. She reminded Gianiji on more than one occasion that he was not the Chief Minister of Punjab any more but the Home Minister of India. But Gianiji was irrepressible. When Mrs. Gandhi chose him over Narasimharao for Presidentship, many observers felt it was to stop his meddling in Punjab that he was sent to Rashtrapati Bhawan. Gianiji stayed impetuous all along. One can never forget his quip *'Pappu khilono se khel raha hai'*, when Rajiv Gandhi tried to usher in computer age. It was Pandit Nehru who had chosen him in the first instance to lead a revolt against the ruler of Faridkot, then Mrs. Gandhi who nurtured him to be the Chief Minister of Punjab. Even Sanjay Gandhi helped him to get a grip on chief ministership. Then again Mrs Gandhi pushed him up to become the President of India. He very conveniently forgot that he owed political life to three generations of Nehru-Gandhis. Nihangs conferred the title of Mahasikh on him.

Sardar Darbara Singh and Giani Zail Singh vied with each other so disastrously that they blocked a settlement between the Nirankaris and the Damdami Taksal. The Nirankari Chief was said to be prepared to abide by the conditions laid down by Sant Jarnail Singh. However, Sardar Darbara Singh in his anxiety that the credit for this compromise should go to him alone, pushed Giani Zail Singh into a tight corner and thus succeeded in scuttling the whole plan of compromise.

Misuse of every organ of Government to further or to maintain a leader's hold on the state has led to systematic undermining of the edifice of orderly governance. Mr. B.K. Chum, Special Correspondent of the *Indian Express*, Chandigarh commented as follows on the fall of Darbara Singh Ministry and imposition of President's Rule in October 1983:

"Over the period some evil genius in it (the Congress Government of Punjab) evolved a theory of Controlled Chaos in the mistaken belief that it would ensure its continuity in power. These well wishers forgot that a 'Controlled Chaos' invariably leads to uncontrollable events in politics".

A government, which seeks to perpetuate itself by creating Controlled Chaos is devoid of ethics and commonsense. The pursuit of such a moronic policy by the Government of Punjab was bound to end in a disaster and this policy of Punjab government pushed the Hindus and the Sikhs of the state over the precipice.

- 12 -

The Central Government Sleeps over the Secessionist Activities

Though it may sound incredible, yet the fact remains that the Government of India did not stir even its little finger, when the secessionist activities started in the Union Territory of Chandigarh. Such inaction bespeaks ill of Central Government's subsequent anxiety and their reprimand of the duly elected government of Punjab, under Sardar Darbara Singh. No Punjab Government could be held responsible for the persistent Sikh secessionist activities growing in the Union Territory of Chandigarh it being administered by the Union Ministry of Home Affairs.

As already described in Chapter 8, the early Khalistan Movement started from the city of Chandigarh. The Young Sikh Association had its headquarters at Chandigarh.

On 6th August 1978, the Young Sikh Association and other splinter groups merged and assumed the historical name of Dal Khalsa. It located its headquarters in Gurudwara Akal Garh in Sector 35, Chandigarh. It proclaimed as its objectives:

1. To protect Sikhism from its opponents, that is, the purity of the Sikh religion i.e. Sikh fundamentalism.
2. To establish Khalsa Raj.

All the workers of Dal Khalsa, retired bureaucrats espousing the country Khalistan, roamed about freely preaching the gospel of secessionism. The meetings calling for formation of Khalistan were held in Panchayat Bhawan, a government building. On 1st February, 1981, a Seminar of senior Sikh sophisticates was held in the Panchayat Bhawan.

The forum meeting was presided by Syed Abdullah Bukhari, Shahi Imam of Delhi. It called upon the Government for the creation of Khalistan.

On 20th January 1980 a seminar was held by Dal Khalsa under the aegis of Dr. Jagjit Singh Chauhan, the so-called President of Council for Khalistan at Chandigarh.

The 54th Sikh Education Conference was held at Chandigarh in March 1981. It called for Punjab to be admitted as a member of the United Nations Organisation on the analogy of the Uzbeks.

When the Prime Minister addressed a public meeting at Bassi in Patiala Distt. during 1972 elections to Punjab Vidhan Sabha, the Dal Khalsa distributed pamphlets championing the cause of the Sikh Homeland among the audience collected by the Congress. Intelligence personnel were present there in large numbers but those distributing those pamphlets were not apprehended.

Gajender Singh and Harsimran Singh had inscribed "Khalistan to safeguard Sikhism" on the walls in the Sector 17 & 22 of Chandigarh in March 1974.

Amender Singh, the most active member of Dal Khalsa, was an employee in the Punjab government at one time. A government servant is not allowed to carry out anti-government and anti-national activities. Similarly, Harsimran Singh was close to all the important people in Chandigarh. His name was kept on the waiting list for a government job.

Nor were the activities of Council for Khalistan with its headquarters in the Golden Temple, Amritsar, checked by the Government of India. The Council issued Khalistan stamps and Khalistan passports printed in Canada and freely distributed them in Chandigarh, Jallandhar and Amritsar for publication in the print media. The Ministry of External Affairs did nothing to counter the activities of the Council for Khalistan in Canada and the U.K. When the Punjab government requested for some action in U.K. and Canada, the venerable mandarins of Ministry of External Affairs sitting in their airconditioned rooms in the South Block, New Delhi sniggered at the anxious supplications of Punjab officers who went to meet them.

It can rightly be said that the authorities in Chandigarh and New Delhi through their avowed apathy to activities of Dal Khalsa and Council for Khalistan probably wanted Khalistan to come into existence in double quicktime.

– 13 –

Darkness at Noon

This chapter deals with terrorism in Punjab in the pre Operation Blue Star period.

While examining the Sikh Ethos in Chapter 5, it was shown that the brave Sikhs took to arms whenever they perceived a threat to their religious identity. Terrorist tactics adopted by the Arabs, the Red Brigade in Europe, I.R.A. in Ireland also came to be adopted by the Sikh terrorists in Punjab. Actually, the analogy of terrorism in Punjab is very close to that of the I.R.A. who has been waging terrorist campaign on behalf of the Irish Catholics against their co-religionists i.e. with Protestants for centuries.

Punjab, once synonymous with communal amity, harmony and agricultural success, had come to present a picture of distrust and violence not known in the annals of post-independent India. The militant siege of this thriving state had emanated from communalism, which had come to mar the amity of the state in less violent manifestation since 1950 when the Punjabi Hindus, under the influence of Arya Samaj and Jan Sangh, disowned Punjabi language, thus laying the foundation of communal carnage of 1980s. This communalism would have died but for the naked political opportunism of the worst order indulged in both by the Congress and the Akalis. This communalism was nurtured and fuelled by the myopic policy of political expediency by these two parties.

Before the expiry of the first year of Sardar Darbara Singh's Ministry in the State, foundations for Sikhs confronting various communities and involving the State apparatus came to be laid by one article published in the daily *Partap* (Urdu) of May 1981 by one Jaswant Rai, painting Guru Gobind Singh as a luxury loving potentate than a Warrior Saint, who as the tenth Guru had given the Sikhs a new identity and imbued them with courage to fight oppression and discrimination, one of the basic radical traits of the Khalsa.

I found this article in a very bad taste and it shamelessly outraged the religious feelings of the Sikhs. Under the law, a prosecution could be launched by the government alone. Thus, I sought the sanction of the Chief Minister to launch the prosecution against Shri Jaswant Rai and the proprietor of *Partap*, Shri Virendar. I later came to know that Sardar Darbara Singh had been cultivating Shri Virendar as a counterpoise against Lala Jagat Narain, the proprietor of *Hind Samachar* group of publications. So Sardar Darbara Singh disagreed with me and no action could be taken against the offenders.

As a rejoinder, Sardar Sukhjinder Singh, a member of the Akali Working Committee, and an ex-Minister in the Akali Ministry, wrote an article criticising the role of Hindu Rajas of Himachal area against Guru Gobind Singh at Anandpur Sahib.

In the meanwhile, the All India Sikh Students Federation (AISSF) demanded that the city of Amritsar be declared a sacred city and the use of cigarettes, meat and alcoholic drinks in Amritsar be banned.

The Akalis also passed resolutions demanding that the Government of India should declare Amritsar city as sacred as in the case of Banaras and Hardwar. They further demanded that, in the trains coming to Amritsar, smoking should be banned.

When these demands were made public, the Hindus of Amritsar city adopted a perverse stand and took out a procession on 29th May, 1981, claiming that it was their right to smoke and opposed the Akali and AISSF demand in this regard. The attitude of Hindus was such as not to appeal to any rational being. The Hindu processionists had raised slogans derogating the proponents of the anti-tobacco agitation.

The Hindus claimed that it was their birth right to smoke, and opposed any ban on smoking and drinking of liquor and eating of animal meat. This stand of the Hindus of Amritsar was reminiscent of similar stand of the Punjabi Hindus claiming that they did not know Punjabi language and they spoke Hindi in their day to day life and misleading the State Reorganisation Commission in 1956, thus filling the Akalis with a bitter conviction that the Punjabi Hindus' communalism was ineradicable, whatever the Sikhs did to build Punjabi culture and purify Punjab's life.

Sardar Gurcharan Singh Tohra did not want to show his hand yet, so he egged on Sant Bhindranwale to take out a procession in retaliation to Hindu demonstration. Bhindranwale, AISSF and Dal Khalsa activists took out a procession on 31st May marching through the main markets of Amritsar. The processionists raised provocative communal slogans and the most provocative act was that the Jatha of Sant Jarnail Singh displayed their fire-arms, which included a number of 319 rifles but most of the demonstrators brandished swords. Police was on the horns of a serious dilemma: if they had intercepted armed Jatha, it would have resulted in exchange of fire and serious casualties including those of some innocents. So the police let the procession pass but dealt firmly with the dispersing crowds, which tried to put tobacco stalls on fire. As usual, the Akalis lashed out against Punjab Government. Hindus, on the other hand, accused the police of showing weakness. Akalis wanted police to open fire, so they could find a cause to ignite fires of agitation. Shri Prem Bhatia, Editor, Daily *Tribune* wrote in his paper on 24th June 1981:

"Grave government provocation is presumably what the Akalis and their allies in the Dal Khalsa and AISSF are hoping for. Nothing helps an agitation based on passion or a sense of injustice more than the use of excessive force. Incidents of violence result in death or serious injuries to the agitators. An Akali leader said, "What we need are a few dead bodies presumably brought down by police bullets. We can then deal with Darbara Singh and Indira Gandhi." Police had decided not to oblige the Akalis.

MURDER OF LALA JAGAT NARAIN

It is generally believed that terrorism in Punjab began with the murder of Lala Jagat Narain, Editor, *Hind Samachar* chain of dailies. However, the fact is that the militant era in Punjab was inaugurated earlier by Talwinder Singh Parmar's gang of motorcyclist desperadoes. Originally, Talwinder Singh had belonged to the Village Panchatta in District Kapurthala. He had migrated to Canada. He succeeded in bringing arms and money into India. He had purchased a couple of jongas and motorcycles. His personal jonga bore the banner line "Jo Ade so Mite", that is, whosoever confronts this Canadian Akhand Kirtani Sikh will be destroyed. Talwinder Singh's speciality was baptising ex-Naxalite Sikhs to form his killer gang. He had baptised one Tarsem Singh of village Kalasanghian, District Kapurthala. Tarsem Singh was a crack shot and with the help of three Head Constables of Punjab Police, namely Sewa Singh, Gurnam Singh and Amardeep Singh, took to selected killings of Nirankaris. In 1970's, Head Constables Sewa Singh and Gurnam Singh used to organise the audience of constabulary for Sant Jarnail Singh Bhindranwale in Faridkot Police Lines itself. The gang of Tarsem Singh, Head Constables Sewa Singh, Gurnam Singh and Amardeep Singh came to be known as a "Khooni Jatha" for eliminating the heretics among the Sikhs and the Nirankaris. The first victim of this Khooni Jatha was Shadi Lal Angra, President, Municipal Committee and Nirankari Pramukh of Anandpur Sahib. He was shot down by the ex-Naxalite Tarsem Singh.

Next victim was Master Gurcharan Singh of Kot Shamir of District Bhatinda who had allowed his feet to touch the holy *Guru Granth Sahib*. His drunken folly was made public by his devout wife who had raised hue and cry. Tarsem Singh, Sewa Singh and one Surjit Singh shot him dead on 18th August, 1981 while he was riding a bus. The era of motorcyclist terrorism started in Punjab in this manner.

Dal Khalsa had carried out sustained campaign of hatred against Lala Jagat Narain for his anti-Khalistan posture as well as his appearance as a defence witness in the murder case against Nirankari Chief. While killing minor Nirankaris had been taken upon by the Akhand Kirtani Jatha, Sant J.S. Bhindranwale's followers had taken upon themselves the liquidation of what in terrorist parlance is called the "strategically important targets".

After killing Baba Gurbachan Singh at New Delhi on 24 April, 1980, the turn of Lala Jagat Narain, who had been outspoken in his articles against Khalistan and Sikh revivalism, had come. He was gunned down while returning from Patiala to Jallandhar via the Grand Trunk Road (G.T. Road) on the evening of 9th September, 1981, in pursuance of a conspiracy as meticulously hatched as the one for the murder of Baba Gurbachan Singh. Fortunately, one of the murderers of Lala Jagat Narain was arrested after a chase by the police while the remaining two had managed to escape. Murder of Lala Jagat Narain had created great resentment among Hindus.

World Sikh Convention - Charter of 45 Demands

Sant Longowal called World Sikh Convention on 26th July, 1981 at Manji Sahib, Golden Temple. It called for acceptance of Anandpur Sahib Resolution, declaring Sikhs a separate nation and removal of discrimination and grievances of Sikhs.

The last resolution was moved by S. Parkash Singh Badal. The conference presented a charter of 45 demands. Sant Harchand Singh Longowal disclosed that he would wait till 31st August 1981, failing which Dharam Yudh would be launched with first demonstration at Delhi on 7th September. Some of the 45 demands were straightforward and simple and should have been accepted but neither the Punjab Government nor Government of India paid due attention nor were the Akalis invited for talks. When 31st August passed, Akalis started preparations for demonstration at Delhi on 7th September, 1981. Police Chiefs of Punjab and Haryana were summoned to Delhi and told that Akalis should be discouraged to come to Delhi, particularly those who would entrain without tickets as well those who misused road transport. A large number of AISSF workers entrained at Amritsar without tickets.

Nachhattar Singh (he belonged to village Rode of Jarnail Singh Bhindranwale), the accused arrested from near the site of murder, was put to intensive interrogation who stated that the murder was committed by Swaran Singh, a nephew of Sant Jarnail Singh Bhindranwale, and also one Dalbir Singh. He also gave details of conspiracy involving Sant Jarnail Singh Bhindranwale to arrange this murder by unknown, unconcerned youth, his nephew Swaran Singh *s/o* Jagir Singh and Dalbir Singh the proclaimed offender in the murder case of Nirankari Guru Gurbachan Singh. Parsan Singh was to provide transport. The fault of Lala Jagat Narain was that he had been depicting Sant Bhindranwale as an aggressor in the clash of 13th April, 1978, at Amritsar between Akhand Kirtani Jatha, followers of Sant Jarnail Singh and Nirankaris. Nachhattar Singh had originally been a Naxalite and had earlier murdered one Ajaib Singh, but was acquitted of the charge of this murder. Nachhattar Singh, after his stint as a Naxalite, had turned into an opium smuggler. Knowing his past career as Naxalite, Political murderer and Opium smuggler, he was cultivated to carry out the mission. Nachhattar Singh had heard Sant Bhindranwale praising Ranjit Singh and Kabul Singh for eliminating Nirankari Baba Gurcharan Singh and further that anyone who carried out his entrusted mission could not be arrested and the families of absconders were paid Rs. 1500/- per month by the Panth and when suitable occasion arose Santji would weigh Ranjit Singh and Kabul Singh in gold. The families of these were offered Siropas, which inspired Nachhattar Singh to carry out the mission. Attempts were made earlier to murder Lala Jagat Narain at Kurkshetra on 29-31 July without success. Second attempt at Malerkotla did not succeed because the motor cycle had run down battery and the front tyre got punctured at the crucial moment. However, they had been able to monitor the car numbers of Lala Jagat Narain. The third attempt was to be made at Yamuna Nagar on 19.8.81 but Lala Jagat Narain did not turn up. Gurmukh Singh, proclaimed offender in Nirankari Baba murder case, appeared on stage at Bhikhiwind on 2nd and 3rd September, 1981 and Sant Jarnail Singh Bhindranwale said no one could touch anyone who formed his Jatha. Santji told Sangat that nothing had happened after the murder of 'Bachna' and nobody would be touched by police who joined his Jatha. Lala Jagat Narain was to visit Patiala on 9th September 1981 when this mission would be completed. Nachhattar Singh was driving the motor cycle, Swaran Singh and Dalbir Singh armed with .32 bore and .455 revolvers were on the pillion, with which they killed Jagat Narain between Ludhiana and Phillaur. Nachhattar Singh further stated that he had no personal grudge against Lala Jagat Narain and he had joined in the commission of the crime in pursuance of the inspiring instructions of Sant Jarnail Singh.

Above is a summary of the disclosures made by Nachhattar Singh during his interrogation. It discloses the methodology of the mission created and entrusted and also rebuts the Akali allegation that the accused had been framed by police.

ARREST OF SANT JARNAIL SINGH

After the above disclosures, Ludhiana police had no option but to seek warrants for the arrest of all the accused and the conspirators.

Sant Jarnail Singh was camping at village Chandu Kalan, District Hissar on 12th September 1981. A meeting was held between Punjab and Haryana Chief Ministers at the residence of the latter. As decided in the meeting, police contingent was sent to village Chandu Kalan to effect the arrest, since it was apprehended that Sant and his followers may offer armed resistance. However, when the Punjab Police contingent arrived, the Santji had already fled. His followers brought police under fire so that it could not chase the Sant. In this cross fire, some vehicles of the Jatha and some religious pothies were burnt.

The question is: who had informed Santji that police was arriving? Even if it is believed that Jallandhar Radio in its evening news bulletin had referred to the issuance of warrants of arrest, the escape cannot be linked to it. Again, Santji was to weigh Kabul Singh and Ranjit Singh in gold for murdering 'Bachna' why should he himself flee and seek sanctuary in the Gurudwara Gurdarshan Parkash Mehta? What does his abscondence indicate? Why did he always seek sanctuaries in Gurudwaras? Actually, Punjab Police had been betrayed by someone. Who is that person? Evidently he did not want Santji to be touched.

On 13th September, 1981, I received a phone call from the Home Minister of India, Giani Zail Singh to reconsider the question of arrest of Santji. I told him that police was bound by Court orders. By morning of 13th September, Bhindranwale had found sanctuary in Gurudwara Gurdarshan Parkash and police force had returned without success. Chief Minister Darbara Singh called a meeting with DIG, CID, late J.S. Anand and me to consider the future course of action. The Chief Minister was told that police was legally bound to arrest Santji in pursuance to the warrants and since Gurdarshan Parkash was not a historic Gurudwara and had been built only recently, we may consider police should enter it if it became necessary to do so, though police should not enter sanctum sanctorum of any Gurudwara. The Chief Minister argued that he would have to resign if the police entered any Gurudwara. He recalled how Bhim Sen Sachar had to resign in 1956. I told the Chief Minister that I too was not in favour of entering Golden Temple, which is the holiest of holy places for Sikhs as well as for Hindus like myself. But a distinction between a Gurudwara associated with great Gurus and a Gurudwara built a couple of years back may have to be made. Shri. J.S. Anand intervened to say that none from Punjab police would enter any Gurudwara. I said I knew how to have legal orders carried out. Nonetheless, the Chief Minister remained adamant. He found support from Shri J.S. Anand and said he would make moves to induce Sant Bhindranwale to surrender. Shri J.S. Anand offered to go to Mehta Chowk and speak to Santji. But when Shri J.S. Anand presented himself before Sant Bhindranwale at Gurdarshan Parkash, the latter refused to talk to him as he had used scissors on his beard. Thus, our DIG., CID., returned crestfallen. However, political emissaries, who went on behalf of Punjab Chief Minister, were more successful. Ultimately, Sant Bhindranwale agreed to surrender on 20th September, 1981, provided he was arrested by an Amritdhari Sikh Officer, and was kept in custody of only Amritdhari Sikh Officers. Thus, a Sikh Superintendent of Police, who had been baptised by Bhindranwale himself, was detailed to effect the arrest and escort him to Ludhiana. In the meanwhile, most incendiary speeches were delivered in the Dewans held daily at Gurudwara Gurdarshan Parkash and basest passions were sought to be whipped up. Large crowds started gathering. On the request of the brave Sr. S.P., Amritsar, Shri Ajit Singh Atwal, reinforcements were sent to Mehta Chowk to deal with the situation and also D.I.G., Jallandhar Range, Sardar B.S. Dhaliwal, (who later became Director General of Punjab Police under Akali Ministry and was replaced by Shri J.F. Ribeiro), was asked to camp at Mehta Chowk. Before surrendering to police, all the Akali leaders except Sardar Parkash Singh Badal, reached Gurudwara Gurdarshan Parkash and delivered fiery speeches. The most irresponsible speech was made by Jathedar Santokh Singh of Delhi who was considered very close to the Central Government at Delhi. Whose game, and what game, Jathedar Santokh Singh was playing, remains an inscrutable mystery till today.

The inevitable happened. The infuriated crowds attacked police camp with swords and firearms and set police vehicles and tents on fire as soon as the car of Shri Bhindranwale and his favoutrite S.P. had left Mehta Chowk alongwith him. Police under Shri Ajit Singh Atwal, showed great forbearance and courage and appealed to the fanatics to stop this insensate firing and arson. But to no avail. They had become inebriated with the fiery speeches they had heard during the Dewan. Consequently police had to open fire in self-defence. Result: a number of police officers and men injured and seven of the mob dead. The saddest part was that the D.I.G. camping only one km away never bothered to visit the scene and guide the police.

Violence had not ended; rather it had just started. On the night of September 20, 1981, 3 Sikh youths on motor cycles went on indulging in indiscriminate firing with their stenguns in the Jallandhar market. Four innocents were killed and 12 injured. Next night similar violence occurred at Tarn Taran when Sikh youth indulged in indiscriminate firing killing one and injuring 13 including 2 Sikhs. The police met success in tracing the culprits from one single fact: the culprits had used a special type of .38 bore wad cutter of white chrome metal ammunition.

The empties bore the words "REM". It was found that this ammunition was either with the Air-Force personnel or was imported. Working on the theory of the ammunition having been imported, police arrested one Agriculture University Ludhiana worker Surjit Singh, who acknowledged his role in procuring the ammunition and supplying it to Babbar Khalsa group of Canadian Talwinder Singh Parmar and his gang of Tarsem Singh Kalasanghian and Head Constables Sewa Singh, etc. Jathedar Talwinder Singh had been the brain behind all the crimes listed below:

1. Master Gurdarshan Singh Kot Shamir was shot dead on 18th August 1981 by Head Constable Sewa Singh of Govt. Rly. Police, Tarsem Singh and Surjit Singh.
2. Tarsem Singh, Head Constables Amarjit Singh and Gurnam Singh had shot down 4 persons on the night of 20th Sept. 1981 at Jallandhar (the day, Sant Bhindranwale was arrested).
3. Mohinder Pal, Ex-sarpanch of village Panchhatta (the village to which Talwinder Singh belonged) was shot dead by Tarsem Singh and Head Constable Wadhawa Singh.
4. On 16th Nov. 1981 evening Shri Prahlad Chand of Kapurthala was shot dead in his tea shop by Tarsem Singh.

Earlier Tarsem Singh had gunned down Shadi Lal at Anandpur Sahib. The victim's fault was that he was a Nirankari Mukh.

Thus, by third week of November, all the major crimes perpetrated by Babbar Khalsa had been worked out.

VISIT OF PRIME MINISTER ON 22nd SEPTEMBER, 1981

But before the story of what happened to Talwinder Singh and others is told, it is necessary to unfold here how Sant Bhindranwale came to be released. Things had been happening simultaneously and rapidly. The Prime Minister thought it fit to visit Chandigarh and sound public opinion on the happenings in Punjab. I conveyed to the quarters concerned that if one police firing and two shoot out cases (of Jallandhar and Tarn Taran) would induce the Prime Minister of India to make a personal study, its impact would not be salutary in dealing with the situation. However, she arrived at Chandigarh on 22nd September and stayed for a little more than two hours and met persons of different shades of opinion including Akalis. When I met her, I told her we were not afraid of any inquiry and I myself would initiate move for a judicial inquiry. She looked relieved. Soon after her departure, I told the Chief Minister that P.M. was keen for a judicial inquiry into Mehta firing and I would be sending a request for the same. Accordingly, I drafted a note and terms of reference for the commission of inquiry. Punjab Government entrusted the judicial inquiry to Justice P.S. Pattar, a retired Judge of the Punjab High Court. Government was keen to entrust inquiry to a Sikh Judge so that the impartiality of the Commission of Inquiry was not under doubt. From the news carried in *The Times of India* and *The Tribune* of 10th May 1984, it was learnt that the Commission had justified police firing. Prabhash Joshi, Editor of *The Indian Express* at Chandigarh wrote: "But if Punjab is not in flames today, the state government should share the credit with Mrs. Indira Gandhi, who promptly flew to Chandigarh and defused the situation by starting a dialogue with the opposition, particularly with the Akalis".

RELEASE OF SANT JARNAIL SINGH

A word about the interrogation of Sant Jarnail Singh Bhindranwale is appropriate here. He wanted to be interrogated by an Amritdhari Sikh police officer only. We also thought it better part of discretion to entrust his interrogation to such an officer to avoid allegations of sacrilege, as had been done by him in regard to Chandu Kalan incident. During his interrogation, Santji showed that he was master of Double-speak. He would say that 'Bachna' and Lala Jagat Narain had committed grave sins against Sikh Panth and he as head of Taksal could not tolerate them. Yet, he would plead that he had no hand in their murder. Santji was requested to place his hand on *Guru Granth Sahib* to vouchsafe his innocence so that police could discharge him and other accused. He declined to do so on religious grounds. He was afraid that police had placed tape recorders in the room and he used to search the room very carefully. Large crowds turned up for his Darshan at the rest house where he had been lodged. It was, therefore, decided to take him to another rest house. He resisted this move on the baseless plea that police were moving him to kill him by faking an encounter. Police interrogator was himself a devout religious Sikh who, citing Sikh scriptures, convinced the Santji of his devoutness. He would not harm a small creature, not to speak of harming a Sant like him. With great difficulty, Santji moved to another rest house where police would not have to deal with crowds eager to have his Darshan.

The Director CBI had written to Punjab Govt. that CBI wanted to interrogate Sant Jarnail Singh in regard to the murder of Nirankari Baba Gurcharan Singh. So the Punjab Government requested the Government of India to seek custody of the Sant by moving appropriate court. It is learnt on good authority that the whole of bureaucracy, which included Cabinet Secretary, wanted CBI to apply for securing custody of the Sant but they were overruled by the Home Minister. So we were told by CBI that they would not like to take the remand of the Sant. A perusal of Govt. files can show the unbecoming conduct of the Home Ministry agencies in this regard. So the police sent Sant Jarnail Singh to Ferozepur Jail after seeking judicial remand for him. Crowds started visiting Ferozepur Jail.

In the meanwhile, AISSF had activised itself. Bhai Amrik Singh and Harminder Singh Sandhu thought of a stratagem to spread panic. Harminder Singh Sandhu got in touch with a cracker maker of Meerut. AISSF cadres, after learning the techniques of making crackers and thus understanding the technique of assembling crude bombs, started exploding these at sundry places. The populace, who never had taste of terrorism, panicked. Railway lines were also tempered with by AISSF cadres. In this climate, Sant Longowal called a Shahidi Conference at historic Gurdwara Alamgir near Ludhiana on September 27, 1981. AISSF President threatened Akali leadership that he would denounce them among Sikhs if they did not secure the unconditional release of Sant Jarnail Singh. Posters had already been put up by them in this regard. Akali Dal, which was ultimately to be a silent patron of extremists, announced intensification of their Dharamyudh with effect from the 17th October, 1981 unless Sant Jarnail Singh was released unconditionally by that date. Thus, Akali Dal showed itself as a protector of assassins. Both Punjab Government and Central Government took serious note of the deadline announced by Sant Harchand Singh Longowal who was ultimately called for talks to Delhi. But Akali Dal leader refused to talk unless Sant Jarnail Singh was released. AISSF pressure had been working relentlessly on Akali minds. Verbal consultation took place between Punjab and Central Governments.

It was the view of Punjab Government that if Akalis promised to work for peace, the prosecution of Sant Jarnail Singh could be deferred. S. Darbara Singh was summoned to Delhi. What transpired at Delhi is not known but can only be inferred. To enable Akalis to come to negotiating table, police was told to release Bhindranwale. Police took care not to stop the process of law. SSP Ludhiana made a carefully worded request to the court that for the time being police did not need any custody of the Sant and prosecution for conspiracy would be launched at appropriate time. Thus, Sant Bhindranwale came to be released on the night of 15th October, 1981, from judicial custody at Ferozepur. Jathedar Gurcharan Singh Tohra had already spread the word and a reception for the Sant was organised. He was taken to Gurudwara Gurdarshan Prakash in cavalcade of cars and trucks. Police had to make arrangements that this welcome took place at night only. Had he been released during day time, much larger crowds would have assembled causing law and order problem. After his release, Sant Jarnail Singh made a strange revealation during a public meeting that a Central Minister had called on him in Ferozepur Jail and conveyed him Government's (Central) regrets for arresting him. 'Indeed a miracle in this holy land of miracles' or Santji's Doublespeak?

It appeared that the Central Government was keen to start negotiations with the Akalis. One day after the release of the Sant, Akalis held talks with the Prime Minister on 16th October, 1981. Akalis had emerged victorious in having the serious crime of conspiracy to murder condoned in this way.

This encouraged AISSF to continue their bombings and explosions. Police went after them. Harminder Singh Sandhu was arrested with great difficulty. But the ambivalence on the part of the Govt. had caused demoralisation in police ranks and there was such awe of AISSF that no police officer was prepared to interrogate any of its members or apply to the Court for their remand. With great difficulty police could get out the story from one of them as to how the AISSF had come to acquire the technique of making bombs. Thus, the role of AISSF as a terrorist organisation had been laid bare. In all, 16 explosions were caused by AISSF at various places and the culprits responsible for all, except two, were arrested.

A serious explosion took place in Gurudwara Gurdarshan Prakash on 29th November, 1981. There was scientific evidence to show that the bombs were either being manufactured or stored when the explosion had taken places, sulphur chlorate being the main ingredient used. But Government ban on police entry into Gurudwaras was still in force.

Earlier, Tarsem Singh and Wadhawa Singh wanted in shootout cases, were surrounded by police in the home of one Amarjit Singh Nihang at village Daheru, District Ludhiana on 19th November, 1981. The Police party under Inspector Pritam Singh Bajwa, instead of proceeding tactically, relied on the assumption that the Inspector had shown favour to Tarsem Singh earlier so he would readily surrender. In place of surrendering, Tarsem Singh gunned down Pritam Singh and Constable Surat Singh when they were ascending winding stairs. This enabled Tarsem Singh to escape. After this incident Tarsem Singh and Talwinder Singh decided to leave India. They proceeded abroad via Tarai in UP, Nepal and Bangkok. Punjab Police's request to Interpol for assistance made through CBI for their arrests abroad met with no response and the Canadian and West German Governments gave curt replies to the Government of India with regard to extradition of Talwinder Singh relying on archaic laws. This case also exposed the fact that, not withstanding mouthing cliches of friendship, no Western power was prepared to assist in curbing terrorist activities by their citizens who visited India.

There was a conference of State Director Generals and Inspector Generals of Police in January 1982 in Delhi. The Prime Minister had invited all the delegates at her official residence. She met each Director General separately. Talking to me she said that Hindus in Punjab complained that police was favouring Sikhs. I told her no doubt some police ranks had been infiltrated but we were taking remedial measures. What Arya Samajist press of Jallandhar wanted was that police should raid the hostels attached to Golden Temple. I gave her my assessment that if ever police entered Golden Temple, that would invite unamendable Sikh backlash and ire. She seemed satisfied with my reply particularly since Sikhs had also complained to her of police harassment. I further told her that I would rather relinquish my charge than agree to formal screening of Sikhs in police which communal press wanted to do. No disciplined force can work when loyalty is sought to be destroyed on basis of community alone.

On 12th February, 1982 police arrested Harsimran Singh, Mukh Panch of Dal Khalsa. His interrogation showed how the hijacking of Indian Airbus plane on 29th September, 1981 was planned and how he had been receiving financial aid from prominent Akali leaders.

On 16th February, 1982, the police succeeded in arresting Swaran Singh, nephew of Sant Jarnail Singh Bhindranwale, from a village in District Bhatinda. During his interrogation he disclosed that he worked in some Gurdwaras as a Raagi. Lala Jagat Narain had been writing against Sikhs and he had criticised Jathedar Gurdial Singh Ajnoha, Head Priest of Akal Takht, and Jath. Gurcharan Singh Tohra, President, SGPC as traitors.

He and Dalbir Singh had hatched the plan to punish Lala Jagat Narain. He purchased a motor cycle for Rs. 13,975, but he got the receipt in the name of a fictitious person. Dalbir Singh had brought two revolvers and six cartridges each. Lala Jagat Narain had gone to Patiala on 9th September, 1981, for inaugurating an eye camp. Lala Jagat Narain's Fiat car left Patiala at 4 PM and they pursued him on that motor cycle. He denied that he had fired the revolver. According to him, Dalbir Singh and Nachhattar Singh had fired (though Nachhattar Singh had given a different version exculpating himself). After committing the murder, they had joined Sant Jarnail Singh at Chandu Kalan and told the latter about the murder of Lala Jagat Narain.

Police had worked out all terrorist crimes and arrested culprits. Some of them had fled the country. They were definitely on the run. Newspapers had started taking note of these aspects of the situation. On November 6, 1981, *The Tribune* came out with an editorial entitled 'Khalistan in Canada', The same paper in its leading articles of November 23, 1981, had written of 'Hope of a Breakthrough' though only 4 days earlier it had castigated Punjab Police and its Chief in its leading article 'Police in Disgrace' (November 18, 1981) as a result of shootout at Kapurthala, which police had already worked out but had not publicised as they wanted to nab Tarsem Singh and Talwinder Singh. Media publicity of police success foiled designs to impose President's Rule in Punjab. But it had helped the two conspirators and murderers to escape abroad. By February, 1982, all the cases had been worked out. The Punjab Government called a meeting of Members of Parliament in Kapurthala House, New Delhi on 22nd Feb. 1982 and distributed a paper entitled 'Background of violent incidents in Punjab'. The paper not only disclosed how the conspiracies were hatched and culprits nabbed, it claimed that incidence of crime in Punjab was the lowest as compared to other States, according to statistics issued by Govt. of India itself and that the principle which had guided the state machinery was to maintain communal amity and not to over-react to provocations of those who wanted to see the peace of the state shattered. The Police would not unleash any oppression. Learning that I was in Delhi, the Home Minister Giani Zail Singh called me to his residence. Accordingly, I met him on the morning of February 23. He was very upset that I had entrusted the interrogation of Dal Khalsa Pramukh Harsimran Singh to a Jat Sikh DIG, who was inimical to him. He said that he was the only non-Jat who had become Chief Minister of Punjab and Home Minister of India and the Jat Chief Minister of Punjab and Jat police officers wanted to see him, disgraced. I told him that police in Punjab was not working on caste or religious basis and there was no question of assassinating his character through the revealation made by Harsimran Singh. I recalled to him how police had foiled attempts to malign him when Punjab High Court had asked for tapes of interrogation of Onkar Chand who was Gen. Secy. Punjab PCC when Gianiji was its President and whom Akalis had got arrested in a corruption case and who had made damaging revealations of Gianiji's working. Further, I told him that we had already forwarded to the Home Ministry detailed transcript of Harsimran Singh's interrogation report. He was surprised that it had not been put up to him. I latter called upon Shri T.N. Chaturvedi, Secretary, Ministry of Home Affairs and requested him to put up a gist of Harsimran Singh's interrogation report to his Minister to allay the latter's unfounded misgivings.

The Yamuna Satluj link canal scheme had remained in hybernation till elections to Haryana Assembly were announced in 1982 summer. On April 6, 1982, we got information that the Prime Minister would like to address a public meeting in village Kapuri in Patiala District on the borders of Ambala to inaugurate this work. The atmosphere was terror-ridden and Akalis announced that they would never allow this irrigation project to become operational. So, we had to make foolproof arrangements for her security during the public meeting for which Haryana crowds were mobilised by Haryana Ministers under guidance of Shri Bhajan Lal. The village had a Gurudwara. Dr. Rajinder Kaur, daughter of Master Tara Singh and President Istri Akali Dal, with a few women started bursting crackers inside the Gurudwara. However, the public meeting of the Prime Minister passed off peacefully. Before leaving Kapuri by helicopter, the Prime Minister inquired if police had resorted to firing. I told her that it was a ruse resorted to by Dr. Rajinder Kaur bursting crackers. PM gave a subtle smile.

Now started the Nehar Roko Andolan. Govt. started digging. We barricaded the site tactically and kept police inside to avoid clash with agitators, which could have given a fillip to the agitators. This kept Akali and CPM workers outside the enclosed fenced area. The symbolic digging and equally symbolic satyagraha continued till July 1982. Punjab Govt. was dragging its feet and Akalis were keen to maintain semblance of agitation till the same was shifted to Amritsar in August.

As already stated, police had gained upper hand over the terrorists of Babbar Khalsa and AISSF by February, 1982. However, the respite was shortlived when remnants of Dal Khalsa tried to ignite Hindu-Sikh riots by placing two severed Cow Heads in front of Shiva temple in Katra Ahluwalia and Bazar Kathian, Amritsar. Tension between the two communities started building up. When opposing groups started brickbatting on the afternoon of April 27,. 1982, police had to open fire injuring three persons. Curfew was clamped. Shri R.L. Bhatia, M.P. played a constructive role in pacifying people. A number of policemen had been injured in brick-batting incidents. On investigation it was found that the two heads had been severed at Kharar where bodies of two headless cows were discovered on April 27. Police was able to identify culprits, one of whom was provided transport by SGPC and other with means to escape to U.K.

A piece of cow's tail was found lying near the railing outside Kali Mandir, Patiala on April 30, 1982. Hindus took out a procession. Another procession was taken out by Naujawan Khalsa Dal. To avoid head-on clash between these two processions, police had to intervene and 2 DSPs., 3 Inspectors and a number of other ranks were injured. Investigation of cow slaughter cases revealed that Hindu Suraksha Samiti had the backing of Congress (I) M.L.As. It's president Pawan Kumar was arrested with difficulty: his interrogation revealed that he enjoyed patronage from Congress M.L.As and leaders. Thus, when the Prime Minister happened to visit Adampur from tour of Himachal Pradesh for enplaning for Delhi in the last week of May, 1982, I told her forthrightly that if Congress M.L.A.'s were allowed to sponsor communal violence, it will be very tragic.

Seeing the mischief Dal Khalsa had perpetrated, the Government of India awoke to the need of taking some decisive steps. We were summoned for a meeting in which it was decided that Dal Khalsa and Council for Khalistan be banned. Thus, bypassing the Home Minister, the two organisations were banned from May 1, 1982. Had the Home Miniser been there, he would certainly have vetoed this. His tendencies were well known. It was a mistake not to ban All India Sikh Student Federation, which was hell-bent on subversive activities. One more significant decision was to arrest and detain Sant Jarnail Singh Bhindranwale at Bombay when he visited that place with his armed Jatha. Maharashtra Government was opposed to this plan. Their representative was reluctant to act as it would mean transferring Punjab problem to Maharashtra. Nonetheless, Maharashtra Government was asked to act. A crack unit of India Frontier Force was flown to Bombay to deal with the situation in case the armed Jatha offered resistance. Like Chandu Kalan, the Bombay plan too failed. According to facts revealed by Bhai Amrik Singh during his interrogation, after his arrest on July 19, 1982, the plan failed because the deployments of Maharashtra police and the crack unit from Delhi were too obtrusive and his followers did not want the Sant to be harassed by the Police. So he had left Bombay for Punjab in a Fiat car. It is not correct to say that Giani Zail Singh during his visit to Bombay had arranged escape of Santji.

The fact of the matter is that Santji had a sizeable following in Punjab and Punjab Government did not want this following to be provoked by arresting him in Punjab. But realising that no State Government would muster courage, Punjab Government weighed the pros and cons of taking action against the Sant and AISSF in Punjab itself. Police had precise information that 17 persons of Bhindranwale's Jatha carried licensed carbines .310 rifles, double barrel and single barrel guns and revolvers. They had unlicenced weapons, too. The Government came to the conclusion that a direct confrontation by police would result in a number of casualties and if Santji became a martyr, Punjab would go up in flames. Public opinion by that time was not aware of the extent of murders and crimes being perpetrated by AIISF and that Jatha. No public man was prepared to issue open statement against them as this would have brought his name on the "Hit list". There was also awareness that police itself was neither trained not indoctrinated to take upon itself to battle such an armed band of fanatics who would probably prefer martyrdom than laying arms. I was determined to avoid bloodshed not only of the members of the Jatha but also of Punjab Police. Frederick, the Great had this to say about such a situation: "If you wish to be loved by your soldiers, husband their blood, and do not lead them to slaughter. Do not break your head against unpractical things".

It was, therefore, decided to raise a Company of Commandos under instructors from CRPF and BSF. It was, further decided that we must make such an impressive demonstration of our firepower that the Jatha should prefer to lay down arms. The Border Security Force had four Patrol Cars of First War vintage and if we sought aid from BSF alongwith Patrol Cars which to the laymen looked like tanks, we could intercept the Jatha. A place on Amritsar Mehta Road was selected for encirclement of the Jatha. However, when approached BSF disclosed that they had dismantled those patrol cars. Then it was decided that Army may be approached to provide patrol cars to BSF as it had done earlier. S. Darbara Singh and myself went to Shri Balram Jhakhar who was then working as Speaker, Lok Sabha. He told us that he would take it up with Shri R. Venkataraman who was then working as Home Minister as also worked as Defence Minister of India. It is not clear if Shri Jhakhar spoke to Shri R. Venkataraman or not. The political leaders and Central Ministers concerned were unable to persuade Army Directorate of Operations to sell or lend some patrol cars to BSF. What a state of affairs indeed! Army by its intransigence thus contributed its share in aggravating the situation in Punjab. It is also a sad reflection on working of Centre that the Defence Minister could not persuade the Army to loan 4 scout cars to BSF

In the meanwhile, Bibi Amarjit Kaur, widow of Fauja Singh of Akhand Kirtani Jatha, killed on April 13, 1978 gunned down 4 innocent persons at Patti on 22nd May, 1982. Police investigations revealed that this crime was perpetrated by the same gang, which was responsible for shootout at Taran Taran on September 21. 1981. A number of culprits were arrested. From their interrogation the role of Bibi Amarjit Kaur with the blessings of Akali leaders came to be known. She suddenly went underground and never left Golden Temple premises and surrendered only during Operation Blue Star. She was treated as state guest by Barnala Government because of her relationship with Sant Harchand Singh Longowal. Bibi was released on Oct 2, 1985 by Barnala Government. The leader of the gang was a colleague of Fauja Singh; another Agriculture Inspector Surinder Singh Warrang, who managed to escape to Pakistan. He could have been arrested but action was not taken in time. It was also rumoured that his escape was arranged

Throughout my career I have been opposed to fake encounters. I was of the firm view that if any fake encounter took place, the fires of Sikh extremism would be stoked beyond control. Thus, I had impressed upon all Superintendents of Police to avoid fake encounters at all costs and temptations. However, if there was any genuine encounter, we should deal it tactically and inflict minimum injuries. We had been harvesting a good crop of intelligence by interrogating arrested suspects. However, those in authority above me had different notions. They were of the view that unless the terrorists were liquidated, the Government would continue to be accused of lack of firmness. Thus, those authorities started asking Superintendents of Police, bypassing me, to stage fake encounters. I protested vehemently. They had to give up this policy but I was not forgiven and tendentious news were leaked to the press about my impending transfer. I took this campaign of misinformation in my stride. I may state here that on the eve of Diwali in 1981, when police had failed to arrest or shoot ex-head constables Sewa Singh and Gurnam Singh, we had a night-long meeting at CM's residence in which the Chief Secretary wanted me to quit so that a relation of S. Partap Singh Kairon could take over. I had told the CM and the Chief Secretary, that I would never agree to fake encounters, as was hinted to me, and would apply for leave next day. I reminded of General Wolfe. After the battle of Cullodem in 1745, Wolfe was asked by his C-in-C to shoot an injured Highlander. Wolfe replied, "My commission is at your Royal Highness disposal but I can never consent to become an executioner." I offered to quit. At that point, the CM suddenly went away to his Prayer Room, probably to consult *Guru Granth Sahib*. He told me later that there was no need for me to proceed on leave. The fact is that the Prime Minister was away on tour probably to Fiji and was due to return on the Diwali morning. The Chief Minister wanted that he should be able to report to her that the killers had been arrested or liquidated. To pressurise police to stage fake encounters was not acceptable to me. Hence, my offer to quit. The second time I offered to quit was on the question of screening Sikh constabulary and to condemn people on the basis of religion, a highly repugnant notion to me.

It was decided to arrest Bhai Amrik Singh at Ludhiana in the first week of July, 1982 as he had gone about threatening police station staff everywhere and carrying armed men in his jeep aping Sant Bhindranwale. He was out to spread terror. We moved our commandos and a CRPF company to Ludhiana where he was to appear in a court of law. On the appointed day, he failed to appear. I apprised Chief Minister of our failure and was astounded to hear from him that he had cautioned Amrik Singh to desist visiting Ludhiana in view of the dragnet laid by police. I was baffled as to why Chief Minister did not want us to succeed against AISSF. I had noted that with the arrest of Swaran Singh, nephew of Jarnail Singh Bhindranwale in February 1982, the Sant had started criticising Sardar Darbara Singh openly and stridently. It was clear that by arresting Swaran Singh, police had exploded the myth that none related to Bhindranwale or anyone, who had gone to his 'Sharan', could ever be touched by police. I wondered if any unspoken pact had been broken by police by arresting Swaran Singh. My misgivings got a new spurt when the Chief Minister Sardar Darbara Singh had candidly stated that he had warned Bhai Amrik Singh. I also started entertaining doubts if we could ever have a decisive edge over the militants. I talked this matter with concerned authorities at Delhi. They advised me that there might have been a communication gap and I should continue with my work in Punjab.

Thus, when the Chief Minister was away to Simla, Bhai Amrik Singh was arrested by Amritsar Police on July 19, 1982. He was informed only after he was arrested. There was every possibility he could have been tipped off. Police also arrested his other companions. This infuriated Sant Bhindranwale who shifted his headquarters to Guru Nanak Niwas, the same day and announced a programme of Jathas courting arrests daily till Bhai Amrik Singh was released: the Sant wanted to repay the debt he owed to Amrik Singh who had successfully secured his release in October, 1981. The strength mustered by Sant for his Jathas was inconsequential. However, Santji was adept at threats as well as emotional blackmail by which means he first won Jathedar Gurcharan Singh Tohra and later Sant Harchand Singh Longowal to his side, who shifted the site of his Dharam Yudh from Kapuri to Amritsar. Golden Temple has always fired the Sikh imagination to massive actions. Thus, on the call of Sant Harchand Singh, large numbers turned out to court arrest daily.

I was of the view that after arrest we should release these volunteers at some distance away from Amritsar. However, I was overruled by political leadership on the wrong advice of Punjab Home Department that their jails had not enough holding capacity. Once the peaceful morcha was taken over by Longowal, Sant Jarnail Singh Bhindranwale and AISSF provided new impetus to terrorist activities. On August 4, 1982, one Gurbux Singh wanted in murder cases hijacked Indian Airbus flight to Lahore. The plane was refused permission to land at Lahore. Accordingly, it landed back at Amritsar. Gurbux Singh was taken into custody and he confessed how the plan to hijack was blessed by the sponsors of terrorism.

On August 20, 1982, Punjab Chief Minister was to inaugurate a Girls Higher Secondary School at Rahon when a grenade was thrown in the school compound injuring the Chief Minister and Education Minister Harcharan Singh Ajnala and some others. One of the culprits for this outrage was killed next day by Jalandhar police in an encounter. CID knew fully well who was behind all this. No action was authorised by the senior authority.

The same day one Manjit Singh alias Museebat Singh, an electrician of Putlighar, Amritsar, hijacked IA flight from Jodhpur to Lahore. Again Lahore authorities did not permit it to land. It landed back at Amritsar and Museebat Singh put forth usual demands on behalf of Sant Bhindranwale. Punjab Police Commandos carried out a successful operation and Museebat Singh was gunned down without any harm coming to any passenger. His death put a stop to hijackings for some

We had been exploring possibilities of using high tech gadgets in dealing with Jarnail Singh Bhindranwale and other militants hiding in hostel complex of Golden Temple. One of the techniques thought of was to instal certain undetectable cameras in the vicinity of this complex to photograph each person going to meet Sant Bhindranwale in or coming out. The consideration of this and other allied plans were known to only three persons in Punjab; myself, an IAS officer who is still serving, and the Chief Minister. To my dismay I found the plan had been disclosed in a distorted manner that we were planning to plant bombs in the room occupied by Bhindranwale and Sardar Randhir Singh Cheema. Ex-PWD Minister in Akali Ministry, was made to issue a public statement, which was carried by vernacular press of Jallandhar. This was the last straw to break my will. I was convinced no police plan to deal effectively with Sant Bhindranwale and his cohorts will be allowed to succeed by Punjab Government for purposes of their own.

So I requested the Secretary, Ministry of Home Affairs, to shift me from Punjab. I happened to meet the Prime Minister to whom also I repeated my request and added that the morcha launched at Amritsar was being converted into a mass movement and she should ask Punjab government to release Akali volunteers. She asked about the next course of action. I submitted to her that Sardar Swaran Singh enjoyed respect among Akali leaders and he was a consummate negotiator. If he could be persuaded to mediate, a solution may emerge. She was kind enough to consider my submissions.

When I left Punjab to assume the charge of Director General, Border Security Force at Delhi, terrorists were lying low and police had gained the initiative. Once the Akali volunteers were released in mid-October, 1982, situation seemed to return to normalcy. Sardar Swaran Singh and Harkrishan Singh Surjeet CPI(M) had assumed the role of mediators and a compromise was on the anvil. I remained busy with arrangements for Asiad Games but was at times consulted on Punjab. It is a pity that when the whole compromise had been worked out, a member of the Prime

Minister's family intervened to sabotage the whole package. It is a matter for historians to research whether it was the Prime Minister who changed her mind or Rajivji was made to advise her contrarily. I know something because we were told to keep the BSF aircraft ready to fly to Amritsar in an early November night. That plan was suddenly cancelled.

Till mid November, 1982, Sant Bhindranwale and Longowal were hopeful of resumption of talks. Actually Sant Bhindranwale was showing signs of fatigue. Some Akali leaders had faith in me because despite persistent efforts from some quarters, I had refused to send police in hostel area of Golden Temple. They were also aware that I had never been a party to any fake encounter and had actually opposed this disastrous and unethical course of action. So an emissary from their side met me at Delhi in mid-November and requested me to ask authorities to resume dialogue and provide a face-saving formula to end the agitation both by Bhindranwale as well as Akalis. I conveyed it to the authorities concerned since meeting PM again and again at that stage was not desirable. It appeared as if the earlier Akali intransigence had been replaced by Government intransigence. Then Bhajan Lal Government in Haryana started searching every Sikh coming to Delhi on the eve of Asiad Games. Who had asked Bhajan Lal to do so? An answer to this can unravel some mysteries. It hardened the attitude of Akalis and infuriated Sant Bhindranwale. Fuel was added to fire by the resumption of the policy of fake encounters. Punjab Government committed another mistake. They made some officers Superintendents of Police in charge of Amritsar District who were not known for integrity. I remained aloof as BSF was assigned onerous duties in connection with Non-Aligned Meet (NAM). We achieved success not only in keeping Punjab extremists away but also confined foreign commandos in their respective houses who were foolishly brought in large numbers to Delhi by two warring non-aligned countries.

In the first week of February, 1983, I received information that Akali Dal had concluded that Central Government was not going to give them a single concession and they should intensify their struggle. I happened to be in Guwahati in mid-February when the Prime Minister halted at the airport for change of her aircraft. I apprised her of Akali thinking and plans and suggested that if she could have separate talks with Shri G.S. Tohra, the agitation in Punjab could be brought to an end. She showed her disinclination and suggested meetings at some other level. Accordingly, I arranged one such meeting. Nothing concrete emerged because decisions were being taken at a different level by those who had no inkling of Sikh ethos or Bhindranwale's machinations nor any idea of Punjab Government's weaknesses.

National Police Academy, Hyderabad, had invited us for witnessing passing out parade in April 1983. On April 25, 1983 I had returned from Hyderabad but the Home Secretary had stayed back. Though it was a Sunday, at 11 AM. I got a call from Amritsar that Shri Ajit Singh Atwal, D.I.G. had been gunned down at the steps of Golden Temple, Amritsar. Prime Minister was away to Rajasthan on a tour. I apprised Cabinet Secretary, Shri C.R. Krishnaswamy Rao Sahib of this dastardly murder. No action was taken to pursue the murderers. S. Darbara Singh and his Director General of Police maintained that they had sought permission from Delhi to enter hostel area of Golden Temple to arrest culprits but the same was refused to them. Who had taken this decision when the PM and Home Secretary were away? The death of this brave officer went unavenged and no proper investigation was held. Shri Atwal had been inveigled into visiting Golden Temple by a Police Officer and a Brigadier who claimed to have links with high ups. Why no action was taken against them remains a mystery?

On August 6, 1983, Bhai Amrik Singh, who had been in custody at Gurdaspur Jail, appeared for his trial in a court at Amritsar. Due to poor police arrangements or in connivance with them, he was whisked away by co-terrorists from the court premises in the presence of police and taken to the sanctuary of Golden Temple. This ended all hopes of settlement as he was more megalomaniac than Sant

Bhindranwale and shrewder than anyone in the coterie surrounding of Bhindranwale. Soon after that, 6 Hindu passengers were gunned down on 6th Oct. 1983 near Dhilwan on G.T. Road to give a new turn to the violent campaign. Delhi decided to impose President's Rule. Those of us who understood Sikh psyche had advised avoiding direct confrontation between Delhi and Sikhs. A Sikh Chief Minister, whatever his designs, was to be preferred as a buffer. However, our advice was overruled. Ouster of Darbara Singh was celebrated not only in Punjab, but also in Delhi, by his opponents. Then began a procession of Governors and their Advisors to Chandigarh. With each serious incident, they were changed like dirty linen. No coherent policy was evolved. Earlier in October, soon after the imposition of President's rule, a suggestion was made that a para-military force should strike hostel area with the help of commandos and certain equipment which had been built by them. But the decision makers again fumbled. Seeing this state of affairs, I was feeling restless and circumspect. But I kept myself busy with the security arrangements for the Commonwealth Heads of State Meet (CHOGM) at Goa.

Sant Jarnail Singh and his Jatha moved out of hostel complex and occupied Akal Takht on December 15, 1983. Seeing this, a para-military organisation, which always prided itself on secret missions and ultimately let down the Government, came out with a plan to occupy hostel area and the langar in Golden Temple. Thinking that I knew something about the complex, I was consulted. I had two objections. What was the objective? Sant had left. Again one company was too inadequate and would be slaughtered by fire from Akal Takht and adjoining buildings. At last, in mid- February, 1984, I was able to have the plan abandoned and thus saved the para-military force from charges of amateurism and slaughter of their men.

LAST MINUTE PARLEYS

In April, 1984, I was asked to take up secret parleys with Sant Bhindranwale. Bhai Amrik Singh's baneful and obstructive influence was at work and I could foresee that I would not succeed in my mission. We were told by Sant Bhindranwale that a certain Minister and I should come for talks to Golden Temple. Our proposal was that Damdami Taksal should come to Circuit House, Amritsar and we will guarantee their safe conduct. Bhai Amrik Singh insisted on our going into Golden Complex. This plan also had to be abandoned. Where was the guarantee that the Minister and I would not be taken hostages? The mediator in this case was a cousin of Bhindranwale and had come from Canada. It was learnt later that he was wanted by Canadian Police in connection with a trumped up murder charge slapped by his own wife. Human infidelity is appalling as I was told she had engineered his arrest with a view to capturing his enormous property. I failed in Peace Mission which the Prime Minister had entrusted me with. She too was disappointed but was aware of the enormous risks involved.

Once in Akal Takht, Bhindranwale launched fortifications drive of Golden Temple on the advice and plans of retd. Maj. Gen. Shabeg Singh, who had been dismissed from service on certain charges, and a retd. Brig. Mohinder Singh resident of Amritsar. It was clear that Santji had decided on giving a positional battle from within. Security forces and Sant's desperadoes came to exchange fire almost every day. The sanctity of Golden Temple was being violated and devotees were afraid to go to the Temple. Sandbagging of defences was visible to any visitor as also the pockmarks caused by exchange of serious nature.

On April 29, 1984, the BSF was asked to surround Gurudwara Keni Kaur and Gurudwara Singh Sabha and Gurudwara Alaksar at Moga whence militants were firing constantly and had killed a number of civilians. The BSF were given the task to enter the Gurdwaras on May 2, 1984. Knowing how decisions were changed at last minute, I had cautioned the I.G. commanding the BSF to re-confirm with me at 3 A.M. on May 2, before entering the gurdwara. My assessment proved right. At midnight I was called for a meeting and asked to tell the BSF not to enter the Gurudwara at Moga. I told the officers assembled that the orders to enter

Gurudwara would not be revoked and I had made final arrangements. They pleaded that the political solution was being sought and this entry had in any case to be called off. This conclave of the seniormost bureaucrats ate their own words and almost pleaded helplessness. My anticipation had thus come true. When my Inspector General rang me up at 0300 hours as already decided, I told him of the new decision and asked him to order the commandos back to their base. I have narrated this incident to show that decision making at the highest level was marked by confusion and suffered from the evil of countermanding one decision after another. On May 3, we got all the three Gurudwaras vacated and recovered large quantity of arms and ammunition.

In May, 1984, incessant daily exchange of fire between security force and Sant Bhindranwale's entrenched men had become a dangerous routine. Seeing the situation deteriorating, I put forth two proposals: One of these involved expenditure of foreign exchange wanted by a man who used to meet Mr. Z.A. Bhutto in Jail during black days of General Zia's oppressive rule. The sanction came late. Unfortunately the man had lost his son and delay on his part became unavoidable.

On Sunday May 13, 1984 afternoon, the Prime Minister called 3 officers, including me, for final consultations. I told her that in place of holding group discussions, she should hear us individually so that secrecy and legal aspects remained intact. On raising of legal issue, she demurred and agreed. I do not know what the gentleman from Chandigarh told her. But what I told her was that we should not enter Golden Temple and we could deal with Sant Bhindranwale from outside since I knew the topography of the place intimately. After hearing us one after the other, she asked me to discuss the plan with the Secretary who was the third member of the group. However, that man had no control over the organisation, which had the capability to help best carry out the task I had in my mind. That organisation's head admitted that he had the capability but pleaded inability to carry out the task because of fear of ultimate exposure. I again said that it was a feasible plan since I had information from very reliable Akali leaders who differed with Sant Bhindranwale. That day, the organisation, whose budget runs into hundreds of crores refused to help carry out the task. It appears, it was only after that, that a decision was taken to send the Army into the Golden Temple. Since I was opposed to such a move, I was no more associated with these decisions. Soon after, I learnt that the projection was to clear Golden Temple of the armed insurgents within four hours. The operation was named Blue Star. This four hour theory seems to have mesmerised all the decision makers and the die was cast. The very Government, which had refused permission to the police to enter Gurdwaras in deference to the sentiments of Sikhs as stated by Shri P.C. Sethi, Home Minister during a debate in Rajya Sabha, had been persuaded to send the army into Golden Temple. Verbal brilliance of top brass and the assurance of swiftness of army action as proposed swept off all the logic built on historic examples and data. Results are for all to see.

OPPRESSIVE LAWS

Our rulers showed misplaced faith and zeal for the efficacy of draconian laws. They thought that severer the laws, easier it would be to deal with the problem. Thus, there was a spree of legislating black laws such as Terrorist and Disruptive Activities Prevention Act (TADA) 1985, which provided for the identities of the witness to be kept secret and permitted only one appeal to the Supreme Court. This Act enabled police in Punjab to resort to indiscriminate detentions and let loose a reign of terror of their own. This also enabled unscrupulous elements in police to mint money by threatening detention and prosecution on flimsy grounds. This rapacity and reign of police terrorism was bound to alienate people and that is why during Lok Sabha elections in November, 1989, the villages en masse voted for candidate sponsored by extremists. This is not to say that the whole segments of voters were not terrorised openly by the militants who made liberal use of dire threats and display of their sophisticated weaponry. Gun in Punjab, as elsewhere, has been greater pervertor of our electoral process. Whom are we deluding by putting forth slogans of democratic uprightness? Repressive laws not only alienate people, but corrupt the enforcers badly.

The 59th Amendment to the Constitution, which enabled the government to suspend operation of Art. 21 of the Constitution, is the blackest mark in our legal jurisprudence. Art. 21 reads as under "No person shall be deprived of his life or liberty except according to procedure established by law". The Congress during Emergency of 1975 had this Article suspended and lost the elections of 1977. Two ordinances were issued for amending the National Security Act in April and June 1984. On July 14, 1984 another ordinance was issued entitled the Terrorist Affected Areas (Special Courts) Ordinance.

The National Security Act Amendment Ordinance No.5 amended section 8 of the National Security Act substituting '15 days' for 'ten days' for serving grounds of detention whereas the Supreme Court of India had laid in a reported decision that the grounds of detention should normally be served alongwith the order of detention. The effect of the amendment was that a detinue would remain in Jail for fifteen days without knowing grounds of his detention, which deprived him of challenging his detention by moving Habeas Corpus petition.

In the case of persons detained before April 13, 1985, it has been provided that a detinue can be detained for a period of 2 years instead of 1 year as laid down earlier in Section 13 of the Act.

Again under section 10 and 11 of the un-amended Act, the case of a detinue was to be referred to the Advisory Board within 3 weeks of his detention and the Advisory Board was required to submit its report within 7 weeks of the detention. Amended section provided that the case of a person detained before April 3, 1985, may be submitted within 4 months instead of 2 weeks of his detention and the Advisory Board may submit its report within 5 months and 3 weeks of the detention. Thus, a detainee covered by the amendments has perforce to undergo detention even if his detention was eventually found to be without justification by the Board.

Again, amended Section 5-A provides that even if a detention order is based on several grounds, law would assume that detention was made separately on each ground, so that the order of detention will be valid even if only one of the several grounds was valid and tenable.

The Terrorist and Disruptive Activities (Prevention) Act 1987 (TADA) scraps provision of trial as in Criminal Procedure Code and prescribes enhanced penalty. Section 6 provides for Designated Courts, Place of Sitting (Sec.10), Procedure and Powers of Designated Courts (Sec.14) and Protection of Witness (Sec.16). Thus, a trial under TADA is an extra-ordinary trial and nullifies proceedings under CrPC. The question is: do procedures outlined amount to denial of due process of law?

Though the 59th Constitutional Amendment was not made use of, was it fair to suspend the operation of Article 21 in this cavalier fashion?

The Government showed a penchant for legislating extreme measures but, in the face of public criticism, it made a hasty retreat. This happened in case of creating Safety Belt on Punjab border, too.

POLITICAL EXPEDIENCY

The sole guiding principle, which moulded the style of governance was political expediency. Rajinder Sareen claims that in a paper submitted by him much earlier. He had delineated the course of future events in the manner in which they unfolded and yet no action was taken.

The reality is that whether it was Sardar Partap Singh Kairon, Shri Ram Kishan, Giani Zail Singh or Sardar Darbara Singh, every Congress Chief Minister of Punjab, like his Akali counterpart, had a two point programme: self-preservation and self-promotion. Every measure, every instrument of government, every plan for upliftment of any section of the population were to sub-serve these two priorities. If necessary, moral homilies and secular and religious platitudes were also to be pressed in to subsume these two objectives. Power had to be acquired and retained at all costs. The worsening situation in Punjab over decades was subjected to considerations of political expediency. It is this expediency which compelled Akalis to produce the explosive mix of religion and politics. Prabhash Joshi, Editor, *The Indian Express*, Chandigarh wrote: "Akalis just cannot reduce religion to a matter of personal faith, they need it to retain their hold on their base in the peasantry and use it (religion) as a weapon to fight."

The Armed Forces, unlike police, are trained to use maximum force and to destroy the enemy. When country's own peoples are invaded in a confrontation with the military machine, the question is: can citizens, Nagas, Mizos and Sikhs or Kashmiris be treated as enemies to be destroyed by the army? General J.N. Chaudhary had warned against the over-use of armed forces to aid civil authorities. He had said, "When the people are alienated from the military, the military themselves get incorrect ideas about their importance in relation to their constitutional role and position." Another Senior army general was of the view that the system had dragged the armed forces to pull politicians' chestnuts out of the fire.

Well informed commentators of military history have voiced the fears that, if over-used, the military machine would be reduced to a rabble like the rest of the armed constabularies.

It really happened in Ahmedabad and Baroda when mobs started defying Army since it had lost its effectiveness due to having been deployed for months, on internal security duties. The mutiny in the wake of Operation Blue Star is an eloquent testimony against our use of army, paramilitary and police forces as well as use of our excellent army for political purposes. Both the political and military leaderships should heed what General Andre Beaufere, who led Suez Operation in 1956, has to say: "All too often throughout history, people thought to solve a highly involved political problem by launching a military operation. Such an operation had no prospect to succeed, if not carried out against a favourable political background".

-14 -

Foreign Armed Commandos and the NAM Meeting in Delhi

The Non Aligned Meet was held in Vigyan Bhavan, New Delhi in March 1984. The security arrangements for the Meet were sought to be entrusted to BSF. As Director General BSF, I protested the verbal orders Government conveyed to me. I told Shri TN Chaturvedi, the Home Secretary, that this duty is not germane to the charter of duties of the Border Security Force as this force was created primarly to guard Indo-Pak border. He argued that it was the prerogative of the Government to entrust any duty to its paramilitary forces. I remained adamant and told him that ad-hocism for an armed force was not acceptable since we go into security mode after detailed preparations.

He went and reported to the Prime Minister that I was being difficult. The Prime Minister told Shri Chaturvedi that he should tell Birbal Nath that this was an order from Shrimati Indira Gandhi. Accordingly, he again summoned me to his chamber, which was located one storey above my room in the North Block. He told me that this was not the order of the Government of India but that of Shrimati Indira Gandhi. I remained quiet and came back to my room. There was nothing more to protest about. I devised my plans for the areas surrounding the Vigyan Bhavan and provided for all round defence of the Vigyan Bhavan by locating several Brengn posts in flower-decked sand-bagged posts. Gen. Zia-ul-Haq, President of Pakistan, was so impressed that he asked our Prime Minister to send to him the Director General of the

Security Force as he was impressed by the defence arrangements and the turnout of the BSF. As desired by Shrimati Indira Gandhi, our IG Administration KK Zutshi and I called on General Zia at his Suite in Oberoi Inter Continental Hotel in New Delhi.

Another serious complication arose threatening bloodshed as Iran and Iraq, both were at war at that time, had brought 200 Commandos each with their delegations respectively. Thus, New Delhi was swamped with armed commandos located in the Embassies of Iran and Iraq respectively. This happened due to the inadvertence of the Ministry of External Affairs. The Government of India asked the Army to disarm these commandos. The Army refused point blank. They argued that to disarm such a contingent, they needed a Brigade for a tactical confrontation. There was no such Brigade in and around New Delhi. The nearest place where such a Brigade was available was Agra. This time Shri MM Wali, the then Home Secretary, asked me to take over this onerous duty. I also pointblank refused since such an operation could result in bloodshed. He apprised the Prime Minister on telephone. I was summoned to 1, Akbar Road office of the Prime Minister. When I entered her chamber, I was shocked to see Shrimati Indira Gandhi slumped in her chair. She said, "So you have also decided to desert me in this critical hour and disgrace me in the international community." I said I was sorry. After talking to her for some time, I came back to my office. I knew that the Border Security Force had to untangle this problem since it was the question of the prestige of the country, and its Prime Minister. I requested Maj. Gen. Ishwarya to leave Vigyan Bhavan and meet me. He was in-charge of our training Institutions. I told him, we must close all the training Institutions for a while and transit all the personnel under training to New Delhi immediately, by any means of transport available. We had four Dakotas, rail and surface transport. Accordingly, we collected about 1000 armed well trained BSF personnel by 10 pm the next morning. We surrounded the Iraq and Iran Embassies by 11 pm. We stopped people from going in and coming out of the Embassies. Maj. Gen. Ishwarya and I first called on the Iraqi Ambassador to India. I told His Excellency that the Republic of Iraq had committed a serious breach of International Law by bringing in armed personnel to New Delhi. He remained quiet. I told him that the Embassy had been completely shut down by the armed BSF personnel and we will not allow anyone to come in, nor go out. Then he said that he would ask his commandos to surrender their arms if we could similarly secure the surrender of the arms of the Iranian commandos. I told him that the Iran Embassy was already under siege of the BSF and after securing the arms of his commandos, we would be calling on the Ambassador of Iran, too. On getting this assurance from me, he got the arms that the Iraqi commandos had and locked them in a hall in the Embassy. We sealed the lock and posted BSF sentries at the entrance at the locked gate. Then we proceeded to the Iranian Embassy where we called on His Excellency the Ambassador of Iran. When he came to know from us that Iraqi arms were in our custody, he immediately agreed to surrender the arms and placed them in our custody. Thus ended the gruesome threat to the Non Aligned Meet.

– 15 –

The Great Betrayals

The Prime Minister, Mrs. Indira Gandhi, was betrayed by all of us upon whom she had depended for a clean operation against the terrorists entrenched in the Golden Temple, Amritsar.

First of all, I will take indictment against myself. Some criticised me on the ground that I should not have left Punjab in Oct. 1982, since I had contained the movement, which was running at a low ebb at that time. All other terrorist crimes had been worked out and from August 1981 to September 1982, only 13 persons, including two policemen, were killed. However, we did not seek publicity, and did not beat any drum. Some people complained that the Punjab police was inactive those days. No, certainly not. The incidence of terrorist crimes in this period was the lowest in the blood spattered era of terrorist violence in Punjab. Our low profile was deliberate strategy to stop the proliferation of terrorism and avoid a communal divide in Punjab. The police performance had been quite solid rather than flamboyant encounters and publicity. Anyone acquainted with Sikh psyche knows that it is dangerous to challenge the Sikhs by flaunting success against their bravado. Once a Sikh is challenged, he immediately gets into a competitive mode and the vendetta continues over generations.

So far as my leaving Punjab is concerned, I had to request for transfer. I had found I could not mount any major operation without informing the democratically elected government. I did not believe in spectacular fake encounters. After the shoot-out at Patti in May, 1982, the Chief Minister had been running to New Delhi complaining that I was not giving a free hand to the District Police Chiefs to deal with the limited number of extremists. The fact is, I had certainly forbidden the District Superintendents of Police from staging any fake encounters in their anxiety to curry favour with the Government. I may reiterate here that on the eve of Diwali in October 1981, when police had failed to arrest their own force members - Head Constables Sewa Singh and Gurnam Singh - responsible for two shoot-out cases, I was obliquely advised that I may stage an encounter to flaunt Police success in dealing with the terrorists. I had declined to go along the advised way and promised to put in my papers next day. The Chief Minister had also given a thought to my objection and agreed not to press me for such an action. I was firmly of the view that the shoot-out at Patti in May 1982 was a reprisal against a fake encounter, which was staged earlier in one district on orders from Chandigarh, bypassing me. I was never against any genuine encounter but I was totally opposed to any encounter staged to please someone who had failed to understand the ground realities.

Stray incidents of terrorism against Nirankaris were taking place. The Court had acquitted many against whom cases of terrorism were registered. Nirankaris were known to be responsible for killing 13 workers of Akhand Kirtani Jatha and two of Damdami Taksal on the Baisakhi day 1978, and that these two fundamentalist organisations were bent upon killing the same number of Nirankaris in what they misconstrued as 'meting out justice' to the guilty. They could any time turn this into reprisals against police, whom they considered responsible for staged encounters. This cycle of 'vengeance' killings of Nirankaris and those whom Damdami Taksal and Akhand Kirtani Jatha considered responsible for fake encounters snowballed into the fury of fundamentalist terrorism against police and the government in 1983. Thus, I was at loggerheads with Punjab Government from May 1982 to September 1982. My objection to the policy was both ethical as well as pragmatic.

The Punjab Government had adopted, for myopic and moronic reasons, what has been called the policy of "controlled chaos" to maintain their hold on Punjab. I, as Director General of Police, Punjab, could not be a party to this type of adventurism. I had to act according to law and my professional principles. I could not allow perpetrators of heinous crimes to roam about the state with armed gangs, obstructing the course of justice. At the cost of being repetitive, I may say that we had decided to arrest Bhai Amrik Singh, the President of All India Sikh Students Federation at Ludhiana in June 1982, when he was to appear for evidence in a court of law. However, on that day Bhai Amrik Singh and his armed band failed to turn up at Ludhiana. When I narrated the facts to the Chief Minister, he chuckled and non-challantly told me that he (the Chief Minister) had got in touch with Bhai Amrik Singh and advised the latter not to visit Ludhiana on that day.

What a wonderful situation it is when the Chief Minister advises a criminal how to evade his arrest! During a visit to New Delhi, I had apprised Director, Intelligence Bureau and the Cabinet Secretary, of the role of the Chief Minister in ensuring police failure in arresting Bhai Amrik Singh. Ultimately, we did arrest Bhai Amrik Singh in July 1982, when the Chief Minister was away to Shimla. The policy of the Punjab Government to keep Punjab in a state of 'controlled chaos' may appear Machiavellian to some, but it was indeed a self-defeating manoeuvre. This was proved true when terrorist violence intensified in 1983. Again, we had decided to keep 24 hour surveillance on the place where Sant Jarnail Singh was staying. This was to ascertain the number of people who visited him and the number of arms held by them. We were to instal some equipment for this purpose. Some details were leaked out by Punjab Government and it was said that a bomb was to be planted in the room of Santji. Under these circumstances, my request for a change from Chandigarh was fully warranted.

Whereas my seeking transfer from Chandigarh in 1982 was justified in all respects, my failure to oppose Operation

Blue Star more vigorously rankles me even now. I was not in favour of this operation and might have succeeded in preventing it if I had made a success of two covert operations, which I had projected. But neither of these could be put into action. The first project entailed an expenditure of two million dollars. Unfortunately, the government sanction for this came very late.

After May 20, 1984 when I had the last detailed discussion with the Prime Minister and still opposed the use of military option, she also started distrusting me. I was summoned only in July 1984 when the Prime Minister had decided to lend her healing touch to the Punjab situation.

As desired by her, we contacted some Sikh leaders and arranged their separate meetings with her. The wound inflicted on Sikh psyche by the operation Blue Star could not be healed in one or two meetings. Before her healing touch could take effect, the tragedy had struck on October 31, 1984.

So far as operations are concerned, I need not dilate on the reactions and forces unleashed by "Operation Blue Star." All these are public knowledge by now. But I have to comment on the Prime Minister's perception of Punjab situation in the pre-operation, Blue Star period. One fallacious impression I have to rectify. The impression is that she was anti-Sikh and for this reason she allowed Punjab situation to deteriorate to justify the ultimate use of army in the holy shrine of Golden Temple. This allegation against the Prime Minister prevailed among Sikh intellectuals and general populace in Punjab in June and July 1984. I came across a specimen of this when a prominent Sikh lady politician from Punjab, who was to assume great power in post-Beant Singh period, during a visit to me in my office in North Block started crying: her sobbing was so acute that I feared she may collapse. With great difficulty, I steadied her. But she persisted in her allegation that the Prime Minister was anti-Sikh and she had resorted to Operation Blue Star to placate Hindus.

We are all captives of our beliefs, which we come to acquire by information that we accumulate and our experiences gleaned over the years. While the Prime Minister was not anti-Sikh, I found she was anti-Akali. She had told me in May 1984, while peace parleys with Sant Jarnail Singh Bhindranwale were going on, that she would never allow Akalis to come to power in Punjab as they were in league with separatists. I tried my best to de-programme her but she was not open to argument in this matter. I do not know how she had come to acquire this opinion about Akalis. I do not know, if her opinion of Akalis was based on any intelligence inputs or was the result of her "intuition". But this opinion of her was an insurmountable obstacle in obtaining peace through negotiations.

The Prime Minister was betrayed by the failure of Police and the Army in delivering results by their destruction of those whom they considered to be enemies of the State. Army's operation "Rosewood" led hundreds of Sikh youth to flee into Pakistan and, in due course, after their training and arming by Pakistan, they infiltrated back into Punjab as desperate soldiers of Khalistan.

I have discussed here the operational failures. There were other failures and betrayals arising out of India's past policies.

– 16 –

Operation Blue Star

Operation Blue Star was a tragedy and a blunder of dimensions which defy proper description. Even if there was some semblance of justification for use of army against heavily armed insurgents entrenched in the Akal Takht, there was no justification whatsoever for Operation Rosewood. Why should army go on a witch-hunt in the villages, search houses and round up the Sikh youth, since there was no armed resistance in the villages? We have an excellent army which is renowned for valour and professionalism, but there has to be circumspection in using them against civil populace.

In Operation Blue Star, our jawans and officers gave on excellent account of their valour, yet the planning of the operation was defective from the beginning. The army top brass, impelled by ambitions of their own, misled the government to permit the twin operations, that is, Blue Star and Rosewood to go on at the same time. This brings us to the primary roles of army and the substance of those roles. We should not have treated Bhindranwale and his group as enemies to be destroyed, but some wayward youth only to be tamed. The fact, is that whenever army has to deal with large segments of sensitive populations, it has resulted in misfortune.

Bangladesh would not have come into existence but for brutalities committed by Pak Army under their professional generals on the sensitive people of East Pakistan. Similarly secessionism in Punjab owes its growth to Operation Blue Star and Rosewood. The fact is that army is not trained to fight with their countrymen. They are trained to fight alien armies whom they seek to destroy. Thus, they think in terms of foes and friends only. Whenever they are given a task, they apply the same formulation. Let me reproduce from *US Military Review*, May 1977 as to what military role is when summoned to the aid of civil power. It reads as under:

"The concept of the application of force in a domestic operation is the anti-thesis of the traditional mission on the battlefield: the destruction of enemy forces. Here the conception is 'Zero Kill'. This requires a measured response. Suppression is an act imposed upon people, whereas restoration is the act of returning a condition to a desired former state. The latter is the true objective of the Control force. The operation is not a contest of relative strengths. The successful accomplishment of a mission to restore order in a domestic situation, disturbance without bloodshed or injury to the perpetrators is a noteworthy military achievement, consistent with the traditional role of the soldier in this free society. This is the implied task of every such mission".

Does, not the Operation Blue Star stand professionally self-indicted? In place of using a rapier, the army used the bloody bludgeon. Then where was the justification in detaining women and children? Again to make a prestige issue of not releasing such persons is the manifestation of a regimented mind, which fails to see things beyond the drill square. The wisdom of old saying that an army should be always ready but never used cannot be over emphasised.

Again professionally how can a direct assault on a fortified and well defended position be justified? Is indirect approach as advocated by Liddell Hart not universally accepted military doctrine? In his study of military campaigns spread over thirty centuries, John Laffin says, that there have been only six campaigns on the basis of direct approach (of course he was not aware of Chinese tactics).

Let me quote him from his book *Links of Leadership, Thirty Centuries of Command*: "A competent commander should do anything rather than commit himself to a direct approach. A direct approach causes a stalemate which becomes more insoluble".

Army's Operation Rosewood in Punjab countryside and villages was totally unjustified. The countryside was not in rebellion so that it had to be pacified by Army, which it went on to police. Whatever the doctrinal foundation of the Operation Rosewood, the Army by taking policing of border villages pushed the harassed Sikh youth to cross over into Pakistan. Much before Operation Blue Star, the Army had taken over the duties on Indo-Pak Border. BSF had been placed under Army's operational control. The Army failed to seal the border, since BSF could not act on their own and Army orders regarding policing of borders were amateurish. Operation Rosewood has left a bitter legacy among rural Sikhs and it continues to rankle in their hearts even now.

B.H. Liddell Hart (*The Other Side of the Hill*, pp. 35, 36, East Prussia, Blomberg) had experimented with new forms of tactics, which more realistically recognised the existing superiority of modern defence, and sought to turn this to advantage the other way — as an offensive aid. Instead of attacking a strongly defended position, one might lure the enemy out of position, draw him into making a rash advance or hurried assault, catch him in a trap, and then exploit his disorder by delivering one's own real stroke – in the more deadly form of a riposte. The bait might be created by luring withdrawal or by a sudden swoop that threatened the enemy's communications. The potentialities of this "baited move" combining offensive strategy with defensive tactics – like sword and shield – had struck me in the course of my study of Sherman's campaign in Georgia, and in subsequent books I had eleborated its application to modern warfare. It was Blomberg's particular interest in this idea, which first brought us into contact.

'Again, all warfare is based on deception. Hence, when able to attack, we must seem unable; when using our forces, we must seem inactive; when we are near, we must make the enemy believe that we are away; when far away, we must make him believe we are near. Hold out baits to entice the enemy. Feign disorder, and crush him.'

'There is no instance of a country having been benefited from prolonged warfare.'

'It is only one who is thoroughly acquainted with the evils of war that can thoroughly understand the profitable way of carrying it on.'

'Supreme excellence consists in breaking the enemy's resistance without fighting.

Thus the highest form of generalship is to baulk the enemy's plans; the next best is to prevent the junction of the enemy's forces; the next in order is to attack the enemy's army in the field; the worst policy of all is to besiege walled cities.'

'In all fighting, the direct method may be used for joining battle, but indirect methods will be needed in order to secure victory.'

'Appear at points which the enemy must hasten to defend, march swiftly to places where you are not expected.'

'You may advance and be absolultely irresistible, if you make for the enemy's weak points; you may retire and be safe from pursuit if your movements are more rapid than those of the enemy.'

'All men can see these tactics whereby I conquer, but what none can see is the strategy out of which victory is evolved.'

'Military tactics are like running water; for water in its natural course runs away from high places and hastens downwards. So in war, the way to avoid what is strong is to strike what is weak.

Water shapes its course according to the ground over which it flows; the soldier works out his victory in relation to the foe that he is facing.'

'Thus, to take a long circuitous route, after enticing the enemy out of the way, and though starting after him, to contrive to reach the goal before him, shows knowledge of the artifice of *deviation*.'

'He will conquer who has learnt the artifice of deviation. Such is the art of manoeuvring.'

'To refrain from intercepting an enemy whose banners are in perfect order, to refrain from attacking an army drawn up in calm and confident array—this is the art of the studying circumstances.'

'When you surround an army, leave an outlet free. Do not press a desperate foe too hard.'

'Rapidity is the essence of war; take advantage of the enemy's unreadiness, make your way by unexpected routes, and attack unguarded spots.'

SUN TZU, *The Art of War*—500 B.C.

'The most complete and happy victory is this; to compel one's enemy to give up his purpose, while suffering no harm oneself.'

BELISARIUS

'The whole art of war consists in a well-reasoned and extremely circumspect defensive, followed by rapid and audacious attack.'

NAPOLEON

'All military action is permeated by intelligent forces and their effects.'

CLAUSEWITZ

'By indirections find directions out.'

SHAKESPEARE, *Hamlet*, Act II, Scene I

FALL OUT OF OPERATION BLUE STAR

Everyone expected Sikh backlash in response to ill-conceived and badly executed Operation Blue Star. It had three calamitious results: First, it wounded Sikh psyche beyond repair. Alienation of Sikh womenfolk and teenagers, older Sikhs' anger and anguish remained subterranean leading to various conspiracies, which cannot be revealed here, but culminated in the assassination of the Prime Minister Indira Gandhi.

Second manifestation was mutiny and desertion by Sikh troops at a fairly large scale. Border Security Force wireless network found several army messages floating about desertions and mutinous acts by Sikhs soldiers in J & K, Rajasthan and some other places. Pakistan must have also monitored and garnered them gleefully. When BSF placed those messages before the Government, there was a gasp of horrified disbelief. However, the fact of mutiny cannot be glossed over. Not only Sikh troops refused to partake of meals at several places, but a mutiny took place in Sikh Regimental Centre, Rampur, which resulted in shooting of Brigadier Puri on June l, 1984. Three convoys of mutineers proceeded to Amritsar but were intercepted in Bihar and UP and a number of them lost lives in a skirmish near Jaunpur.

Sullen Sikhs of 18 Sikh at Miran Sahib near Jammu succumbed to the taunts of their womenfolk and 80 of the mutinees were intercepted near Dina Nagar (Gurdaspur Distt.) Punjab. Similar situation arose in 14 Sikh when nearly 127 Sikh troops with their arms and ammunition deserted unit lines in vehicles shouting slogans against the Prime Minister. Their vehicles were intercepted in Maharashtra itself. It is not the purpose to describe every mutinous act, but to emphasise that the army top brass, while planning operation Blue Star, had overlooked the crucial importance of explaining the necessity of the Operation to their own men, who underwent emotional trauma of the worst type and also the reaction of their mothers, wives and daughters who taunted them to rise against what they came to perceive as unforgivable sacrilege of their holiest shrine. It is estimated that 2800 troops had deserted or mutinied.

A large number of Sikh families had thronged Golden Temple as the martyrdom day fell on the June 5, 1984.

Major General K.S. Brar (a Jat Sikh of the lineage of Sant Jarnail Singh Bhindranwale, who was also a Brar) and Ranjit Dayal, Chief of Staff to General K. Sundarji of Western Command claim that they had made several appeals on public address system to the pilgrims to leave the Golden Temple premises. Observe Mark Tully and Satish Jacob, "The hostel complex was eventually evacuated in the middle of the attack on the Temple itself. During the rescue operation, many innocent people were killed, many were injured and many were wrongfully arrested." According to *Probe India*, August 84:

"On the morning of June 6, the Golden Temple Complex was like a graveyard. Bodies lay around in the buildings, on the Parikarma, in the sarovar... I myself carried the bodies of three soldiers on my shoulders. Each regiment conducted the funeral rites of their Jawans.

"The civilians, who had died, about 1500 of them, were piled in trollies and carried away. Many bodies were thrown into the rivers.

"The battle was tragic one. I couldn't eat anything. Food made me sick. I used to just drink lots of rum and go to sleep. I am glad now to be relieved of my duty in Amritsar."

Again, Khushwant Singh is quoted to have said to Ajit Kaur, after his visit to Amritsar:

"Three hundred bullets have hit Sri Darbar Sahib, a blind musician was sitting inside and was hit there by a bullet. ... the carpet on which his blood had been spilt could not be cleaned. It was wiped, washed and scrubbed but the flies would again come to the spot. Also the stench got worse day by day .... "

"I wonder pools of blood have been created in our hearts. No matter how hard we try to mop up the spill, there is no way to clean the blood that has soaked in. Time will perhaps wipe or wash away the blood but the spots will be there for ever. The smell of blood will gradually become a stench. The flies of boiling anger and helpless rage will again and again visit the same spot of blood."

The repressive laws enacted rescinded the Fundamental Rights enshrined in the Indian Constitution with regard to Punjab, a part of the ongoing slaughter of their human rights. It began in a systematic manner with Operation Blue Star when indiscriminate arrest of women, children and old persons was made within the precincts of the Temple buildings. The charge sheet filed in regard to this Operation by Special Police Establishment, Delhi acknowledges this fact vide paragraph 7. The same is reproduced below:

"On June 5, 1984, the terrorists and others entrenched in and around Golden Temple Complex were asked at 16.30 hours and onwards to come out and surrender by 17.30 hours by making announcements over public address system. The announcement was made in Punjabi from three different places and within the hearing distance of persons inside and around Golden Temple Complex. The announcement was met by shouts of pro-Khalistan slogans like "Khalistan Zindabad", "Lad ke Lawange Khalistan" and intermittent bursts of fire. However, in compliance of aforesaid announcement 119 men, women and children surrendered at PS Kotwali by 17.15 hours."

Again, was force used during Operation Blue Star restrained enough or was it exercised in accordance with Geneva Convention?

Amnesty International takes an extreme view of situations, yet the following portion from their report of 1985-86 on Punjab deserves attention and is reproduced below:

"The State of Punjab", says the report, "which, since 6 October 1983, had been under direct (President's) rule by the Central Government. The two draconian amendments to the National Security Act (NSA) permitting detention without trial for up to two years of persons suspected to be involved in acts prejudicial to the defence or security of the state, and requiring the courts when releasing a detainee to rule that all (as opposed to some) grounds for detention are invalid: the Terrorist Affected Areas (Special Courts) Act allowing trials in camera, shifting the burden of proof on the accused, and restricting appeals only to the Supreme Court within a reduced 30 days period; the brutal torture and cold-blooded murder of innocent Sikhs following the army action in the Golden Temple" - all come in for Amnesty's criticism.

It further states: " Amnesty International's position vis-a-vis violence, whether by the State or by private groups, is unambiguous. The organisation, as a matter of principle, condemns the killing or torture of individuals detained by anyone, including opposition groups, and recognises that the government has a responsibility to bring to justice those responsible for violence." Unfortunately, Amnesty International's methods of quiet persuasion appear to be becoming increasingly ineffective as is evident from the record of its correspondence with the Indian government. Not only were repeated requests for clarification regarding some of the disturbing trends in human rights compliance coolly ignored, but when the organisation informed the Foreign Minister in April 1984 of its intention to send a delegate to India to meet professionals involved in the protection of human rights, it was informed that a visa for such a visit could not be granted. No reasons were, of course, assigned for the refusal."

Regarding Jodhpur detenues, Amnesty International reported: "Thousands of Sikh men and women were arrested during and after Operation Blue Star in June 1984. The government released most of them during that year and by January 1985 announced that 379 of them, who remained detained under the provisions of the National Security Act, would be tried by a Special Court established under the Terrorist Affected Areas (Special Courts) Act, 1984, Justice C.S. Tiwana, investigating the conditions in which 60 of them had been held before taking to Jodhpur Jail, found that their initial detention had been illegal since they had not been brought before a magistrate within 24 hours of arrest as the law requires."

Thus, Operation Blue Star was a military blunder and unmitigated disaster for the women folk, children and the old who were unduly detained.

– 17 –

The Prime Minister is Assassinated

PLEASE DO NOT READ THIS CHAPTER IF YOU
HAVE NOT READ CHAPTER 1, CAPTIONED
WHY READ THIS BOOK

My wife was on a visit to Canada and was staying in a Jat Sikh family in Toronto in June 1984, when operation Blue Star took place. She told me on phone that Sikhs in Canada were outraged by the army action in the Golden Temple. She had heard several of them planning to assassinate the Prime Minister for her military operation in Darbar Sahib. I conveyed this to the quarters concerned; however, I was rebuffed by the reply that I should not interfere in others' work.

The central issue was that once the Sikhs in the Army, which is more disciplined than the police, had mutinied, the chiefs of the police forces should have anticipated similar reaction in their police forces. Since police of several states had been rocked by mutiny in 1979, they should have seen beyond sullen masks, which their Sikh subordinates had been wearing.

On October 31 morning, there was Raising Day Parade of CRPF in their camp at Jharoda Kalan on the outskirts of Delhi. During the parade, the then Director Intelligence Bureau, Sri R.K. Kapoor, was sitting by my side and Sardar Buta Singh who was then Minister of Works and Housing was addressing the parade when the driver of Shri Kapoor brought him a signal received on his car radio. The Director of Intelligence Bureau left immediately. Any question to Shri Kapoor for his leaving like that would have been indiscreet. In the meanwhile, his driver had informed other drivers that

Smt. Indira Gandhi had been seriously injured when her own guard had opened fire on her and that she had been rushed to the All India Institute of Medical Sciences. Thus, as soon as Shri Buta Singh stepped down the rostrum, most of us came to know of the tragedy and rushed back to Delhi.

With her death I felt as if a part of my being had also died. I respected her because she was a true lover of nature and a highly compassionate individual. Whenever I saw her in hills, she looked lost in the pageant of clouds, in the beautiful cascading rivulets, the carpets of flowers and the changing rainbow of colours. She was, nay, indeed, a fanatic in her love of nature. At times, it looked if her only religion was love of plants, flowers, rivers and skyward rising hills. When I think of her death, I feel overwhelmed by her various images and roles. My mind reels when it recalls her refusing to ride a docile pony and her insistence on riding my horse, named Rustam, who was very headstrong and my fear that in this jungle of Mashobra, she may injure herself trying to tame this animal. However, she had come prepared. She soon produced a handful of biscuits from her jacket and fed Rustam.

Then she caressed his neck. In a couple of minutes, the wild animal was putty in her hands. She rode him in utter silence with a smile, which seemed to mock my fears and my following her in the gorgeous jungle of Mashobra, that wet morning of July 1959. Then my mind switched to May 1967 and her coming to Dachigam forest sanctuary six miles out of Srinagar in the face of opposition from the Chief Minister, Shri G.M. Sadiq, and his security advisers on the ground that some Pak infiltrators might be lurking in the jungles or on the slopes of hills snuggling the Dachigam bungalow or in the burning jungle atop us due to the folly of Military Police Battalion, which was sent to block infiltration routes, her gazing on the blazing jungle and her telling Shri G.M. Sadiq that it was a glorious sight though she regretted the loss of trees and Shri G.M. Sadiq looked blank not knowing how to react to this unpredictable Prime Minister. After their departure, she asked me if there were really any Pak infiltrators around. On my saying "No", she enquired how could I be so sure. I replied we had reconnoitred the entire area up to 10 km. and our patrols were still out. On this she remained quiet as if she had come only to see how the infiltrators could operate so close to Srinagar and see our armed reaction to them.

In the afternoon I was told that the Prime Minister would go out for a walk. (Impromptu, as she used to do at Mashobra eight years back), my dropping Shakespeare's Hamlet and grabbing my 9 mm. pistol and descending down to the bungalow. She making enquiries about the security arrangements BSF had made for her security because she could not see anyone in uniform near the bungalow within her sight. My telling her that adequate number of sentries were around. Her expressing surprise as none was visible. My then taking her to a blossoming shrubbery and her being surprised to see that there was a dug out sentry post and an armed sentry with binoculars on duty. Her remarking that the Chief Minister was right in telling her that proper security arrangements were not possible in this secluded jungle bungalow. Her inquiring about wild animals and my telling her that my jeep was attacked by a wild boar in the early morning that very day. Her, then suddenly starting down the narrow valley and my following her clutching my loaded pistol lest any cobra or some wild animal pounced upon us in that narrow pebbled jungle route, the dark shadows suddenly growing, hills aglow with the rays of the setting sun, and on our left across the fast running stream the burning jungle having turned into smouldering embers. A chilly wind hit us, her pulling the lapels of her furred long coat and her entering the bungalow where the rooms were lit by the burning wood. I remember my saluting her and leaving for my tent.

Her taking another walk next afternoon and insisting on crossing the fast flowing (East to West) stream. Her suddenly wading the water bare foot and my jungle shoes saturated with icy water and sloshing. Then her walking up the hill and as the hill arose her feeling the strain; her taking a seat on a rock and my mind being swamped by fears as there were not adequate deployment across the stream and there being only two patrols in the area. Actually, none could visualize that this frail looking lady would be entering bare footed in the icy water constantly flowing from the glaciers one could see at the end of the valley.

My mind reeled with thousand of her images left on it during my service to her over a long period.

She wrote me once to arrest a BSF officer who had been found poaching in Rajasthan. She refused to visit Punjab in December 1980 to lay the foundation stone of Ranjit Nagar near Phillaur on the banks of Satluj, as four or five trees in the forest near Phillaur were felled to make a helipad for her landing. Indeed when she made her visit, she travelled on dusty roads from Ropar to Nakodar and Phillaur till late night to her great inconvenience and hazard.

In November 1983, the Conference of Heads of Commonwealth Governments (CHOGM) was held in New Delhi. These heads of the governments had to take a break and Goa was selected to be their Retreat.

During this break at Goa, a very unpleasant event took place. Every head of the government had been assigned a young Personal Security Officer trained and briefed by the Intelligence Bureau. Mr. Lee Yuan Kew, the Prime Minister of Singapore, was a jogging buff. He went jogging every morning and evening. On the first day of his arrival, the Prime Minister of Singapore went out jogging on the shore. He was, I think, 65 years old at that time. While the Prime Minister of Singapore at his age was swift and adroit in his jogging, the young Indian Personal Security Officers lagged behind to the shame of us all present on duty.

Next day early in the morning, Mrs. Indira Gandhi had gone deep into the sea cruising on a powerful motorboat. When she returned, she was wearing salwar kamiz with her tresses swept back by the sea wind. When she alighted, she looked ruffled. A number of people were watching and they clapped seeing her alighting in her beautiful apparel. She then looked upon me with a stunned expression and asked me why a namby pamby weakling P.S.Os. had been attached to the Singapore Prime Minister. I respectfully told her that I had nothing to do with the P.S.Os and was not concerned with their training or assignment. She then angrily enquired what remedial steps I had taken. I told her that the problem had been sorted out by our putting a placard at 1 Km. point away on the shore saying that the shore beyond was not sanitized and advised the visitors not to proceed beyond that point. So in the morning, Singapore Prime Minister had not gone beyond that point and the Personal Security Officer no more puffed and presented a spectacle of misery. She faintly smiled and proceeded to her suite in the hotel.

She had the magnificent obsession of making India impregnable in matters of security. In the period 1982 to 1984, I had the privilege to meet her frequently. Our meetings generally lasted about 15 minutes. In the first ten minutes, intelligence and security matters were discussed. In the last 5 minutes, she inquired about the new books having arrived in the book stores of Delhi. She used to say that as the Prime Minister of India she felt like a prisoner as she could not even visit a book shop and browse through the newly arrived books, something she always wanted to do.

She was a reticent person. She could listen to you with interest if you talked about nature and spiritual matters and the books, both new and the ancient.

She was fond of quoting from various scriptures according to her disposition of the hour. Evidently she had made a thorough study of various spiritual disciplines. My knowledge of various scriptures was limited. One day after listening to her quoting Buddha I said that I was her disciple as Ananda was to Buddha. She remained quiet for some time and then told me that I ought to know that if one meets Buddha on a road, Buddha has to be killed.

Her interest in Zen Buddhism was immense. She often cited from *Zen Flesh, Zen Bones* by Paul Reps.

She had apparently studied Hinyana Buddhism in detail. She was a shrewd reader of human nature. However, she had such a faith in her own charisma that she never attended to the details of the task assigned to various officers. She was confident that once she had made her wishes known, the bureaucrats would automatically comply with her wishes. This does not happen when a counry like India is to be administered. Firstly, the people want no change and feel safe to wallow in the status-quo. Secondly, everyone puts out a performance according to his/her standards, which may not be high. Thus, the results to her various directions were mediocre and sometimes disastrous.

She again and again expressed her desire to pass out of this world while serving the poor of India and thereby the world. In this regard, she quoted Swami Vivekanand, the great saint of Ramakrishna Order, who had made it his mission of life to serve God in man: "May I be born again and again, and suffer thousands of miseries so that I may worship the only God ... above all, my God the wicked, my God the miserable, my God the poor of all races, of all species ... " Yet she had developed an obsessive ambition that the world ought to recognise her work for the poor and her services to the down-trodden. Those who knew this obsession of hers and pandered to her obsession, secured undeserved rewards. Some said that she was craving for Noble Prize for Peace to be awarded to her. Those who knew about her obsessive ambition exploited her weakness in this regard.

Indeed, Mrs. Indira Gandhi was an enigma and her paradoxical stand on certain issues remains a great mystery till this date. Her enigmatic attitude was the result of the contrasts making her personality: she was earthy yet ethereal; a pagan who enjoyed all the delicacies of the world offered by variegated flora and fauna, yet a highly spiritual individual who never wanted to harm a single living being; a person who was paragon of the exquisite beauties as well as the sordid realities of the political world!

She used to say some time that very few are really alive and generally the living corpses wear flowers to gather some fragrance about them. When I saw her body wrapped in flowers during state mourning, I was reminded that she had been a flower, which blossomed in India to fill this land of somnolence with fragrant thoughts and exquisite colours of courageous endurance.

HAM JANATEN HAIN BULBUL KYA HAl
TERI HAQIQAT
DO PAR LAGE HUE
HAIN IK MYSHTE KHAKH KE BAS

The investigation of this dastardly murder was entrusted to a special Investigating Team (SIT) headed by an IPS officer from Andhra Pradesh, Sri Anandaram. The supervision of the investigation was entrusted to Sri Shiv Shankar, the Minister of Law and Justice and Sri Arun Nehru the Minister for Internal Security. Sub Inspector Beant Singh and Satwant Singh had riddled her body with service weapons bullets. Beant Singh was killed by the ITBP guard on duty. Constable Satwant and Kehar Singh were held guilty by the Supreme Court. Sri Anandaram was good enough to consult me during various phases of investigation since I had come to be regarded as knowledgeable about Punjab. At one stage, the question of prosecuting Shri R.K. Dhawan and impeaching the highest Constitutional Authority of India was also considered. These courses were wisely abandoned because we had to prosecute the real culprits and not be swayed by peripheral evidence. But the issue remains: whether Mrs. Gandhi's assassination could have been avoided. Only history will pronounce the final verdict.

It is remarkable that on October 30, 1984, she delivered a public speech in Bhubaneshwar which was prophetic:

"I am here today", I may not be here tomorrow. I do not care whether I live or die. I have lived a long life and I am proud that I spent the whole of my life in the service of my people. When I die, I can say that "every drop of my blood will invigorate India and strengthen it."

The fact is that she had been tempting death by interfering with her security. To her what was important was the image.

Death is always tragic and the peculiar circumstances under which the charismatic life of Indira Gandhi was snatched away left every one numb with unspeakable sorrow.

Dr. G.V. Kulkarni has mused as follows on the issue:–

"In the nectar lake of religion some one poured
The deadly poison of separatism
Priyadarshani became the victim
Was that inevitable?
Was that unavoidable?"

This might be directed to the claim of Army top brass that they would overrun defences round holy Harmandar Sahib erected by criminals like Sahib Singh and a crazy Brig Mohender Singh in 5 hours.

It is urged that the Government of India should constitute a Court of Inquiry of three Retired Chiefs of Army Staff to find out whether Gen. Krishnamurti Sunderji, GOC Western Command, had a well thought out Operation Plan.

1. Whether this plan was based on proper reconnaissance of the Bhindranwale Defensive Posts.
2. Whether any Aerial Survey of Akal Takht and Harmander Sahib defenses had been made.
3. Why did the Army Brass misled the Prime Minister that Bhindranwale's resistance can run over in 5 hours.
4. Why did they press Artillery and Armour to destroy Akal Takht.
5. Did they not know that there would be thousands of pilgrims inside the holy Harmander Sahib during those days.
6. What were the briefings to various officers and ranks.

– 18 –

Resentment against Authoritarian Rule of Prime Minister Shrimati Indira Gandhi and Evolution of a Plan to Weaken the Same

Chandigarh is a miracle of a city planned by Le Courbosier. It has vistas of highways lined by superb flowering trees. A city of wide spaces and open vistas, Punjab and Haryana have claimed this prize city as their capital respectively and shed blood to get possession of this maiden city. Never before had such a city existed in India.

It is the city of bureaucrats and politicians, both scrupulous and unscrupulous. It is the city from where Sardar Partap Singh Kairon, Chief Minister of Punjab, in 1950s trounced Akalis among Jat Sikhs, their base. His wife and sons went on a spree. Sardar Partap Singh was followed by Comrade Ram Kishan during the epic years 1963-1965. Then the days of Congress were over and Akalis took the reins of the government.

In such salubrius ambiance of lust and love, commitment to service of people and frenzied quest for power at Delhi prospered with manic speed.

In the 1970s Giani Zail Singh was the Chief Minister of Punjab and Shri Bhajan Lal happened to be Chief Minister of Haryana. It was natural that they should have good and friendly relationship. They consulted each other as how to weaken the autocratic rule of New Delhi so that more autonomy was available to them in their respective provinces.

This friendship resulted in the escape of Sant Jarnail Singh Bhindranwale from village Chandu Kalan (Haryana) on 12th September 1981.

When apprised of these murmurings, Shrimati Indira Gandhi merealy quoted Corso:

> "What makes a people huddle so?
> Why can't they be universal?
> Who had smalled them so?
> This is serious! I do not mock or hate this; I can only smell some mad vast conspiracy?"

– 19 –

Blood-Bath for Khalistan

In 1987, Prof. Darshan Singh Ragi was appointed Chief Priest of Akal Takht by the extremists of the Damdami Taksal and All India Sikh Students Federation. While the Panthic Committees were calling the shots in Punjab from their sanctuary in Pakistan, Tat Khalsa led by Avtar Singh Brahma, Khalistan Liberation Army headed by Aroor Singh and Khalistan Armed Force (KAF) led by Sher Singh Sher perpetrated murders and kidnapping.

New Delhi Government went on appointing Commissions under Hon'ble Justice K.K. Mathew and Hon'ble Justice Venkatramia to award Chandigarh to Punjab in lieu of a few thousand acres of land from Punjab to Haryana. Despite expenditure, despite fanfares of publicity, nothing came out of these Commissions nor that of the Eradi Commission, on the sharing of Ravi-Beas waters among Punjab, Haryana and Rajasthan. Thus, the Rajiv-Longowal Award remains unimplimented till today. The proceedings of Judicial Commission appointed in November, 1984 anti-Sikh riots, the Justice Rangnath Misra Commission were held in camera. It examined 128 witnesses and 3500 affidavits. After this Commission, a number of other Commissions and Committees were formed but hardly a guilty person was brought to book for a long time — a case of sheer lack of will power.

In the meanwhile, ding dong battle between the terrorists and police in Punjab continued. Manbir Singh Chehru, Sukhdev Singh Sukha, Avtar Singh Brahma continued to kill and boast of their killings. Now they are all dead. Most formidable of them was General Labh Singh alias

Sukhdev alias Sukha of Khalistan Commando Force, who had been dismissed from police and had gone on killing the families of policemen. In the meanwhile, Panthic Committees' desperadoes on orders of Pak Inter Services Intelligence went on killing rural Hindus to force them to migrate out of Punjab.

The grand design was to have Khalistan demographically, if not politically. Terrorists went on striking with ease and immunity in rural areas whether it was Lalru in Patiala Distt or Fatehabad in Haryana. Mao Tse-Dong had said that when the guerillas controlled the countryside, cities would collapse on their own for want of food and other amenities for which they were dependent on the villages. Earlier Gandhiji had said; "if the village perishes, India will perish too". Thus the strategy devised by the ISI to secure migration of non-Sikhs from the Punjab countryside was well thought out and was executed as a well orchestrated plan.

Killing of bus passengers had started as early as the first week of October 1983, near Dhilwan in Kapurthala Distt., which had caused the downfall of Sardar Darbara Singh Ministry. Bus killings went on becoming more and more gruesome since 1985. Killing of passengers in Muktsar (July 6 1987), Fatehabad Hissar Distt. Haryana (July 7 1987) conjure up scenes of inhuman brutality. Indeed the entire series of gruesome murders of prominent personalities beginning with Lala Jagat Narain (September 9, 1981), DIG A.S. Atwal (April 25, 1983), H.S. Manchanda (March 28, 1984), Shri Ramesh Chander, the fearless son of Lala Jagat Narain (May 12, 1984), Lalit Maken and his wife Gitanjali Maken (July 31, 1984), Sant Harchand Singh Longowal (August 20, 1985), Arjun Dass (September 4, 1985), Gen. (Retd.) A.S. Vaidya at Pune on August 10, 1986 were perpetrated to send a signal to the minority of Punjab that they should migrate out of Punjab so that *de facto* Khalistan was available to the terrorists and their new mentors in Pakistan.

In early 1987, the Surjit Singh Barnala Ministry of Punjab was lauded by New Delhi rulers. It was said that this Ministry was the most benign and popular after Maharaja Ranjit Singh's golden rule in Punjab. People in Punjab sniggered on these fulsome tributes by those who should have known better because it were the people who bore the brunt of terrorism and unprecedented corruption unleashed by -vay of extortions. The same rulers who had extolled Barnala Ministry had no compunction in dismissing the same on May 10, 1987, with a view to gain advantage in the elections due in Haryana the next month. Can there be anything more cynical?

During Governors' Rules, the number of terrorists' depredations mounted sharply and Shri Jaswant Singh of BJP wrote in the *Seminar* of May, 1988: "There is one other cruelly debilitating factor. Rajiv Gandhi's vaccillations have left all in the Punjab completely perplexed. A hero of the Punjab (Barnala) of one morning is termed as incompetent the next day and dismissed. A wanted terrorist overnight converted into the new arbiter of Punjab destiny and elevated. Why, therefore (indeed how) ought an ordinary police constable fight his individual battle with the terrorist?"

It was the dithering of New Delhi rulers in the face of Punjab's grim tragedy, which turned vibrant Punjab into a charnel house.

An offer of peace was made by the militants in June, 1986, which could lead to a negotiated peace in Punjab. The militants were prepared to lay arms and ensure peace in Punjab on two simple conditions. With all my experience of Punjab terrorism, I thought it to be the most opportune moment to arrive at peace. A decision could be taken only by the Prime Minister. I found that it was not as easy to meet him as was the case earlier. However, I ultimately talked to him briefly during the Independence Day, 1986 reception at the Rashtrapati Bhawan and told him of the offer. He promised that he would give me early audience. Finding the matter was getting delayed. I wrote to his Secretary, Shri V. George. Ultimately on October 30, 1986, I was given hearing by two bureaucrats. I followed up the matter by writing to the Secretary to the Prime Minister. There was no response.

The Govt. availed the services of Darshan Singh Ragi, late Acharya Sushil Muni and Jasbir Singh Rode (nephew of Sant Jarnail Singh), for negotiating with the militants. All these moves were for putting up a facade of reasonableness. Trilochan Singh Riyasti paid for his sincerity with his life and all others were jettisoned to the limbo of oblivion.

The high priests of Akal Takht went on rousing the masses to religious frenzy in favour of Khalistan. They were released and negotiations were started with these very protagonists of Khalistan. Similarly, Atinder Pal Singh and his co-conspirators in the assassination of the late Prime Minister Mrs. Indira Gandhi were released and the leadership of the militants was got transferred to them in the hope that they will be more pliable. They went on spitting venom and fire proving that the New Delhi rulers were gullible. In the elections of 1989, the alleged murderers made a clean sweep. This happened after the success of Operation Black Thunder in May 1988. The benefits of the success of this operation were frittered away in futile cajoling and mollycoddling of those who had prided themselves in fostering secessionism and rabid communalism and sought U.N. intervention for Khalistan and openly prayed U.S. and other foreign interventions.

A study of the following statistics will show that in the years beginning 1981 to 1993, 11,666 civilians and 1425 policemen fell victim to the Pakistan inspired terrorism.

	1981	1982	1983	1984	1985	1986	1987	1988
Civilians	13	13	75	359	63	520	910	1949
Policemen	2	2	21	25	10	46	100	125
	1989	1990	1991	1992	1993...	1997		
Civilians	1168	2484	2591	1519	45	55 (between March 14 & July 10, 1997 due to bomb explosion etc.)		
Policemen	166	399	368	144	14			

Sikh history mentions "ghullugharas" with abhorrence. Does the killing of thousands of civilians, of whom Sikh were in large number, and 1425 securitymen, out of this number the largest being of Sikh officers and men, not constitute the Ghullugharas of 1980s and 1990s? Those who incited misguided youth to violence and patronised assassins by holding massive Bhog ceremonies and awarding medals to the assassins' families, have to introspect and answer the question themselves? If Akalis have come to power now through elections, it is due to sacrifices of thousands of civilian and security men, who in the performance of their duties laid down their lives fighting the most inhuman terrorism in the era of any nation-state except Ireland. If Sardar Parkash Singh Badal is the Chief Minister today, it is due to the fact that Sardar Beant Singh, the Congress Chief Minister of Punjab, was a relentless fighter against terrorism and his assassination on August 31, 1995, proved that the Chief Minister of a State is the right and the only instrument for successfully fighting foreign inspired or internally created terrorism. Shri Beant Singh proved that in the case of Punjab, while he was the Chief Minister between 1992 to 1995.

– 20 –

The Assassination of Shri Rajiv Gandhi

General Elections were due in 1991. In this connection Shri Rajiv Gandhi went on an election tour to Sriperumbudur on May 21, 1991. He was assassinated by an LTTE cadre named Dhanu, the human bomb who had tied an explosive round her waist. This assassination was in consequence to a criminal conspiracy which was unearthed by a Special Investigation Team headed by Shri RD Kartikeyan. As a result of this investigation, many people were apprehended, tried and are now undergoing sentence. The Government of India ordered a Commission of Enquiry under Justice JS Verma, then a sitting judge of the Supreme Court.

The terms of references of the Verma Commission were as follows:

"The Commission shall make an inquiry with respect to the following matters:-

(a) whether the assassination of Shri Rajiv Gandhi could have been averted and whether there were lapses or dereliction of duty in this regard on the part of any of the individuals responsible for his security;

(b) the deficiencies, if any, in the security system and arrangements as prescribed or operated in practice which might have contributed to the assassination.

The Commission may also recommend corrective remedies and measures that need to be taken for the future with respect to the matters specified in Clause (b) of paragraph 2 above."

Shri Rajiv Gandhi was the bravest Prime Minister which India ever had. He believed in confronting the danger rather than skirting it. When the interference in day to day administration by the President of India was rife, Shri Rajiv Gandhi took the course of confrontation than eschewing the same as was done by his mother. His assassination sent shock waves not only in India but all over the world. He was termed JF Kennedy of India, and not in vain. His contribution in modernising India and its economy are lauded even after a decade. He empowered the rural community by giving a constitutional status to Panchayati Raj. His assassination was the result of linkage between the Punjab terrorists and the LTTE insurgents. The latter had resented his induction of IPKF into Sri Lanka.

The Government of India constituted a judicial commission to go into the assassination of Rajiv Gandhi under Justice JS Verma of the Supreme Court of India. The Verma Commission findings were hotly debated both in Rajya Sabha as well as in Lok Sabha of India. Detailed proceedings are available in the following books:

1. Lok Sabha Debates 20-30 July, 1991
2. Rajya Sabha Debates 12-14 May, 1993
3. Lok Sabha Debates 12-14 May, 1993
4. Lok Sabha Debates Aug 24-26, 1995
5. Lok Sabha Debates Aug 3-6, 1998

– 21 –

MC Jain Commission Report into the Assassination of Shri Rajiv Gandhi

MEMORANDUM OF ACTION TAKEN ON THE INTERIM REPORT OF JAIN COMMISSION OF INQUIRY SUBMITTED ON 28.8.1997

The Government of India appointed a Commission of Inquiry consisting of Shri Justice M.C. Jain, retired Chief Justice of the High Court of Delhi by Notification S.O.No. 545(E) dated August 23, 1991. The terms of reference of this Commission were:

"The Commission shall make an inquiry with respect to the following matters: -

(a) The sequence of events leading to, and all the facts and circumstances relating to, the assassination of Shri Rajiv Gandhi at Sriperumbudur (other than the matters covered by the terms of reference for the Commission of Inquiry headed by Shri Justice JS Verma):

(b) Whether any person or persons or agencies were responsible for conceiving, preparing and planning the assassination and whether there was any conspiracy in this behalf and, if so, all its ramifications."

2. The Commission submitted its Interim Report to the Government on 28.8.1997. The Interim Report deals, as per the commission, with the 'sequence of events' which is the first part of the first term of reference of the Commission.

The Report contains a narration of events and observations/ conclusions drawn therefrom. It does not contain any separate set of recommendations. The Interim Report is in 17 Volumes; the main Report is in four parts consisting of 8 Volumes as under: -

Part – I :	Commission and its Proceedings (Vol. I and II).
Part – II :	Threats to Shri Rajiv Gandhi and his security (Vol. III and IV)'
Part – III :	Growth of Sri Lankan Tamil militancy in Tamil Nadu (Vol. V, VI and VII)
Part – IV :	Indo-Sri Lanka Agreement: Evolution and its Aftermath (Vol. VIII).

The remaining volumes contain copies of the exhibits, documents, statements, etc.

3. Prior to the appointment of this Commission, the Government of India had appointed another one man Commission of Inquiry consisting of the Chief Justice of India Shri Justice JS Verma, then a sitting judge of the Supreme Court, vide notification S.O. No.356 (E) dated the 27th May 1991.

4. The terms of reference of the Verma Commission were as follows:

"2. The Commission shall make an inquiry with respect to the following matters: -

(a) Whether the assassination of Shri Rajiv Gandhi could have been averted and whether there were lapses or dereliction of duty in this regard on the part of any of the individuals responsible for his security.

(b) The deficiencies, if any, in the security system and arrangements as prescribed or operated in practice, which might have contributed to the assassination.

3. The Commission may also recommend corrective remedies and measures that need to be taken for the future with respect to the matters specified in clause (b) of paragraph 2 above."

THE SCOPE OF INQUIRY OF THE JAIN COMMISSION

4. In the Interim Report of the Jain Commission of Inquiry (Vol. I and II), there are observations regarding the scope of inquiry of the Commission and reasons for delay in completion of its work.

5. About the scope of the inquiry, the Commission has stated in para 3.21 (page 63, Vol. I) of its interim report as follows:-

..."Having regard to the terms of reference, the commission has jurisdiction to inquire into all aspects of the assassination, including responsibility of person or persons or agencies in the assassination and whether there was any conspiracy for the same and that the commission can inquire into all the sequence of events leading to the assassination of Shri Rajiv Gandhi."

The Commission has arrived at conclusion in Part-II of the Interim Report regarding the adequacy or otherwise of the assessment of threat to late Shri Rajiv Gandhi and of the security provided to him and the issue of withdrawal of SPG protection. It is noteworthy that these matters were within the purview of the Verma Commission of Inquiry. As stated above, the terms of reference of the present Commission of Inquiry specifically excluded the matters covered by the terms of reference of the Verma Commission of Inquiry.

6. The Verma Commission of Inquiry submitted its Report on 15.6.92 and the Report along with Memorandum of Action Taken thereon was placed before Parliament on 23.12.92. Later, certain modifications were announced and published in the Gazette of India on 27.2.1996.

The findings of the Verma Commission of Inquiry were mainly that the Government's decision of 30.1.1990 was prompted more by the lack of proper perception or the requisite will than the stated difficulties in extension of SPG cover to Shri Rajiv Gandhi. The Commission also had come to a conclusion that the decision to withdraw SPG, without provision for a suitable alternative for his proximate security, reducing the level of protection to him, was unjustified. Action has been taken by the Government on the recommendations of the Verma Commission of Inquiry. Accordingly, no action is now called for in respect of the matters which have already been covered by the Verma Commission of Inquiry.

7. Regarding furnishing of documents and evidence on the part of SIT/CBI, it was the considered decision of the Government, on legal advice, that nothing shall be done which may delay or disrupt the trial of Shri Rajiv Gandhi assassination case before the Designated Court at Chennai. The Commission asked for the records of this case for which the Designated Court did not give permission and had also issued an order under section 16(3) of Terrorist and Disruptive Activities (TADA) Act prohibiting the disclosure of any material. In the meantime, SIT/CBI had, as early as on 2.2.95, offered to share all its records with the Commission on confidential basis. This offer was made on more than one occasion. Finally, with the permission of the Designated Court, the records were submitted to the Commission in June 1996 for its perusal only, as desired.

Conclusions

While analysing the threats emanating from various hostile forces, to the life of Shri Rajiv Gandhi, what stands out is that several anti-national forces active during the period 1984 to 1991 nurtured ambitions of assassinating Shri Rajiv Gandhi for strategic reasons. In many instances, these elements colluded and agreed to work towards this common objective. The Sikh extremist-LTTE-ULFA-LTTE and ULFA-Sikh extremist links are some such examples. Whereas the threat perceptions have provided crucial information in terms of links between various hostile forces, whether any of these links or any other unknown links actually worked at tandem to hatch the conspiracy, which ultimately culminated in the assassination of Shri Rajiv Gandhi, requires to be enquired into in depth.

The decades of 1980 and 1990 were particularly tumultuous for India. Till the assassination of Smt. Indira

Gandhi, the threat perceptions for the Prime Minister were not assessed to be so grave as to require deployment of highly and technically trained manpower exclusively for the protection of the threatened individuals. The assassination of Smt. Indira Gandhi galvanised the security agencies and brought into sharp focus the vulnerability of those public personalities, who due to the decisions taken by them in official capacity in national interest became objects of enmity of the secessionist and terrorist forces operating in the country. Shri Rajiv Gandhi inherited from his mother a grave threat from Sikh extremists even before he became the Prime Minister. As Prime Minister of India, he was drawn into taking several hard decisions against terrorism from the very beginning. Recognising this threat, in 1985, an exclusive security force called the Special Protection Group (SPG) was raised for him.

With the gradual induction of sophisticated arms, explosives and weaponry in the subcontinent during the eighties, the security scenario changed drastically. Beyond the Northwest borders of India, Afghan Mujahideens and their sympathisers in Pakistan had acquired highly sophisticated weaponry and explosives. Much of this supply was being diverted and came into the hands of Indian secessionist elements such as the Sikhs and the Kashmiri militants. Series of bomb blasts in North India and several assassinations of threatened personalities notably Sant Harchand Singh Longowal, Lala Jagat Narain (September 1981) and his son Ramesh Chander (May 1984) in Punjab, Lalit Maken in New Delhi and General Vaidya in Pune underscored the need for streamlined intelligence machinery and responsive and effective security systems to be brought into implementation.

By early eighties the tentacles of Sikh terrorists had spread all over the world. Uncovering of a plot in the USA hatched by these elements for the assassination of Shri Rajiv Gandhi and Shri Bhajan Lal in the USA in 1985 was one such indication. During this period, the international network of these terrorist and secessionist organisations became highly organised. The intelligence reports of the period clearly indicate that Sikh terrorists based abroad were not only engaged in propaganda, but alsó in large scale mobilisation of arms, induction of arms training to their cadres and in building up liaison with other terrorist organisations.

Beyond the Southern borders of India, the problem of Sri Lanka assumed alarming proportions in the early eighties. The ethnic riot of July 1983 in Sri Lanka had a direct impact on India. During the course of the decade, Sri Lankan Tamil terrorist groups, particularly the LTTE acquired extremely sophisticated weaponry and explosives. Their repeated acts of violence in Sri Lanka as well as Southern India, in Tamil Nadu, made them extremely potent security hazards for the Indian dignitaries.

The LTTE had the most extensive international network among all the terrorist organisations operating at the international level. The LTTE possessed a highly evolved propaganda machinery abroad, notably in London and Paris; they were owning a fleet of commercial ships used for smuggling arms and contrabands from the international arms market to Sri Lanka; They had an extensive communications network worldwide and were actively engaged in getting their cadres trained to carry out terrorist acts in many countries. (This has been dealt with in detail in another chapter.)

In the Northeast, United Liberation Front of Assam (ULFA) emerged as a leading terrorist secessionist group with considerable expertise in handling arms and explosives. This group, despite periodic crackdowns, continued to pose a fairly high degree of threats.

During the entire decade of eighties, there were intelligence reports of a growing nexus between these terrorist organisations. The common theme of this nexus was the annihilation of their commonly perceived enemy — Shri Rajiv Gandhi. There is sufficient evidence in the form of intelligence reports, which have been discussed earlier in this chapter, to this effect.

Evidence placed before the Commission also indicates that certain outside powers were also behind stoking the flames of militancy in India, abetting the hostile terrorist elements in their plans to bring harm to the life of Shri Rajiv Gandhi. In the reports available, which have been referred to earlier in this chapter, there are clear indications of the hostile attitude of a section of Sri Lankan Government who was opposed to the Indo Sri Lankan Accord and the induction of IPKF. Similarly, information existed of hostile attitudes of a section of Pakistani Government and its security and intelligence agencies towards Shri Rajiv Gandhi. However, this issue pertains to the second part of the terms of reference of this Commission and has been dealt with in this chapter only as a passing reference with the limited objective of bringing out the threat perceptions to Shri Rajiv Gandhi.

These prevailing conditions of the time made Shri Rajiv Gandhi the most threatened Indian in recent times. The level of threats to him was unprecedented and ever increasing.

There is overwhelming evidence to indicate that threats to the life of Shri Rajiv Gandhi increased after he ceased to be the Prime Minister. Threats to him were unparalleled irrespective of the fact whether he was the Prime Minister. Indications were clear that forces inimical to him were looking for the slightest opportunity to strike. Even after he ceased to be the Prime Minister in 1989, threats to him were perceived to be higher than those of the incumbent Prime Minister, Shri VP Singh.

Exh. 267 – A comparative threat assessment report prepared by the R&AW on perceived threats to the incumbent Prime Minister, Shri VP Singh and the former Prime Minister, Shri Rajiv Gandhi – is a confirmation of the extremely high level of threat faced by Shri Rajiv Gandhi.

While assessing the threat to the Prime Minister Shri VP Singh, this report stated that there did not exist any information regarding any specific threats from any of the extremist elements abroad, whether from the Sikh extremist organisations or from the JKLF or from any other organisation of Kashmiri expatriates from POK or from Nepali groups or from any of the Tamil or Sinhalese extremists groups of Sri Lanka or from the Anand Marg against Shri VP Singh.

On the other hand, speaking of the threat to Shri Rajiv Gandhi, the report is categorical that threat to Shri Rajiv Gandhi from the Sikh extremist organisations was continuing to be very high despite his leaving office. The reasons for this were assessed to be the continuing threats from those Sikh extremist elements abroad who had vowed, after Operation Blue Star, to avenge the operation by having Mrs. Indira Gandhi as well as her entire family physically eliminated. The Sikhs also held Rajiv Gandhi responsible for the anti-Sikh riots after the assassination of Mrs. Gandhi and also for the hanging of Satwant Singh and Kehar Singh. The R&AW assessment also pointed out that there was a growing nexus between the Sikh extremist organisations abroad and the JKLF and other organisations of Kashmiri expatriates from the POK as well as the LTTE. All these organisations shared a common anger against Shri Rajiv Gandhi.

The most compelling indication of the under-estimation of the threat potential to Shri Rajiv Gandhi by the Intelligence Agencies appears to be their threat perception assessment vis-s-vis the LTTE. By all standards, the LTTE had emerged by then as the most formidable terrorist group in the subcontinent. A terrorist outfit that could fight a sustained full-fledged war with the Indian Army for over two years and still survived cannot possibly be under-estimated. The implications of sensational assassinations carried out by the LTTE in Sri Lanka – notably those of Sri Sabaratnam of TELO in 1986 near Jaffna, A. Amirthalingam of TULF in 1989 and Ranjan Wijeratne, Defence Minister of Sri Lanka in March 1991 at Colombo – could not possibly have escaped the Agencies. The systematic manner in which the leaders of the rival militant groups such as Sri Sabaratnam of TELO in Kondavil in 1986, the capability of the LTTE to strike at will in India was confirmed after the brutal assassination of K. Padmanabha of EPRLF and 15 others in Madras on June 19, 1990. The cyanide cult of the LTTE and the readiness with which its handpicked cadres, called the 'Black Tigers', embarked on suicide missions should have been reasons enough to have been extremely wary of the LTTE. In India, the rabid anti-

Rajiv Gandhi sentiments of the LTTE were well known. It is indeed appalling that this incriminating information was so grossly under-estimated by the Intelligence and Security Agencies and by Central Governments.

The tenets of the security considerations have been comprehensively propounded by the security experts in their evidence before the Commission. One of the quoted security tenet has been that no security system is foolproof; the threatened person becomes particularly vulnerable to an attempt by a determined killer. The remedy to this should be to create as many barriers as possible between the assassin and the target in order to deter a determined attempt. In three instances, we have seen that the determined potential killers of Shri Rajiv Gandhi could not execute their plans. Two of these attempts were made during election meetings of Shri Rajiv Gandhi in Shahdara and Faridabad in May 1991. Earlier, in July 1985, Harjinder Singh Jinda could not make an attempt on Shri Rajiv Gandhi outside Ram Manohar Lohia Hospital when Shri Rajiv Gandhi went there to see the dead body of the assassinated leader Lalit Maken due to the security around Shri Rajiv Gandhi. In the case of providing security to Shri Rajiv Gandhi, especially from such rabidly determined killers as the LTTE, the implementation of this tenet was conspicuous by its absence. This is a subject matter of security cover and has been dealt with in details in the succeeding chapter.

While conducting an inquiry into the sequence of events leading to the assassination pertaining to the security aspect, a very significant consideration, which requires to be emphasised is the fact that extremely grave threats to the life of Shri Rajiv Gandhi existed even before he became the Prime Minister of India; the level of these threats increased dramatically during the period he remained the Prime Minister and further accentuated after he ceased to remain Prime Minister. This fact alone made his security considerations stand on a singular footing - unparalleled so far and not comparable to any other high dignitary.

Brutal assassination of his mother, Smt. Indira Gandhi, by her own security guards, underscored the need to immediately devise foolproof methods to ensure effective security for Rajiv Gandhi. This thinking finally led to the creation of SPG in 1985, which was conferred a legal status as an armed force of the Union in 1988. The creation of SPG was recognition of the fact that under existing threat scenario from LTTE, there was an essential requirement for creation of a highly trained, compact and special force to provide proximate security to the VVIP.

SPG is the best proximate security system available in the country. The training, motivation and physical fitness of SPG personnel are superior to those in any alternative security system. The techniques of proximate security and technology deployed by the SPG are highly specialised and exclusively geared to ensure the best possible proximate security liaison and composite functioning of close Protection Detail. The SPG also has an edge over other proximate security systems as far as legal protection and the power to overrule in security matters are concerned. All these features make SPG a formidable and exclusive Proximate Security System.

It was possible to have provided SPG protection to Shri Rajiv Gandhi after he ceased to be Prime Minister by amending the SPG Act, which could have been easily achieved, operational constraints of SPG having to simultaneously providing protection to the incumbent Prime Minister as well as the former Prime Minister could have been overcome at that time in the manner in which they were overcome in 1991 when SPG Act was amended and its protection was extended to several former Prime Ministers and their families at short notice.

It cannot be outrightly said that the SPG was not in a position to meet the requirements of the security of the Prime Minister and the ex-Prime Ministers simultaneously as is evident from the opinion of Director, SPG in which he stated that in case SPG is ordered to continue to provide security, necessary arrangements would be taken care of.

It appears that the extension of SPG Act or continuation of SPG protection to Shri Rajiv Gandhi was not in contemplation from the very beginning.

What weighed at all levels is that under the law, SPG is meant for the Prime Minister alone and cannot be provided to ex-Prime Ministers; SPG was facing operational difficulties on account of paucity of manpower. It was decided that the security of Shri Rajiv Gandhi should be handed over to the states and Union Territories without regard to the fact that he continued to face the highest threat, which no other dignitary was facing, and without regard to the threat, which may be there at a given time, place and situation. The question of Rajiv Gandhi's security was not at all considered in its true and correct perspective.

At all the three levels i.e. security agencies, bureaucrats and the cabinet, it was not thought whether Rajiv Gandhi would remain secure in the hands of the states/ UTs concerned without a specialised body for proximate security. Vital factors were totally overlooked, especially the grave nature of LTTE threats to Rajiv Gandhi. As ex-Prime Minister had become an easy and soft target, more vulnerable to attacks from such determined and deadly elements.

The possibility of raising another specialised force, which could be called by any other such name, was examined. As central protection force or special protection force was not examined though it was suggested by some bureaucrats who thought of putting together a 'Nucleus Force' or special force, etc. Director, SPG Shyamal Datta has deposed that such a force could be created comparable to SPG under MHA circular dated 14.05.1985. But no importance was attached to this aspect. The VP Singh Government turned a deaf ear to the protests made subsequently after cessation of SPG cover on 09.02.1990. Amendment was suggested but was not given due consideration. Some such system should have been devised whereby the Centre could have provided adequate and effective security comparable to SPG with exclusive responsibility for proximate security to Shri Rajiv Gandhi exercising full control over the same and not leaving it to the States.

The Intelligence Bureau, which was responsible for devising an effective and adequate security scheme for Shri

Rajiv Gandhi after he demitted office of the Prime Minister, followed a flawed perception that threat to Shri Rajiv Gandhi had automatically decreased after he ceased to be the Prime Minister, which was contradicted by their own threat perception reports. The fallacious threat perception was contrary to, and inconsistent with, the inputs received by the IB; in the report of IB, the LTTE had been placed in the category of unspecified quarters; such a calibration of inputs was nothing short of misrepresentation on the part of IB, which may have resulted into misleading of the consideration of question of the security to be provided to Shri Rajiv Gandhi.

It was known that militancy and terrorism have been adopting latest devices. LTTE is known to be the deadliest organisation with cyanide culture and suicide squads. No one faced any threat including the Prime Minister or the President from such a deadliest organisation. Thus, Rajiv Gandhi was the most highly threatened person in the country and became more insecure after demitting office in comparison to even the incumbent Prime Minister and the President. The sources of his threats were many and deadliest. If the alternative security scheme provided to Shri Rajiv Gandhi was thought adequate for such a highly threatened person, then why in 1985, SPG was at all created. There was no need of SPG. Such a security scheme could have been devised even at that time. But the Government thought that Shri Rajiv Gandhi would not be safe if left to the States. So a central force was created for his protection.

It also appears that no study of the actual operation of the alternative security scheme was ever made. It did not go into consideration that LTTE had already spread its network. The Tamil population and the State Government of Tamil Nadu were sympathetic to them, which was reflected in the entire State Administration including the police machinery. In June, 1990, Padmanabha had been assassinated in Madras by the LTTE and the killers had made good their escape from Tamil Nadu coast to Jaffna.

It also did not go into consideration that during the election days particularly, the visits of Shri Rajiv Gandhi would be more frequent and even in interior areas and countryside. Hectic tours would be undertaken and several public meetings would be held in a day. Would such a specialised proximate security system be available to him at all the places on the same day? This did not go into consideration.

The IB authorities have stated that the charter of IB does not extend to oversee, control or supervise the implementation of the scheme. IB has no authority or jurisdiction over security in operation anywhere. But such reports can be called or field units can send such reports, which may require rethinking on the security system. If Blue Book is not implemented by the states for the Prime Minister in the absence of SPG, would it not be in the charter or domain of the IB to propose for setting up any Central Force for the security of the Prime Minister.

What stands out clearly from the above sequence is that there appears to be a continuous, deliberate under-estimation by the IB of the threat perception assessment to the security of Shri Rajiv Gandhi, which implies that the IB deliberately misrepresented the facts pertaining to the threat perceptions relating to his security on the basis of which decisions were to be taken, regarding the nature of security to be provided to him. No study was conducted at any of the three levels, i.e. Intelligence and security agencies and bureaucrats and the political executive to ensure a system of inbuilt, systemic implementation in the scheme.

Incontrovertible evidence of possession of sophisticated weapons and explosives by various militants of Sri Lankan Tamil Groups based in Tamil Nadu has come to the notice of the Commission by way of a detailed list of weaponry, ammunition and explosives seized in a statewide operation code named "Operation Tiger" carried out by Tamil Nadu Police on 8th November 1986. The LTTE cadres, led by Sivarasan, one of the key accused in the case relating to the assassination of Shri Rajiv Gandhi, went about their job undeterred and managed to carry out the assassination of Shri Rajiv Gandhi.

– 22 –

The Vaulting Ambition of a Few Politicians Results in Dastardly Assassination of Shri Rajiv Gandhi

George Bernard had said, "Politics is nothing but a man sitting on a heap of dirt and his rival standing beneath the heap and dragging so that he can ascent the same heap and be dragged."

This applies complete to the Indian political scene. V.P. Singh dragged Rajiv Gandhi off the heap and sat there. Before that he was Defence Minister in the cabinet of Rajiv Gandhi. When the Government of India signed a deal with Bofors of Sweden, he started crying wolf. He could gather sufficient wind to drag the gullible public of India with him, thus dragging Rajiv Gandhi off the heap. Nobody asked him what he was doing when the deal was signed. He brought Bofors scandal to the Indian polity and spread so much virulence in the short period when he was on that throne, that its viciousness is haunting the country even now and may linger on, to surface now and then, again viciating the polity in one way or the other.

There are countless other characters which, though projecting themselves as the messiah of the people, did untold harm to the country. They are countless: Giani Zail Singh, Darbara Singh including, the then Chief Minister of Haryana, their chief secretaries and their cronies, who succumbed to the power they had suddenly acquired in the strife-ridden State.

All of them created their own chessboards and played their own chess games, unmindful of the harm they were bringing to the social fabric of the State — the State, which year after year, for two millennia, had absorbed onslaughts from all types of marauders, but never rended from within and had stayed in tact. As for their police chiefs and their CID chiefs, all of them were honest, upright officers, not having any personal agenda of their own. Still, no one can go against the wishes of a chief minister. I could not. I decided: enough was enough. I volunteered and got a transfer. The rot lingered on.

Another character who played his part to the hilt was Giani Zail Singh. Perhaps Pandit Nehru had erred in judging his man when he picked him to lead a revolt against Maharaja of Faridkot. Indira Gandhi selected him to go to the Assembly, made him the Chief Minister of Punjab, Home Minister of India, and President of India. Even then he didn't stop interfering in Punjab politics, which ultimately led to her assassination. After making Rajiv Gandhi the Prime Minister, he started ridiculing him. His quip, 'Pappu khilono se khel raha hai' again stuck in the minds. This coupled with Bofors Scandal led to Rajiv's downfall.

He could have lived. The innate dislike VP Singh had developed for him led to withdrawing Rajiv's security cover, which was not wise considering the threat perception and earlier attacks on him at Raj Ghat and in Sri Lanka.

The rest is history. Down the ages, no dirt heap has been found to be stable. It is always slippery.

– 23 –

Pakistan's Audacity and India's Pusillanimity

Pakistan's complicity, aid and active abetment to Punjab terrorists were suspected since early 1983. However, no intelligence agency in India had come across concrete evidence. In early 1984, Border Security Force got irrefutable information that Pakistan was using Rangers (Pakistani counterpart of Indian Border Security Force) to supply arms to the Punjab terrorists. Unfortunately the Agency, which is responsible for collecting intelligence abroad, would not confirm. Nonetheless, the Government of India was convinced of the authenticity of BSF reports and the Pakistani High Commissioner in India was confronted with evidence. However, Pakistan went on brazening with lies denying her involvement in Punjab imbroglio.

Soon after the Operation Blue Star and Operation Rosewood in June-July 1984, the Sikh youth under religious frenzy and oppression let loose in the villages, started crossing over into Pakistan for refuge and training to avenge what they perceived as humiliation caused to Sikh pride. BSF again was the first to receive information on crossings and establishment of training camps within Punjab (Pakistan) after these military operations. Again, the same agency tried to raise hackles on the issue. Nevertheless, the Government of India was convinced that there were as many as 35 camps, where Sikh youth were being fed on imaginary tales of Government's barbarous treatment meted out to Sikhs by Indian security forces. Blatant lies were told and, after such brain-washing, they were imparted training in the use of firearms, laying of booby traps, use of mines, ambush of patrols and creating caches of arms.

Pakistan came into existence because of communal violence that Muslim League under the leadership of Mohd. Ali Jinnah had unleashed. The Direct Action ordered by M.A. Jinnah on 16th July, 1946, had turned Calcutta into a charnel and the putrid corpses had convinced the tired Congress leadership, that they had no adequate answer to the gene of frenzied violence, which Muslim League could conjure up by one such call.

Thus, when Pakistan came into existence on 14th August, 1947, Pakistani leadership was still imbued with the belief that the Congress rulers of India could be frightened into submission through their successfully tried techniques of unleashing barbarous violence. Hence, the invasion of Kashmir in the last week of October, 1947. That was a miscalculation on the part of Pakistan. Now the Congress Government, instead of flacid Congress Sewa Dal, had the Indian army at their disposal, and they ordered the army to resist this aggression. Ever since the Kashmir misadventure, Pakistan rulers had come to realise that they had to fine-tune their intimidatory tactics against India.

This is not the place to unfold the entire tale of Pakistani intelligence agencies' plans to destabilise India through covert operations. However, unless we examine their evolution and their experimenting with innovative tactics, we cannot understand their murderous role in Punjab for the last one decade. In this decade of torment in Punjab, the Pakistani Inter Services Intelligence (ISI) has played a crucial role. How did it succeed? Here are the pertinent facts.

The ISI came into existence in 1948, that is, soon after the formation of Pakistan itself. In its infancy, ISI was to be headed by an officer of the rank of Brigadier only. It became an important organ of the Pak Army under Field Marshal Ayub Khan. Although this outfit has officers from Pak Air Force and Pak Navy and some elements of Paramilitary forces and police, yet it has always been headed by Army Brigadiers and Generals. During 1965 Indo-Pak War, ISI was headed by

Brig. Riazat Hussain, who explained ISI failures in its missions by alleging that President Ayub had turned ISI into a political outfit. When General Yahya Khan came to power in 1969, ISI was placed under Lt. General Ghulam Ilahi and, when Z.A. Bhutto became President of his country in Dec. 1971, he found ISI a convenient tool for his political manoeuvering. In his book *If I am Assassinated,* Bhutto mentioned that this arbitrary intelligence organisation had not only ably assisted him in re-organising intelligence services, but also in the political and bureaucratic revamp at the federal level.

When Soviet troops intervened in Afghanistan in December, 1979, ISI, headed by the Lt General Jilani got its chance of life to bare its fangs. ISI came to forge alliance of disparate groups and co-ordinated the politico-military factions on behalf of Afghan guerrillas. Salig Harrison of the Carnegie Endowment said in an article published in the *Washington Post* in Feb. 1989 that President Zia had converted the ISI into a Pakistani style blend of the CIA, the Federal Bureau of Investigation (FBI) and the Iranian SAVAK. In addition to collecting foreign intelligence, he systematically built up a vast ubiquitous apparatus inside the country for serving as a powerful weapon against his political opponents".

The expansion of ISI organisation and its objectives took place under Lt. Gen. Hamid Gul, who headed the organisation from March 1987 to May 1989. Under Lt. Gen. Hamid Gul, ISI formed a close nexus with CIA (US) in their common task of arming Afghan insurgents and sharing of intelligence. It was ISI's clout with CIA that made ISI to lay down major parameters of Afghan policy. When Benazir Bhutto rode to power after general elections in November 1988, after the death of Gen. Zia-ul-Haq in an air crash on 17th August 1988, she found ISI "not only implementing the policy but making it". Under US pressure, Pakistan continued to pursue forward its policy in Afghanistan and ISI became the main Pakistani instrument in the arena of international power games. ISI is known to be the US tool for influencing Pakistani power structure. Under Lt. Gen. Hamid Gul and Maj. Gen. Asad Durrani (Aug 1990 to March 1992). ISI came to be identified with Islamic Jehad in Afghanistan and Kashmir. While ISI had been putting its weight in Afghanistan and Kashmir, it had already started taking an aggressive interest in Punjab affairs since mid-1983 and started training Sikh militants soon after the Operation Blue Star in June 1984 and has not stopped providing training and operational guidance to Punjab militants ever since.

Defying pressures from its patron, USA, Pakistan has been still maintaining training camps at the following places:

OPPOSITE PUNJAB

Three camps still operating were, (i) Husan Abdul near Punja Sahib (ii) Faizal town Lahore and (iii) in a cloth mill in Faizlabad.

OPPOSITE RAJASTHAN

Training camps flourished at proper Hyderabad and Thana Bulla Khan (Hyderabad).

All the major leaders of Sikh militants had their hideouts secure shelters in Pakistan; Gurbachan Singh Manochahal, head of Bhindranwale Tiger Force of Khalistan, Wassan Singh Zaffarwal of the Khalistan Commando Force (KCF), and Sukhdev Singh Dassowal, head of Babbar Khalsa International, all operated from Pakistan. The "Panthic Committee" of Dr. Sohan Singh not only provided targets to terrorists but also came to control social life in Punjab. It also "ordered" how and in "Gurumukhi alone", Punjab should carry out its administration.

It was ISI, which guided the formation of Panthic Committee and Sarbat Khalsa at Amritsar on January 26, 1986, when Surjeet Singh Barnala government was in saddle. The terrorist outfits of this Panthic Committee of Baba Gurbachan Singh Manochahal - Bhindranwale Tigers Force of Khalistan (BTFK), Khalistan Commando Force (KLF) of Gurjant Singh Rajasthani, Dashmesh Regiment of Khalistan and Manjeet Singh, All India Sikh Students Federation – all functioned from Pakistani soil and received guidance from Pak intelligence agents. When Dr. Sohan Singh, who had retired from the post of Director of Health Services, Punjab, in 1974, saw that Baba Manochahal had started hobnobbing with a certain Minister of Government of India, he himself migrated to Pakistan, was warmly received and advised by ISI. The militant outfits owing allegiance to his Panthic Committee, that is, Babbar Khalsa (Bhai Sukhdev Singh Babbar), KCF (Paramjit Singh Panvad), Khalistan Liberation Force (Gurjant Singh Budhsingwala), AISSF (Daljit Bittu), BTFK (Bhai Sangha), ISYF (Tarsem Singh) Babbar Akali Dal (K.S. Narang), all operated from Pakistan, killing thousands of Sikhs and Hindus. The Panthic Committee headed by Wassan Singh Zaffarwal, with its constituents KCF (Zaffarwal), Dal Khalsa, AISSF (Butter Kahlon) as well as AISSF (Mehta Chawla) and International Sikh Youth Federation (Lakhbir Singh), all operated from Pakistan and escaped to it after committing depredations in north India. The fact is that in 1991 it was Islamabad, which was ruling Punjab (India) and Chandigarh, ordering Indian print media what to publish and what not to publish, what broadcasts to be made from All India Radio Jallandhar and Chandigarh and what not, which programmes, Doordarshan would present from Jallandhar and stop showing which programmes, that nameplates would be only in a particular script, that what trades would be permitted and what trades prohibited. The writ of New Delhi had ceased to run in Punjab and adjoining areas. It was Islamabad, which was ruling these areas through it surrogates, i.e. the Panthic Committee. When Indian writ was confined to paramilitary forces, police and Armed forces in Punjab, what was New Delhi doing ? It opened talks with militants. What a brave response! It called the sabre-rattling, firebreathing leaders of militants for talks with the Prime Minister who was going by the advice of the intelligence agencies. He went to the negotiating table from a position of weakness because he heeded the advice of so-called counter terrorism experts of the intelligence agencies, who had advised him that he would usher in an era of peace and tranquility in Punjab if he gave in to the whims and caprices of the so-called leaders of militants.

The most damning indictment of Pakistani patronage of terrorism in Punjab is to be found to the revelations of Dr. Sohan Singh and Dr. Jagjit Singh Chauhan.

After his arrest at Mohali on 4th November, 1993, Dr. Sohan Singh told the police that he had first visited Pakistan from February 1990 to April 1991 when he had met Hekmatyar of Afghanistan and planned to instal a Radio Station to be used jointly by the Punjab and Kashmir militants for anti-India propaganda. He again visited Pakistan in March 1993. He admitted that all militant outfits under the umbrella of his Panthic Committee, that is, the Babbar Khalsa International (BKI), the Khalistan Liberation Force (KLF), the Sikh Students Federation (Daljit Bittu Faction) the Bhindranwale Tiger Force of Khalistan (S. Rachpal Singh) and the Khalistan Commando Force (Paramsingh Panjwal) operated from Pakistan, killing Dr. Rajinder Kaur, daughter of Akali leader Master Tara Singh, the Chairman of Bhakra Beas Management Board, Major General Kumar, the Chief Engineer of Sutlej Yamuna Link (SYL) Canal, Akali Leader Mr. Balwant Singh who had been Finance Minister in Surjeet Singh Barnala Ministry and partially successful attempts at murdering Jagdev Singh Talwandi, Gurcharan Singh Tohra, the Youth Congress leader Mr. Maninderjit Singh Bitta. Bus passengers'massacres, as well as the massacres of migrant labourers, were designed to drive the minority community out of Punjab.

Dr. Jagjit Singh Chauhan told Shekhar Gupta and Nirupam Subramaniam of *India Today* (November, 1993, pages 65-67) that he was disillusioned with Pakistani assistance. According to him, it was Z.A. Bhutto who had met Dr. Chauhan in New York in 1972 or 73 and asked him to start Khalistan movement. He also declared, "Several leaders of Sikhs are still there (Pakistan) and all they (Pakistan) have given Sikhs is less than gobar (rubbish)".

Pakistan Rangers, who guard Pakistan border, actively helped Sikh terrorists infiltrate, exporting terrorism to Punjab from 1987 to 1993. There were 148 incidents of firing into the Indian territory by the Rangers to facilitate the infiltration of ISI trained terrorists.

The author had suggested to the then Prime Minister that Pakistan understands only one language, that is, tit for tat. Pakistan must be made to realise, I told the Prime Minister, that it cannot break India through this proxy war and we should activate Punjab border by an aggressive posture. The Prime Minister was awestruck at my suggestion. According to him, Pakistan being a nuclear power could not be taken on by India. Mind it: I had not suggested war but only an aggressive posture.

In August 1965, when Pak agents infiltrated Kashmir under the code named 'Operation Gibralter', India had to cross international border in Punjab posing a threat to Lahore. In 1971, when PAF raided the Indian Air Force bases on the evening of 3rd December, India had to launch a full scale attack in the East as well as in the West. Pakistan believes in using covert force, which can be deterred by a show of overwhelming force by India to make Pakistan realise that it cannot capture Punjab by arming and training Punjab terrorists.

Let me state that in 1949, Pandit Jawaharlal Nehru had made the offer of a No War Pact with Pakistan, that offer was spurned by Liaqat Ali Khan. When tension developed, pacifist Nehru had moved the entire Indian army to Punjab border. The alarming situation as monitored by the USA is recorded in the US *Foreign Affairs* papers, Vol V, *195Q* Page 1407, as follows:

"In reply to my inquiry (The Ambassador Loy Henderson), Bajpai said opening conversations Liaqat had referred to Indian troop concentration at Ambala. Today, just before his departure, Liaqat had again raised this question. Nehru told him it was impossible to make any changes in troop disposition just now." Earlier the U.S. Charge d'Affairs in Pakistan (Wolf) had informed the Secretary of State on March 23, 1950 at 3 P.M.:

"GoP" (Government of Pakistan) regret here to inform Government U.S. of following troop movements which have recently taken place in India towards frontier West Pakistan. Forward movement is continuing:

1. Move of one inf div to area Hissar-Rajasthan
2. Move of one armed brigade to area Ferozepore-Nabha
3. Move of one armoured division to area Meerut
4. Formation of a Corps at Ambala"

Thus the pacifist Nehru had shown a greater understanding of Pakistan psychology than his illustrious successors.

In his book the *Knights of Falsehood* published in 1997, Shri K.P.S. Gill, the former Director General of Police Punjab, under whose inspiring leadership the Punjab Police had achieved a clear victory against terrorism in Punjab, observes as follows (Page 17): "The Inter Services Intelligence (ISI), Pakistan primary agency for covert operations, even today runs a number of terrorist training camps for Sikh militants, including those in Bahawalpur, Sialkot and Lahore; The surviving *sepais* of most of the major terrorist groups of Punjab, including the Babbar Khalsa, The Bhindranwale Tiger Force Khalistan (BTFK), the International Sikh Youth Federation (ISYF), factions of the Khalistan Commando Force (KCF) and the Dal Khalsa, have found sanctuary in these camps." What is the response of India to the low intensity war unleashed by the ISI, and its work is even beyond the review of the elected Government of Pakistan. Thus ISI thumbs its nose against the Pakistani Government. General audacity of ISI and its interference in the political life of Pakistan is palatably clear from the statement of Mirza Aslam Beg, the retired Chief of Army Staff of Pakistan carried by *The Hindustan Times* of 23rd November 1997, where Aslam Beg says that the political cell of ISI, which had distributed Rs. 140 million among political parties, needs to be dandier. Thus, ISI is a government within a government in Pakistan and thumbs both Pakistan and India.

– 24 –

Punjab Terrorism Fails

As against 2591 civilians killed in 1991 and 1519 killed in the year 1992, the number of civilians killed till October 1993 was 45. These statistics eloquently reveal a story of unqualified success against terrorism, which had held Punjab in shackles.

Before we narrate as to how this success was achieved, it will be necessary to understand the nature of terrorism itself.

Bomb explosions in crowded places of work and entertainment in Punjab and Delhi, shoot-outs and assassinations, kidnapping for ransom, abductions and keeping hostages as swaps for release of co-terrorists, hijacking of passenger aircraft and buses may give one the impression that these fiendish acts of barbarism against innocent unarmed civilians are of recent origin only. This is not so. Terrorism is as old as humanity itself.

Terrorism in the form of assassinations has existed over centuries. There have been nearly 65 historic assassinations beginning with that of Philip II, king of Macedonia, in 336 B.C. and Julius Caesar in 44 B.C. Four elected Presidents of the United States have fallen to the bullets of their assassins. India saw assassination of Mahatma Gandhi on January 30, 1948, of Prime Minister Indira Gandhi on October 31, 1984, and the former Prime Minister Rajiv Gandhi on May 21, 1991, in pursuance to conspiracies hatched by religious and other fanatics. In our neighbourhood, Mr. Liaqat Ali, the then Prime Minister of Pakistan, was gunned down by some fanatics at Rawalpindi on October 16, 1951, Sri Lankan Premier S.W.R.D.

Bhandarnaike on September 25, 1959. 1993 saw the assassination of the Ceylonese President Premdasa in busy Colombo itself.

There has been enormous difficulty in defining terrorism because sometime a revolutionary struggle may as well be sought to be snuffed out by branding it as a terrorist movement. U.N. and various governments have spent time and energy to provide a faultless all-comprehensive definition of terrorism, so that activism to secure redress of legitimate grievances and popular upsurge against dictatorship and oppression are not ostracised as terrorism. The British Government in the Prevention of Terrorism Act of 1974 which was promulgated to combat the IRA, defines terrorism "as the use of violence for political ends and includes the violence for the purpose of putting the public or any section of the community in fear."

Generation of fear and dramatising grievances, real or imaginary, have been the motivating force of various forms of terrorism. By manipulating fear, terrorists seek to modify political behaviour in a fashion disproportionate to their numbers.

The U.S. State Department defines Terrorism as follows: "The threat or use of violence for political purpose by individuals or groups, whether acting for or in opposition to established government authority when such actions are intended to shock, stun or intimidate a target group wider than the immediate victims. Terrorism has involved groups seeking to overthrow specific regimes to rectify perceived national or group grievances or to undermine international order as an end in itself."

The above quoted definition does not take into account genuine struggle against a Junta which comes to usurp power. It confers legitimacy on dictatorships self-perpetuating themselves through state terrorism rather than founded themselves on the will of the people. It has to be remembered that sometimes a terrorist group has at its heart a core of legitimacy: For instance, IRA claims to represent the Catholics in Northern Ireland who have suffered centuries of discrimination at the hands of Protestants. Red Brigade claims to seek redress for the oppressed working classes in Milan, Naples and other industrial centres of Italy.

Recognising that every instance of insurgency cannot be an act of terrorism, the U.N. General Assembly has exempted those activities that arise from "the inalienable right to self-determination and independence of all peoples under colonial and racist regimes and other forms of alien domination, etc." from the definition of terrorism. This exemption, from the 1973 General Assembly Report of Ad-Hoc Committee on International Terrorism, is now incorporated as Article 7 of the General Assembly's 1974 Definition of Aggression. International law has also approved certain forms of insurgency.

However, it should be emphasised that the legitimacy of a certain cause does not legitimise the use of certain forms of violence. The ends can never justify the wrong means. That is why on December 9, 1985, the U.N. General Assembly unanimously adopted a resolution condemning all the acts of terrorism as "criminal". Never before had the Assembly adopted such a comprehensive resolution on this issue.

The spurt in terrorist activities has come during our times chiefly because of Palestinian struggle against Israel. Terrorism is the weapon of the weak against the more powerful. Also because fundamentalist regimes in Iran, Libya and Pakistan run a chain of training camps for the terrorists and these governments lends support to the terrorists. Iran is the principal supporter of the Islamic Shiaite's Amal Militia and Libya has contributed vast sums of money and massive quantities of arms to terrorists everywhere. The cult of terrorism embraces mercenaries and drug pedllars, smugglers, soldiers of fortune and ideologues as well. That is why terrorism has never succeeded anywhere in the world as the idealist, the patriot, ultimately comes to lean on the criminal. It has been happening all over the world. Thus, Palestinians also came to lean on criminals of various hues. Their organisations like PLO (Abu Nidal) masterminded December 1983 shoot-outs at EI AI ticket counters in Rome and Vienna and hijacking of Pan Am jet in Karachi; the most dangerous of them all being PLFP, the Popular Front for the Liberation of Palestine which, on Sunday, September 6, 1970 hijacked four aircrafts, one each in West Germany and Switzerland and two in Netherlands. This Sunday is known as Skyjack Sunday in terrorist folklore. These hijackings also showed that terrorism is not the monopoly of males only because AI EI Boeing enroute from Tel Aviv to New York was hijacked by Leila Khaled, a young Palestinian with a successful hijacking behind her and Patrick Arguello, a Nicaraguan leftist. Arguello was killed by the security guards travelling incognito and Khaleda was overpowered. WTA Flight 741 hijacked in West Germany and Swissair DC 8 were ordered to Dawson's Field, an old British airfield outside Amman, the capital of Jordan. Explosives were placed in positions around the aircraft. Then the PFLP demanded the release of prisoners held in West Germany, Switzerland, Britain and Israel. The third aircraft to be hijacked to Amman was BOAC flight 775 from Bombay to London. Though 375 hostages were released in return for release of all Palestinian prisoners by all the governments except Israel, yet three aircraft were blown on 15 Sept. 1970. The Dawson's Field episode served notice on the world that International terrorism had arrived. Punjab extremists were to try similar hijackings in 1980's.

Abu Nidal came to be known as "Mr. Terrorism", first for Syria and later for Mr. Gadaffi. Abu Nidal and his 100 followers were also called "guns for hire".

A number of schools and terrorism advisory services have come up in various parts of USA, Canada and Europe to train terrorists for handsome fees. A team formed by Welsoa and Terpil were suppliers of men and arms to Gadaffi whereas Frank Camper's college took credit for training Sikh terrorists. The Iranian revolution in February, 1979, which overthrew the Shah, brought Ayatollah Khomeini to power, who blessed terrorism and gave religious sanction to kidnappings. It is no surprise that Sant Jarnail Singh Bhindranwale came to be known as Khomeini of Sikhs.

The Irish Republic Army comprises of no more than 300 men and women and yet in 1984 IRA was responsible for 414 terrorist acts: 187 weapons and 3.8 tones of explosives were recovered from them though their terrorist acts were the lowest since 1970. James Adams writes: "The IRA has become such an integral part of Catholic life that it will never be eliminated. There is no senior army officer, policemen or politicians who believe terrorism can be defeated. However, IRA will never achieve its goal... It seems an impossible situation; the violence may continue with both sides fighting a war neither expects to win".

The militants in Punjab have tried to pattern their activities on IRA, PFLP lines with similar results - religion being the motivating force in all these cases. There are periods of lull in all these movements. IRA was comparatively lying low till 1970. Thereafter, they assassinated Lord Mountbatten on 27 August, 1979, by exploding his fishing boat Shadow V and later attempting to assassinate Mrs. Margaret Thatcher, the Prime Minister and her Cabinet colleagues on October 12, 1984 by using explosives in the hotel where she was lodged.

Our world is a world under siege by the network of terrorists, which renders even the mightiest of countries look pathetically powerless. Americans in Iran were held hostage in 1979. 52 of them were released in exchange for the return of Iran's 50 tons of gold. These Americans had remained in captivity for 444 days. The commando operation by the much vaunted Delta force of U.S. had aborted.

Stephen Segaller has called terrorists 'Invisible Armies' because of their ability to melt into the common crowds.

Polish expert J.K. Zowdy says: "Terrorism can flourish in a culture that allows or promotes violence and the effectiveness of the organisation usually depends on the degree to which the cultural values and traditions of a people condition them to use violence". Didn't we find this happening in Punjab?

Generation of fear and imposing the will of the minority group upon the authorities and upon the guardians of state sovereignty remain the objective of most terrorists.

For their purpose they make use of surprise and mobilise weapon of fear. We saw all these elements brought into play by the militants in Punjab and now in Kashmir.

Terrorism is antithesis of democracy since it seeks to replace the will of people by fear and the cult of violence.

One lesson which India has yet to learn is that overwhelming use of force by the State plays into the hands of the terrorists and is always counter-productive. Hence, the alienating consequences in Punjab of Operation Blue Star and Operation Rosewood. Terrorism is no ephemeral phenomenon and countering terrorism is a long war, which requires patience, money and intelligence. Let us remember there is no quick and easy solution to the menace of terrorism. Impetuous leaders and impatient popular parties play into the very hands of terrorists when they seek instant results through application of massive force. Countering terrorism is a long drawn out struggle, which requires not only force but trained forces at that which never fall into the trap of using excessive force.

Terrorists have two objectives. Tactically the goal is publicity and recognition of the so-called grievances. They consider all publicity to be good, that is, bad publicity is better than none. Terrorists appear to succeed as no government can protect everything and everyone, everywhere and at anytime.

Before we close these general remarks on terrorism, it needs to be noted that sometimes terrorists are created by the governments themselves and then used as scapegoat.

Now we can detail the measures which have enabled Punjab and Delhi to have seen restoration of peace.

PUNJAB

For Punjab, nay, for India, terrorism was an entirely new challenge. Assassination and political murders had never been the order of the day in Punjab.

When fundamentalists started terrorist campaign against Nirankaris and soon after against Hindus and Police, the police force was caught unawares by the tactics adopted by modern terrorists.

The police had been trained for traditional police duties and functions. Gradually, the police started equipping themselves with lethal weapons to meet this threat. There were great obstacles in the matter of weaponry and equipment they held. The efficacy of weapons by police could be judged by the frequency of their firing practices and the results thereof. A police force cannot acquire sophisticated weapons only because the terrorists had such sophisticated weapons. The weaponry used by the police has to be approved by the Army. The Army does not approve sophisticated weapons for police. Thus, there was no adequate answer to the A.K. family of rifles that the terrorists had been using. The police was thus out-weaponed and out-trained by the terrorists. Police lost a number of lives including high ranking officers such DIGs, Superintendents of Police and other ranks. It was only when the Police had made sacrifices with their lives that the Army approved the issue of matching weapons to the police. Once these weapons came into the police, the police started making using good use of these in meeting terrorist challenges. Most decisive factor for police morale was the political situation. Who would be the political master in this catastrophic phase in their career and thereafter, they asked? Those who had served Akali Ministries had an ambivalent attitude towards discharging their duties in counter-terrorist operations. They always kept looking back over their shoulders. Akalis could always stage a comeback. Political negotiations with militants dampened their morale. Negotiations were on and off in the year 1989 to 1991 with the result that terrorism swayed this benighted land and the civilian casualties were the highest in those years. On January 23, 1993, Shri K.P.S. Gill, the Director General Police, Punjab said:

"Previously the Police were unable to launch an all-out assault against militants because of the possibility that these militants after negotiations might eventually become their political bosses".

Once the Congress Ministry came to power in Punjab as a result of General Elections of Feb, 1992 the police met the challenge of fundamentalist violence with singleminded devotion. The police had suffered enormously in that their dear ones had been murdered, kidnapped, and they themselves had been humiliated. Thus they had powerful motivation to deal a crushing blow to the various terrorist outfits. In this task they were assisted by the fact that their strength had been augmented. Punjab Police was roughly 32 thousand strong in 1981 and in 1993 its strength had crossed 65 thousand. Their transport had been augmented and most of their vehicles were bullet proofed. The Punjab Police budget rose from Rs. 30 crores in 1981 to Rs. 321 Crores 61 Lacs 35 thousands in 1994. They had raised four commando battalions equipped with automatic rifles and sophisticated weapons in 1992. Their mobility came to be all time high.

When Congress came to power in February, 1992 elections, the police force well armed, well trained, highly motivated and competently led seized the opportunity to decisively liquidate the menace of terrorism. The Chief Minister, Sardar Beant Singh, gave them a carte blanche to deal with terrorism. He extended unqualified support to the police in their war against Pakistan-aided insurgency. One of the decisive factors in this was the success in fencing 336 kilometers of border with Pakistan. At night, the Indo-Pak border in Punjab was well lit by electric lights. Though the Satluj Rangers from Pakistan side still tried to push terrorists in India by opening unprovoked fire on some BSF posts as a diversionary measure, they just could not succeed in view of the obstacle created by fencing the border.

Punjab Police had launched two meaningful schemes, which involved people's participation. Strict responsibility was laid by demarcating areas of responsibility in border districts of Gurdaspur, Majitha, Amritsar, Taran Taran and Ferozepore. Village defence committee members were trained in the use of firearms and equipped with suitable weapons. These committees succeeded because people, particularly Sikhs living in these areas, were by that time sick of the roaming terrorists.

In the post Blue Star era, the people had helped the marauding terrorists because of excesses of security forces, but in the post Operation Black Thunder years, they got fed up with the bands that had not only desecrated the holy Darbar Sahib but had started sexually molesting their womenfolk. The two weapons which have defeated terrorism in Punjab are Sardar Beant Singh's firm stand and terrorists' own misdeeds vis-a-vis womenfolk. The second one has come to be called sexual terrorism by the lumpenised terrorists to whom loot and lust were dearer than the Sikh tenets or the rights of the Sikh community (refer *India Today* Dec. 31, 1992) The leaders of the Panthic Committee wallowed in luxury provided by their Pakistani Masters and from the loot of the districts of the Indian side of Punjab. Their followers felt chagrined that the money they had looted or extorted from their abducted victims was being invested in lucrative trades and properties by their masters. The collapse of terrorism in Punjab was preceded by a colossal collapse of idealism and morality in terrorist ranks. The sexual orgies indulged in by the militants disgusted the Sikh peasantry, which started co-operating with police in eliminating the moronic Sikh youth being exploited by the Pakistan's ISI. That is why Pak ISI operation K-2 to link Punjab terrorists with those of J & K failed miserably. It just could not take off. The killing of Pak agents Intikhab Ahmed Zia and Habibullah dismayed Pak ISI. The killing of Talwinder Singh, the Chief of Canadian Akhand Kirtani Jatha and the father of transforming Punjab's luxuriant land into killing fields since Septtember 20, 1981 the day Sant Jarnail Singh Bhindranwale had offered himself for arrest, was killed in October 1992. It was a decisive blow to the Pak designs upon Punjab.

1992 saw an upturn in counter-terrorist measures. In 1991, Punjabis were a terrorised lot. This is what Shekhar Gupta and Prashant Panjiar had written in *India Today* (January 15, 1991):

"...In a most un-Punjabi like resignation the people have surrendered to the rule of the gun, there is no such thing as a government... if you are a school teacher you learn its new curriculum. No Jana Gana Mana. No Hindi. No skirts, trousers or frocks in your school... And if you work for AIR or Doordarshan, you stop broadcasting in Hindi ... In parts of rural Punjab, particularly along the border, the militants no longer run a parallel government. They run the government."

After the elections of February 1992, people rose with all their power, co-operated with police and freed their land from the brutal octopus of Pakistani inspired and manipulated terrorism.

In 1992, SGPC, which went along their merry game of patronising terrorism denied holidays to their employees on Independence Day (15th August) and Republic Day (26th January). But the tide had turned and they could not stem the wave of peace created by people themselves.

KLF chief, Gurjant Singh Budhsinghwala and Sukhdev Singh, chief of Babbar Khalsa International came to be eliminated though police had to pay a price. 50 police families had been targeted by the terrorists. The firmness in executing Harjinder Singh alias Jinda and Sukhdev Singh alias Sukha, killers of General A.S. Vaidya, on October 9, 1992 had a sobering effect on the fence-sitters. Calls for bandhs given by various Akalis failed to evoke any marked response.

Sardar Khushwant Singh, eminent writer and journalist toured Punjab in Oct. 1992 and wrote two features for *The Times of India*, New Delhi, in which he said "militants are now known more and more as dacoits, looters and goondas".

In reprisal to this feature by Sardar Khushwant Singh, terrorists gunned down 27 in Ludhiana on October 31, 1992. Such attacks had to be expected. Soon the acting chief of the Khalistan Commando Force (Zaffarwal), Gurdas Singh Mansoorwal was killed in an encounter in Ferozepore Distt. The chief of Khalistan Liberation Force (KLF) Nishan Singh Makhu was killed in an encounter on November 15, 1992.

In December 1992, large number of terrorists surrendered to police with their weapons. Prominent among them were Balwinder Singh Babbar, Deputy Chief of BTFK (Sungha) and Lukhwinder Singh Lakha of the Babbar group.

Some carping critics of Beant Singh government had repeatedly emphasised the fact that this Congress government had come to power on minority vote. But this very government organised elections to 93 Municipal Committees and Panchayats of 11,630 villages in Feb. 1993 where the voter turnout was 82.6 per cent. The fact that these elections went off peacefully proved that terrorism no more stalked the Punjab countryside.

Mand is a scrubby piece of land between Sutlej and Beas rivers before they join at Hari Ke Pattan in Taran Taran Distt. This mass of land has elephantine grass which had made it an ideal hiding place for criminals. From here it is easier to operate in Kapurthala, Amritsar and Taran Taran Districts. Militants had found haven of safe base for launching operation from this Mand area. Punjab Police assisted by paramilitary forces cleared this area several times. Each time the militants would escape and return as soon as the police had moved out of the area. Ultimately, one battalion of Border Security Force was permanently located on this inhospitable mand. This solved the problem forever because then the militants never thought of returning to this refuge. This curtailed their depredations in the surrounding districts.

Whenever Punjab Police mounted pressure on militants, they would escape to Rajasthan, Terai in U.P. and Delhi or Haryana. Their having a haven in Terai had surfaced as early as 1982 but Punjab Police reports were brushed aside by the Delhi bureaucrats and no action was taken.

DELHI

Here it is necessary to describe how militants were dealt with by Delhi Police. Whatever happens in Delhi always attracts international attention. We have already described in the chapter Darkness at Noon that how the militants had indulged in shoot-outs and bomb blasts in Delhi.

Terrorism in Delhi was a new problem for Delhi Police since it was raised, trained and armed only for traditional policing. Delhi Police, however, recognised this threat with alacrity and responded to this new menace with professional vigour and insight. It unearthed the gang of Sukhbir Khalsa in 1983 when this gang had caused bomb blasts in Trans Yamuna cinema houses and Palika Bazar and New Delhi Railway Station. In 1984, Delhi Police traced Gursewak alias Babla of Babla gang which had committed bank robberies and dacoities at jewellery shops.

In 1992, there were nine shoot-out cases in Delhi. Police nabbed all the culprits responsible for eight of them.

In an encounter Harbhajan Singh and Rajwinder Singh were shot dead by Greater Kailash Police (1992). Delhi Police also arrested Amrit Pal Singh and Balbir Singh in July 1992. Police was able to arrest Vijay Pal Singh alias Happy and two of his accomplices.

The most dramatic encounter took place on August 11 1992 in Paschim Vihar area. One militant Murta Singh alias Moortu alias Manjeet Singh Fauji and his lady accomplice lived as tenants in one of the DDA flats here. On receiving reports of goings in the flat, police came to inquire and knocked at the front door of the flat. The inmates answered by opening fire. So exchange of fire between the militants occupying the flat and the police who had to take positions in the adjoining buildings started. This exchange of fire continued. Clusters of curious spectators gathered at safe distances.

1993 saw the powerful blast at Indian Youth Congress office at Raisina Road in an attempt to kill Shri M.S. Bitta, President of Indian Youth Congress. Police succeeded in tracing this blast to Kuldeep alias Keepa and Gurcharan Singh alias Chama of KLF. When they were surrounded by police at Ghaziabad (U.P.), they committed suicide by eating cyanide capsules.

In fact, Delhi Police has been able to successfully tackle Khalistan Liberation Force (KLF), Bhindranwale Tiger Force Khalistan (BFTK) and Babbar Khalsa desperadoes who had sneaked into Delhi. The most sensational case was the abduction of Romanian diplomat Mr. Liviu Radu to secure a swap for the release of Harjinder Singh alias Jinda. This abduction was carried out by Dr. Sohan Singh from his sanctuary in Pakistan. The operation failed because Mr. Liviu Radu was released and Jinda was hanged.

In the fight against terrorism, paramilitary forces have also played notable role.

BORDER SECURITY FORCE

Since its induction into anti-terrorist operations in Punjab, Border Security force has accounted for six hundred armed desperadoes. The most important of these was an encounter with Sukha Sipahi alias General Labh Singh who had been responsible for hundreds of murders but had also planned to assassinate the then, Prime Minister Rajiv Gandhi on Republic Day of 1987. He had mastered the technique of causing explosions through remote control for purposes of his diabolic plan. I had conveyed all the details to the Intelligence Agency charged with the task of collecting intelligence for protection of VVIPs. Timely action thus, averted the national catastrophe. Sukha Sipahi was ultimately killed by Border Security Force patrol in 1988 near Dasua-Tanda on Jallandhar-Pathankot road.

Border Security Force has lost 58 of their brave men in Punjab. The arms recovery made by them included 268 AK47, 26AK74 and 18 AK56 rifles.

CENTRAL RESERVE POLICE FORCE (CRPF)

CRPF since its induction in Punjab had more than one thousand encounters. They were successful for accounting for 2542 terrorists and have recovered 5686 weapons. Of these are several hundred AK47 Rifles, Rocket Launchers, Light Machine Guns (LMGs). Since 1983 to 1990 CRPF had lost lives of 90 of their brave officers and men during clashes with various terrorist outfits. CRPF performance in Punjab has been excellent.

THE ARMY

The situation in Punjab would never have improved if army had not extended its expertise and aid to the civil authorities. Army ran a number of training courses for police and paramilitary forces for bomb disposal and dealing with land mines since Pakistan had not only made a generous provision of land mines to the Panthic Committee terrorists but had also imparted training in laying them effectively.

Army in Punjab undertook Rakshak I Operation from May 1990 to Nov. 1990. It created confidence in the rural people and they came to know that the terrorists really were criminals out to loot and commit rape. However, it was Rakshak II which endeared Security Forces to the people and they stopped sheltering the militants, and in fact turned them over to Security Forces.

– 25 –

Will the Guilty Please Stand up and Accept Responsibility

In Chapter 15 it has been shown that the paramilitary forces, the intelligence agencies and the army had failed to carry out clean operations against the terrorists. Indeed, the various organisations involved displayed rivalries and counter productive games of one-upmanship and had been guilty of certain derelictions of duties. The leaders of these organisations will certainly be called at the bar of history to bear their responsibilities.

However, in the interests of justice it is necessary to examine the policies, which led to the creation of the demand for Khalistan and the inadequacy of the system we have adopted to meet such demand and violent situations.

Historically the demand for Khalistan began soon after the, Indian Muslim League adopted resolution demanding a separate Sovereign State for Muslims of India in its Lahore Session in 1940. The same year some Sikhs held a conference at Attari in Amritsar District and gave the call for creation of Khalistan for Sikh Panth. It will, therefore, be clear that the call for Khalistan was several decades old. This call was, however, a meaningless slogan as Sikhs did not constitute a majority even in one district in the country whereas the Muslims, at that time, were in majority in North West Frontier, Punjab, Sindh, Bengal and Assam. Thus, the Sikh cry for parity with Muslims was not accepted either by Cripps Mission (1942) or the Cabinet Mission of later date.

However, Congress Party after accepting the Cabinet Mission proposals retracted and accepted the partition of India on the basis of religion in 1947. With the acceptance of religion as a norm for division, the Congress gave a new impetus to Sikh demand for a separate homeland within India as an autonomous state. When this demand for separate homeland was not conceded, the Sikhs thought that they were being discriminated against by the government (refer action by the Akali Party representatives not signing the Act of Indian Constitution in 1950 and the scholarly but fulminating speech of Dr. Kapoor Singh in the Parliament during the discussion on Punjab State Reorganisation Bill, 1966.)

The politically motivated section of Sikhs pressed for a Sikh homeland ignoring the stark geographical fact that Sikhs were not in majority in any viable geographical area till the fateful year 1966, when Punjab was divided and various areas were given to Haryana and Himachal Pradesh so that Sikhs could be in majority in the residual Punjab. Thus, the slogan of Khalistan was without merit but it continued to breed a secessionist mindset among the Sikhs. Now with the sacrifice of the Prime Minister, Mrs. Indira Gandhi, it has been made clear to the misguided members of this minority community that, come what it may be India will not allow another partition though such a demand may have the support of Pakistan.

It is unfortunate that the Congress having proclaimed from rooftops that on the attainment of freedom, India will be a federation of autonomous states, it adopted a highly centralised Constitution and denied to the states requisite measure of autonomy. This has left a bitter trail in the relations between the Union Government and the States. So long as Congress was in power both at New Delhi and the States, the state Chief Ministers carried out the dictates of New Delhi, but once the monolithic hegemony of Congress was no more there, the regional parties, ruling the States, started resisting and resenting the governance of their states either through legislation in spheres which they considered were, or ought to have been, their domain and imposition of President's Rule over these States through the instrumentality of their nominated governors. A polity working under such strains may carry on but the crucial question is how long and with what measure of effectiveness in the face of security problems?

Terrorism in Punjab having abated, we may study the basic issues that gave rise to the blood soaked chapter in Punjab history.

BASIC ISSUES

To any dispassionate student of Punjab crisis, it would be clear that basic issues are:

1. Sikh grievances arising out of their psyche for historical reasons.
2. Our system of working including working of our Constitution, use of Police, Army, and the decision making being the child finally of pure political opportunism.

It has been shown that Sikhs have always striven for a homeland even when they were in a hopeless minority on the eve of partition of the country. They are a proud people and anyone who tramples over their religious sentiments alienates them and can drive them into a state of insurgency. Prabhash Joshi wrote: "Rebellion against established political authority and fight against real or imaginary oppression are highly respected traits in the Sikh ethos and martyrdom has an irresistible appeal. Readiness to sacrifice everything for the Panth is at once their strength and weakness". P.K. Nijhawan wrote: "We should first agree on a basic fact that Sikhs have a built-in mechanism which makes them willing to offer supreme sacrifice when they perceive any injustice—religious, social or political — being done to their community".

Mr. Prem Bhatia writing about "Sikh psyche" said: "What is it that keeps the Sikh mind on the boil? Sometimes at the simmering level and occasionally at the level of eruption ... we have been far too long with vague, unlisted moans of discrimination, exploitation and injustice with the result that the fictitious or the essentially psychological factors have come to be mixed up with real injuries". He referred then that "the incurable area of the disease is mostly self-induced or imaginary". I have quoted above those who have studied the Punjab problem in depth to show that Sikh ethos cannot be separated from the substance of their grievances. Unless one knows Sikh psyche or ethos he will mishandle and allow a minor or imaginary grievance to become causa belli. It is because of this that Punjab since independence has always been a tinder-box of explosive mix of politics and religion. The manner in which one handles a Sikh grievance is as important, if not more, as the grievance itself. This was fully known to Pt. Jawaharlal Nehru who never agreed to the formation of Punjabi Suba but treated Master Tara Singh and Sikhs with a due sense of deference. He never hurt their pride while declining to concede their demand. But in the subsequent years though the substance of Sikhs demand for a Sikh majority area was conceded, yet the method of handiling their demands, which continued to multiply, was brusque and unceremonial. All minorities are paranoid: a minority complex haunts each minority. Unless it is handled with understanding and sympathy, it ingrains a sense of injustice in the minority which goes on nursing the same. Many Sikh grievances (charters of 45 and later 15) were self-induced and trivial, yet they were handled at Chandigarh and New Delhi in a cavalier fashion. The whole approach has been ad hoc. At one time assassins and conspirators are released and at other times disproportionate use of force wounding the feelings of self-respect of a proud community are undertaken by employing tanks and treating misled Punjabi youth as foes and condoning acts of wrong-doing by state forces. The decision-makers are either arrogantly indifferent to genuine grievances or succumb to imaginary threats.

According to Prof. Arnold Toynbee, "British statesmanship in the nineteenth century regarded India as "Sleeping Beauty". Dr. B.R. Ambedkar has said that this sleeping beauty is a mad maiden having a dual personality - half-human, half animal - always in convulsions because of her two natures being in perpetual conflict. Hence this peaceful land was in grip of extremism in Punjab shorn of all humanity.

The challenge thrown up in Punjab has to be met squarely and unambiguously.

Was it not proposed at one time to hand over the reigns of the government in Punjab to the faction which had called for holding plebiscite on the issue of Khalistan under UN auspices and location of Chinese Consulate at Amritsar? Was it not the height of infantilism and ignorance of ground realities by the government? Again the Chandshekhar government appeasing and applauding the militants condoned the massacres that had taken place.

ANANDPUR SAHIB RESOLUTION AND SARKARIA COMMISSION

Sarkaria Commission's examination of the issue of Centre State relation was totally perfunctory. The demand for a real federal structure cannot be considered seccessionist nor its corollary autonomous state an act of treason as made out by some Congress leaders. Actually this part of the Anandpur Sahib resolution should have been thrown open for a national debate. The concept of federalism as enshrined in the Constitution and as further diluted leaving states with little powers in a pluralist society needs a more earnest consideration. Centre cannot reduce States into vassals by encroaching on their powers bestowed by the Constitution. Our sub-continent encompasses a diversity of ethnic, religious and linguistic groups, palpably heterogeneous and an array of separate cultural entities, which must seek a more meaningful say in their political, economic and social dispensation.

Anandpur Sahib Resolution says:

"The political goal of the Panth, without doubt as enshrined in the commandments of the Tenth Guru in the pages of Sikh history and in the very heart of the Khalsa Panth, the ultimate object of which is the per-eminence of the Khalsa.

The fundamental policy of the Shiromani Akali Dal is to seek the realisation of the birth right of the Khalsa through creation of congenial environment and a political setup".

This goal is based on the Ardas Sikh congregations daily chant: "Raj Karega Khalsa Aki Rahe Na Koi Khabar Hoe sab bache saren jo hoe". It is the view of the fundamentalists and now successionists that this part of Ardas emanates from Guru Gobind Singh Ji. Other scholars maintain that it is a later interpolation. Sardar Kapoor Singh felt that these two lines are "Sri Mukh Wak". However, the practice of reciting this Dohera after the Ardas seems to be of later origin. Bhai Chet Singh, retired Head Granthi of Sri Darbar Sahib, Amritsar, states that this practice was launched during the movement to free the gurdwaras from the control of the Mahants during the British rule in the beginning of this century. According to him, this was the result of a Panthic decision and was gradually adopted by the Sikhs, which greatly helped in enthusing the Sikhs to join the battle against the Mahants. This dohera is a matter of controversy for its import as well. At one end are the people who say that the lines only indicate the rule of the pure and virtuous; on the other end are people like Sardar Kapoor Singh who interpreted this Dohera and even translated it literally as; "The Sikh people shall remain free and sovereign always, none challenging this position. And everyone must eventually accept this position. No matter how unpalatable and bitter it be to them and, behold, peace and safety lie in such a concession or submission."

Thus, Anandpur Sahib Resolution speaks of pre-eminence of Panth. Pre-eminence of any community in a democracy is repugnant. Sikh religion being egalitarian, it cannot be believed that the Tenth Guru who repudiated caste system and selected his Panj Piaras from different castes would ordain pre-eminence based on religion. Be that as it may, suffice it to say that political leadership has been committing a grave error in not examining the issue of more autonomy for States. The Sikh mind luxuriates in the mythologic and wants to dismantle the secularism of Indian polity. This poses a challenge to the secular underpinnings of Indian polity. History of a country is shaped by the methodology by which it responds to the rising challenges. This brings us to examine the adequacy or deficiencies of our system of working.

THE SYSTEM

Although India has a secular, socialist democratic system of governance, it is not the use of idealistic phrases and utopian idiom, which determine the destiny of a people, but how effective they are in running their system. It is an admitted fact that Indian system of governance is sluggish, unresponsive and sometimes counter-productive. We have to examine the quality of a few infrastructures of our system. The Prime Minister Rajiv Gandhi once said that he had tried to change the system but had met resistance and failed. The most powerful man in the country described how his attempts to change the system were failed. The PM was reported to have said: "When I tried to change the system to push it to deliver, I came up against vested interests which just would not let go. Every time I thought I had found a solution, I could not convince those at higher levels, whether in politics or in the administration."

Punjab tragedy had been in the making over decades. It did not erupt suddenly. How did our system respond to the challenge of fundamentalism and secessionalism?

First, how did our system respond to the so-called Sikh grievances? We need not go into the substance of those grievances here because in the deluge of blood, which engulfed Punjab they have lost much of their relevance. In a democratic system, grievance redressal of an ethnic minority is of prime importance. Neglect or drift in this regard result in callous repression.

The fact of the matter is that no serious attention was paid to these grievances. Both Chandigarh and Delhi adopted "do not care" attitude and attempted disruption of Akali ranks than redressal of genuine grievances.

Though at times both the Akalis and the extremists were intransient, yet both had tried to find face-saving solutions. The fate of Akali Government talks particularly in Oct-Nov. 1982 and June 1983 is well documented when at times it was the Government which retracted its steps when even the extremists at certain junctions were keen to come to peace.

They were disappointed when Surjit Singh Barnala failed to concede them some office. They had approached in August 1985 to effect a rapproachement with the government. In turn, I approached Shri Arun Singh who was not prepared to entertain any proposal and was advised to approach the Punjab Governor Shri Arjun Singh directly. The extremists did not trust Shri Arjun Singh as the latter was known for his predilection for Surjit Singh Barnala. In June 1986, they again approached me with two demands only and as a matter of surety they were to guarantee peace for three months in the whole of Northern India before their demands were to be accepted. I conveyed these to quarters concerned. There was no response. When he happened to meet the Prime Minister Shri Rajiv Gandhi on Independence Day Reception at Rashtrapati Bhavan, Shri Gandhi agreed to give time for discussing the matter. However, he was made to meet a somnolent, yawing bureaucrat who could not take any decision. Extremists have their own sources of intelligence and finding that their overtures were spurned, they resorted to murder and pillage.

Thus our system showed singular lack of responsiveness in seizing opportunities when negotiations could terminate the orgy of violence and hate. This failure of taking right action at the right time was due to the antagonists leaning on political expediency and having allowed themselves to be obsessed with the desire to "teach a lesson" to each other.

Now we examine the role of institutions comprising our system and as to how they failed to respond.

Police functions in a given milieu. With the rise of subculture of violence all over the world, the police has been found to be an inadequate instrument for enforcement of peace. Traditional policing could not succeed where violence and lawlessness have become endemic. *New Statesman,* London (Nov 14, 1986) while noting that there was a crisis of law and order ascribed the same to the absence of acceptable authority.

To meet the threat of terrorism, police is an important infrastructural instrument in any system of governance. However, it has been recognised all over the world that police by itself was inadequate in dealing with the menace of terrorism and every country affected by this menace raised its own specialised Services. USA has Delta Force which failed in 1979 operation in Iran and U.K. has SAS. Punjab Police has made supreme sacrifices in stemming the tide of fundamentalism by sacrificing many lives: Ajit Singh Atwal DIG, Shri D.S. Mangat DG lost his own son, Bachan Singh and his whole family were wiped out; the toll runs into hundreds. The guilty party is the one who had failed to provide protection to their own officers and men and families. Guilty are those who had shown inability to provide requisite arms and equipment to police.

There are unscrupulous elements in police also who have taken advantage of the repressive laws, those whose duty was to supervise cannot escape responsibility. In a corrupt system lower and middle rung echelons of police got infected and committed excesses, which should have been avoided. But national leadership never provided ethical guidance to police. On the other hand, they denied arms and equipment for so long to police that security men and their families were singled out and butchered by the terrorists. History is not going to forgive the Government which ignored the threat of terrorism or dealt with it inadequately, for their petty political gains, resulting in the deaths of thousands of innocent Sikhs and Hindus, rape of their wives, daughters and sisters. The political system of India and those who operate it, would stand indicted at the bar of history. It is only the Security Forces, whatever their shortcomings at times, who came to the rescue of thousands of Sikhs and Hindus whom their political masters had abandoned at the mercy of cruel, marauding, looting, killing and raping gangs that had come to rule Punjab in those dark days.

Need for a Comprehensive Judicial Commission

In view of the facts and circumstances narrated in the fore going, it will be in the fitness of things that a Judicial Commission of Inquiry under a retired Chief Justice of India is ordered by the Government of India with suitable terms of reference. The following may be considered for this purpose:

(1) Whether there was collusion between Chief Ministers of Haryana and Punjab which plunged the whole of North India into gruesome anarchy resulting in the assassination of Mrs. Indira Gandhi.

(2) The collusion of the Chief Ministers of Punjab and Haryana in 1970s to weaken Prime Minister Indira Gandhi.

(3) The role played by the Home Minister of India in arranging escape of Sant Jarnail Singh Bhindranwale and his Jatha from Chandu Kalan (Haryana) on 12/13 September and later from Bombay in 1981.

(4) The Role of Shiromani Gurudwara Parbhandhak Committee, Shromani Akali Dal, All India Sikh Students Federations in spreading terror in North India.

Epilogue

By and large Punjab has been a peaceful State except for the terrorist turbulence from part 1982 to 2002—there has been sporadic violence after 2002 but it has been minor, if violence can ever be minor.

Has the unfortunate phase of terrorist crimes come to an end? Have terrorists given up finally? The answer is: Yes, though given up yet they are still hovering in Canada, USA, U.K., Germany and, most important, in Pakistan. It is asked if Punjab will never suffer again from such depredations of two decades. The answer is: it depends upon the Pakistani intentions. If Pakistan decides that Punjab be thrown to terrorism, it will be so as here to fore. Else Punjab can breathe peace, though there are other factors, too, which need to be examined, of which Sikh religious sensibility is the foremost.

There can be problems if the rulers act without foresight and sensitivity. We must remember that whatever we do in a state bordering Pakistan, be it J&K or Punjab, Pakistan will be tempted to meddle. It is compulsive for Pakistan to take advantage of India's troubles. It is for India to deny Pakistan such a temptation.

Porous Indo-Pak Border

Indian border with Pakistan in Punjab (556 km) has unfortunately been porous. It has stretches of ravine border, which is easily fordable. The border on both sides is generally inhabited by smugglers. This enabled terrorists to enter India from Pakistan and return to Pakistan after committing crimes.

When the Prime Minister Mrs. Indira Gandhi approved fencing of border in 1983, the priority was only Indo-Bangladesh border. When Mr. Chandrasekhar became the

Prime Minster, he made strenuous efforts to complete fencing of Indo-Pak border. This fencing has taken away the porosity of the border to an extent. It has to be kept in good state of repair, if the terrorists are to be denied this avenue.

Let us remember there was no fencing when Punjab youth crossed into Pakistan after Operation Blue Star and Operation Rosewood.

After the fencing of Punjab border, the Punjab terrorists made use of Kathua, Samba, Ranbirsinghpura and Rajouri rather generously in Jammu sector. In this, they lighted the path for the Kashmiri infiltrators. But with Kashmir border now getting fenced, this avenue used by ISI, will be closed too.

At present, Punjab border is not only fenced, but also lighted at night. This denies the criminals and terrorists the use of darkness. Thus, the development of border, as it is now, is a factor in favour of peace.

Economic Distress

There is glamour in Punjab. People eat well, dress well and move well. The number of vehicles is large. The number of pacca houses is not small. People spend liberally on alcohol, amusement and litigation. Their holdings are apparently large. There are landlords of name and fame. There are fancy schools and colleges. They spend fortunes to migrate abroad for employment. The number of travel agencies indulging in murky practices is large. Thus, there is a picture of enormous wealth and prosperity, which in reality is phoney.

Underneath this opulence there is a section who are only marginal farmers, whose holdings are small and whose income is piteous and in whose homes food is scarce and amenities rare. The youth of these homes are ready fodder for Damdami Taksal and Pakistani ISI. They are paid a pittance but equipped with a *AK-47* or some other lethal weapon to make them feel intoxicated. Because they have suffered enormously at their home, so when they go on their mission they make good of their economic deprivation, their youth or family, thus there were cases of robbery, smuggling and rape.

The plight of Dalits in villages is harrowing. Dalit youth were equally treck to Pakistan after Operation Blue Star and they participated in all crimes with great fervour.

It has been said that the youth from small holdings invariably made beeline for Arts department in colleges. They had not been properly guided and when they marched into the competitive world of employment, be it police or army they were frustrated. AISSF & ISI made them commit crimes so that they could never return to normal life and waged the Dharmyudh of vengeance instead. The problem of employment among the youth in Punjab is acute and can no more be left to ritualistic remedies.

The Pakistan Dimension

Ever since India and Pakistan attained their freedom from British yoke in August 1947, their relations have been bedevilled by mistrust and bloodshed. After decades of chicanery between the two countries, we hear of confidence building measures (CBM). It is like feeling content with ourselves by wiping blood from the floor after perpetrating murder.

The Punjab problem in 1980s and 1990s was partly manifestation of Pakistani hostility towards India. This problem would not have started if the Delhi rulers were responsive to what was happening in Punjab. Arrogance and insensitivity towards a problem showed a myopic sight.

When a whole arsenal was found in the Golden Temple in the wake of Operation Blue Star in June 1984, it was suspected that this was a Pakistani cargo. But when the arms were examined, it was found that they were of Indian origin. When the unemployed Sikh youth marched into Pakistan to wreak vengeance, they were warmly feted, trained and armed by Pakistan.

When SAARC was held in Islamabad on 16th, 17th July 1989, Pak Prime Minister made an earnest effort to reach some settlement with India. As a part of this effort, she directed Punjabi terrorist training camps to be dismantled. Her efforts was sabotaged by her JSI and as also Indian failure to respond on the familiar argument that any concession will be misconstrued as weakness. Thus, the effort of Mrs. Benazir Bhutto to discard Punjab card remained partial.

The fact of the matter is that if India and Pakistan have to live in peace, they must learn to be good neighbours. It is sad that even at present the heads of all Punjab terrorist organisations: KCF Panjwar, ISYF Rode, Dal Khalsa, Babbar Khalsa and Khalistan Zindabad Force are in shelter with Pak ISI. If they exist today they do so because of Pak ISI. As and when Indo-Pak relations improve, these organisations will be bundled out of Pakistan. Else, they will continue with their menacing posture.

Punjab Government

The tussle between the Home Minister Giani Zail Singh and the Chief Minister Sardar Darbara Singh mushroomed into numberless insecurities. It paralysed the functioning of vital organs of the government and compelled Punjab Government to enter into unprincipled collusion with some terrorists. Could there be anything more dangerous?

The future functioning of Punjab Government will repel or encourage terrorism?

Government of India

One normally believes that Government of India is the paragon of efficiency and equity. No. Its main principle is: be adamant else people may think we are weak. Those who should be supposed to run this vast machine: actually do not know how this machine is run. There would have been no need for Operation Blue Star if certain instruments of governance were used in a correct manner but they were not as there was colossal ignorance.

After Operation Blue Star, Government of India took some steps to assuage Sikh feelings but to no effect. Operation Blue Star is to rankle in Sikh minds for a long time to come.

It is Government of India which freed the conspirators of the assassination of the Prime Minister, Mrs. Indira Gandhi, in violation of the laws of land and tenets of morality, and provided Government aircraft to fly the Chief conspirator from Bhagalpur (Bihar) to Amritsar. It showed how cowardly it was and vainly tried to masquerade its cowardice as statesmanship! (December 1989).

What a Government of India!

The Sikh Separatists

It was Sardar Kapoor Singh who sowed politically the plan of Sikh separatism. He did not reap any results but bequeathed the sturdiest of this idea.

The next man who persisted fondly and nurtured the idea of Khalistan was Dr. Jagjit Singh Chauhan. He spent decades in London to fan hatred and never tired of what he calls Pakistan "perfidy" came back to India and is now settled in Mohali (Punjab). He has floated a political party by the name Khalsa Raj Party. Dr. Chauhan is at present a discredited ideologist who had played a major role in raising the demand of Khalistan and propagating it in foreign countries. We have already dealt with the activities of Ganga Singh Dhillon (USA).

Dr. Sohan Singh who pom-pomed himself as a Sikh intellectual and practical leader is also settled in Mohali. He is 90 years old now. His physical energy is and so in his ebbing his ability to resurrect Panthic Committee, which controlled International Bhindranwale Tiger Force, Babbar Khalsa, Khalistan Liberation Force, Khalistan Commando Force, etc. Militant cadre call him a juda. Militants lodged in Pakistan and foreign countries consider him having compromised and surrendered to the Indian government, thus causing a setback to the movement of Khalistan, which he had once espoused by blood and thunder.

Wadhawa Singh Babbar, chief of the Babbar Khalsa International operates from Pakistan, where his family and about half dozen associates reside. He lives in a safe house on the outskirts of Lahore in Waped Colony. He has hatched several conspiracies to revive militancy through his organisation as also with the operational understanding with Pak Islamic Groups such as Lashker-e-Toeba and Al-Umer. Besides the BK has operational understanding with Khalistan Zindabad Force. Majority of the outrage, which KZF actively committed in Punjab, Haryana, Delhi and J&K through explosions in the buses and trains in late 90s were the combined handiwork of BKI and KZF. Babbar Khalsa was responsible for the killing of late Shri Beant Singh and others and caused injury to many through human bomb, Dilawar Singh in August 1995. Three main accused involved in the late Sh. Beant Singh's assassination, Jagbal Singh, Tara and Parmjit Singh Bhrora escaped from high security jail on the night intervening 21/ 22 January 2004 and are still absconding.

BKI has sympathisers spread over several countries: UK, Germany, Belgium, Norway, Italy, Canada and USA. USA has proscribed it sometime back. To circumvent this ban it has changed its nomenclature. It remains the most dangerous terrorist organised poised to strike in Punjab and elsewhere any time.

The Terrorists Abroad

Some Sikhs abroad have the mistaken notion that religious freedom is incomplete unless it is supplemented by political symbols of freedom. Sikh in India must be liberated. To that end they have mobilised money, weapons, political and media forces.

They have generously contributed to Babbar Khalsa International and other terrorist organisations.

The situation indicates the failure of Indian Government and political organs as well as the foreign governments resolve till they make their anti-terrorist laws comprehensive enough to cover all terrorism covert and overt. Unless it is done, situation will not improve.

If Khalistan Liberation Force, Bhindranwale Tiger Force, Khalistan Armed Force, Khalistan Liberation Organisation, Tat Khalsa, Khalistan Armed Police, Babbar Khalsa International Sikh Students Federation could indulge in inhuman mayhem, it was due to lethargy of foreign

Governments in general and willingness of Pakistan in particular. The strength of these terrorist organisations arose from the mistaken interpretation of Sikhism and spinelessness of Indian Government, which failed on diplomatic and publicity fronts.

The Future

The upheaval that shook the whole of Northern India in 1980's and 1990s and in which 9995 civilian lives were lost and undermined amity, closeness and the organs of governance sowed a harvest of mistrust and hatred. Terrorist violence bred police counter-violence.

The form of terrorism, which Punjab witnessed in the deeds of 1980s and 1990s, would perhaps never be revived unless Punjab terrorists arrived at an agreement with Al-Qaeda for which negotiations so far have not succeeded. Agreement or no agreement, selective terrorism such as assignation and sabotage are likely to haunt Punjab and Northern India from time to time. Numerous terrorist outfits are hibernating on the soil of Pakistan and Western countries and they have to prove their raison d'etre by hiking targets from time to time. Punjab Police is aware of the lurking dangers of this type, but is the political leadership resolute enough to face their challenge hands on and head on whenever required.

Index